FROM THE RICHNESS OF ISLAMIC HISTORY

SOCIETAS
(Series)

BOGDAN SZLACHTA
(Editor)
56

Dorota Rudnicka-Kassem

From the Richness of Islamic History

KSIĘGARNIA AKADEMICKA
Kraków 2013

Reviewer:
Professor Jerzy Hauziński

Editor:
Joanna Michalska-Bartoszek

Layout:
Małgorzata Manterys-Rachwał

Cover design:
Emilia Dajnowicz
Judi Kassem

This publication was subsidized by the Institute of the Middle and Far East
and the Department of International and Political Studies at the Jagiellonian University.

Published in the e-book form plus paper copies.
The primary version of the book is the paper format

ISBN 978-83-7638-340-8

KSIĘGARNIA AKADEMICKA
ul. św. Anny 6, 31-008 Kraków
tel./faks: 012 431-27-43, 012 663-11-67
e-mail: akademicka@akademicka.pl

Online bookstore:
www.akademicka.pl

For my daughter Judi

Table of Contents

Acknowledgements

When people hear about Islamic history even these quite unfamiliar with the issue seem to be naturally aware of the two facts, namely about its richness and its unifying bond, namely the religion of Islam.

The issue of unity and diversity has always fascinated scholars, writers and artists. Islamic civilization, a unique blend of Arabic, Persian, Turkish, Greek, Roman, Indian, Egyptian, Chinese, and constantly acquired new elements constitutes an inexhaustible source of inspiration and offers a wide range of topics to choose for scholarly elaboration.

Although the idea to compose this book was rather spontaneous, I may say that it arose from my up to date scholarly ventures into the world of Islam – my experiences from the Jagiellonian University and McGill University as both a student and a teacher in the field of Arabic philology and Islamic studies. While the narrative, analysis and all the assessments are entirely my responsibility, I have a great pleasure to express my thanks to those whose councel, assistance and support made the work possible.

Special thanks go to the scholars from McGill University and the Jagiellonian University who always encouraged me and supported my scholarly endeavors and to my students whose enthusiastic reception of my courses has been giving me constant motivation to search for themes and ideas to work on.

I owe a very special debt of gratitude to Professor Issa J. Boullata, Professor Donald P. Little and Professor A. Üner Turgay from the Institute of Islamic Studies at McGill University in Montreal and Professor Jerzy Zdanowski from the Polish Academy of Sciences in Warsaw for their scholarly inspiration and support.

I must gratefully acknowledge the financial assistance of Institute of the Middle and Far East and the Department of International and Political Studies at the Jagiellonian University that enabled publication of this book.

My profound thanks go to my family for their constant support and encouragement. Finally, my special thanks go to my daughter Judi whose love and patience was of great help in surpassing all the difficulties related to the project. The beauty of her music at many times has made my constant work not only enjoyable but also possible.

Introduction

Islam is not only a religion but also a culture and a civilization; it features no separation between religious and non-religious matters. For Muslims their religion is not only a system of beliefs and worship but also it embraces all the aspects of the life of its followers: the rules of civil, criminal and constitutional law. The Islamic world and Islamic history are commonly used terms, both in popular public discourse and in academic writing suggesting some kind of coherent unity. Islam is the unifying element in a large and heterogeneous area, which is the Middle East. However, as we have seen, it is not limited to this cultural region. Today the majority of Muslims live east of this area, namely in India, Pakistan, Bangladesh, Indonesia, and Malaysia. Many Muslims also reside in sub-Saharan Africa, in the former territory of the Soviet Union and in Western countries. At the same time, scholars point to the diversity of Muslim societies and the distinctiveness of local cultures.

Great civilizations result from the contributions of many people. This was especially true of Islamic civilization during the Middle Ages when Muslim culture was a blend of Arabic, Persian, Turkish, Greek, Roman, Indian, Egyptian, Chinese and many other elements. The Arabs provided the foundation for this civilization in two ways. One was the Arabic language, which became the language of the government and literature and was adopted by many non-Arabs. Arabic is the holy language for all Muslims. The Qur'ān, the sacred book of Islam is in Arabic. Throughout the Muslim world, even where Arabic is not spoken, the Qur'ān is chanted in its original language. The Arabic call for prayer is heard five times a day in every Muslim town. Furthermore, the Qur'ān, along with the sayings and actions of the Prophet Muḥammad, provide a strong cultural tie among all Muslims. They prescribe proper behavior in the family, as well as in economic and political life. The other foundation was the Islamic religion. The faith proved to be remarkably flexible and tolerant, at least during the first few centuries of its existence. Islam stimulated the search for knowledge and allowed creativity in the arts.

The Islamic era is counted from the year 622, the date of Muḥammad's migration to Medina. Within a little more than twenty years of that date, Syria and Egypt had been wrested from the Byzantine empire and Iraq and Persia from the Sassanian. The rise of Islam marked the inception of a new and extremely important phase in the world's history; while the conquered Byzantine provinces and the old Sassanian empire left a cultural and artistic heritage that was to affect the world of Islam for many centuries. In the vast territories in which Islam was triumphant, two processes – allied but not identical – began to operate, i.e., Arabization and Islamization. Gradually, the Arabic language began to overwhelm the existing tongues. Islamization was less complete than Arabization because substantial communities of Christians and Jews, who were respected and tolerated by Islam as "Peoples of the Book," clung to their faith and survived. However, the spread of Islam was more extensive than that of the Arabic language. Although Persian culture survived both the conquest by the Arabs and their acceptance of the Islamic faith, Persian Farsi language adopted the Arabic script and an extensive Arabic vocabulary. Furthermore, the Turks, although not conquered by the Arabs, were largely converted to Islam in the tenth century. Islamic history primarily focuses on the region where Islam first appeared and flourished. It is in the Middle East, the home of three great peoples – the Arabs, the Persians and the Turks. Its history is one of the interaction of these peoples and their common interaction with the rest of the world, from the seventh to the twenty first centuries.

Islamic studies encompass the study of religion and of Islamic aspects of Muslim cultures and societies. Their scope include the three categories, namely (1) the normative study of Islamic religion generally carried out by Muslims in order to acquire knowledge of religious truth, (2) the non-normative study of Islamic religion, called "Islamic studies" that covers both what is considered by Muslims to be true Islam and what is considered to be the living Islam, pursued both by Muslim and non-Muslim wherever they observe the general rules of scholarly inquiry, and (3) the non-normative study of Islamic aspects of Muslim cultures and societies which, in a broader sense, takes a wider context and approach the "Islamic" issues not from the perspective of the study of religion, but rather from the point of view of history and literature, or cultural anthropology and sociology.[1]

As for the non-normative study of Muslim religion, usually called "Islamic studies," one may distinguish here two categories, namely (1) "Islamic studies" in a narrower sense, which focuses on Islamic religion as the entity itself and (2) "Islamic studies" in a wider sense which deals with data that are part of a given Muslim community and are culled from the Islamic experience but that may or may not posses a religious, i.e., Islamic significance for particular Muslim group.[2]

The development of "Islamic studies" in the nineteenth century was a part of general development of Oriental studies, commonly called "Orientalism." Oriental studies, as pointed out by Waardenburg, "has given Islamic studies a rather positivist" orientation with considerable attention being paid to historical facts.[3] As for the study of Islamic religion, its history has been approached in three ways.

---

[1] J. Waardenberg, "Islamic Studies," in: M. Eliade, C. J. Adams (eds.) [et al.], *Encyclopaedia of Religion*, vol. 7, New York: McMillan, 1987, p. 457-458.

[2] Ibid., p. 458.

[3] Ibid.

A great number of historians, following the example of Julius Wellhausen (1844--1918)[4] in his various studies on the early Islamic period have concentrated on the external history of Islam. The later historians, among them Claude Cohen[5] and Bernard Lewis[6] have demonstrated how much light can be shed on particular Muslim institutions and movements by viewing them against the background of economics, social and political history. As for the third approach, this historical research focuses primarily on what may be called the inner developments in Islamic religion and culture. One should mention here Ignaz Goldziher (1850- 1921),[7] who is credited with his attempts of establishing the basic framework for an intellectual history of Islam. Also Helmut Ritter (1892-1971),[8] whose research was along the same lines, worked on exposing the inner connection among a great number of religious concepts, in particular theological and mystical, as they developed in history.

As underlined by Waardenburg, somewhere between the general historians and the historians of religion are cultural historians of Medieval period, such as Carl Henrich Becker (1876-1933),[9] Jörg Kraemer (1917-

[4] Julius Wellhausen (1844-1918) was a German biblical scholar and orientalist, particularly notable for his contribution to a scholarly understanding of the origin of the Torah. He is credited with being one of the originators of the documentary hypothesis. For his thorough account on 'Umayyad history, see: *The Arab Kingdom and its Fall*, trans. by M. G. Weir, Calcutta: University of Calcutta, 1927.

[5] Claude Cahen (1909-1991) was a French Marxist orientalist and historian. He specialized in the studies of the Islamic Middle Ages, Muslim sources concerning the Crusades, and social history of the medieval Islamic society, with a particular focus on Futuwa orders. For a thorough account of his works see: R. Curiel and R. Gyselen, *Itineraires d'Orient: Hommages a Claude Cahen*, Res orientales (Bures-sur-Yvette), 6, Bures-sur-Yvette–Leuven: Groupe d'études pour la civilisation du Moyent-Orient–Peeters Press, 1994. The Festschrift was published as an honor to his distinguished career. For a complete bibliography of his works refer to: *Arabica*, 43/1 (1996), the issue, dedicated to him.

[6] Bernard Lewis (born in 1916) is a British-American historian and scholar of Oriental studies. He is a Cleveland E. Dodge Professor Emeritus of Near Eastern Studies at Princeton University. Bernard Lewis specializes in the history of Islam and the interaction between Islam and the West. He has published numerous books. For his recent works see: *The End of Modern History in the Middle East*, Stanford, CA: Hoover Institution Press, 2011; *Faith and Power: Religion and Politics in the Middle East*, New York: Oxford University Press, 2010.

[7] Ignác (Yitzhaq Yehuda) Goldziher (1850-1921), more commonly known as Ignaz Goldziher, was a Hungarian scholar of Islam. Along with German Theodore Nöldeke and the Dutch scholar Christian Snouck Hurgronje, he is considered the founder of modern Islamic studies in Europe. For his most famous works see: *Muhammedanische Studien*, 2 vols., Halle: M. Niemeyer, 1889-1890.

[8] Helmut Ritter (1892-1971) was a German orientalist and historian, specialized in studies on Islamic history and editing Arabic manuscripts. For his most famous works see: *The Ocean of the Soul: Man, the World, and God in the Stories of Farīd al-Dīn 'Aṭṭār*, Handbuch der Orientalistik. Erste abteilung, Der Nahe und Mitlere Osten; Handbook of Oriental Studies, trans. by J. O'Kane with editorial assistance of B. Radtke. Leiden–Boston: Brill, 2003.

[9] Carl Henrich Becker (1876-1933) was a German orientalist and politician in Prussia. He is considered one of the founders of the study of the modern Middle East. From his works on Islamic history see: *Christianity and Islam*, London–New York: Harper & Brothers, 1909.

-1961),[10] and Gustav Edmund von Grunebaum (1909-1972),[11] who in his research placed religious developments within the wider cultural frameworks, which were related in turn to political and military history. In addition, one should include the works of Marshall G. S. Hodgson (1921-1968)[12] in which he attempted to present the total history of Islam within a culturally oriented world history.

These three types of historical study are also reflected in the vast number of historical works on particular Muslim communities of the past, studies that present the contemporary history of Muslim societies, etc. In another words, these studies focus on the major points of the Islamic history as outlined by Charles J. Adams in his survey "Islamic Religious Tradition."[13] The main categories are: (1) Muḥammad, (2) the Qur' ān, (3) ḥadīth, (4) law, (5) metaphysical theology, (5) Islamic philosophy, (6) mysticism, (7) Islamic art and architecture, (8) religious institutions and (9) modern developments in Islam. Within the bulk of studies on Islamic history two types of works may be distinguished, namely the one focusing on a particular broader topic, as for example *The Prophet and the Age of the Caliphates, 600–1050* by Hugh Kennedy,[14] *The Middle East: 2000 Years of History from the Rise of Christianity to the Present Day* by Bernard Lewis,[15] and the other including sectional presentation of a few narrow topics which all together give a complex picture exposing the richness of Islamic history with its various currents of development and characteristic features, for example *Gunpowder Empires: Ottomans, Safavids, and Mughals* by Douglas E. Streusand,[16] *Studies on the Civilization of Islam* by Hamilton A.R. Gibb[17] and *An Antology of Islamic Studies* edited by Issa J. Boullata.[18]

---

[10] Jörg Kraemer (1917-1961) was a German historian, especially known for his contribution to the study of Islam within the framework of cultural history. See: *Das Problem der islamischen Kulturgeschichte*, Tübingen: M. Niemeyer, 1959.

[11] Gustav Edmund von Grunebaum (1909-1972), was a well-known Austrian historian and Arabist. From his works on Islamic history see: *Medieval Islam: A Study in Cultural Orientation*, Chicago: University of Chicago Press, 1953; *Der Islam in seiner klassischen Epoche, 622-1258*, Zürich–Stuttgart: Artemis Verlag, 1966.

[12] Marshall G. S. Hodgson (1921-1968) was an Islamic Studies scholar and a world historian at the University of Chicago. For his famous works on Islamic history see: *The Venture of Islam: Conscience and History in a World Civilization*, 3 vol., Chicago: University of Chicago Press, 1974.

[13] C. J. Adams, "Islamic Religious Tradition," in: L. Binder (ed.), *The Study of the Middle East: Research and Scholarship in the Humanities and Social Sciences*, New York: Wiley, 1976, p. 29-96.

[14] H. Kennedy, *The Prophet and the Age of the Caliphates, 600–1050*, London–New York: Barnes and Noble, 1981.

[15] B. Lewis, *The Middle East: 2000 Years of History from the Rise of Christianity to the Present Day*, London: Weidenfeld & Nicolson, 1995.

[16] D. E. Streusand, *Islamic Gunpowder Empires: Ottomans, Safavids, and Mughals*, Boulder, CO: Westview Press, 2011.

[17] H. A. R. Gibb, *Studies on the Civilization of Islam*, Princeton, NJ: Princeton University Press, 1982.

[18] I. J. Boullata, *An Anthology of Islamic Studies*, Montreal: McGill Indonesia IAIN Development Project, 1992.

The purpose of this book, resulting from my up to date scholarly ventures into the study and research of the Islamic world, is to expose the richness of Islamic history by sketching the above outlined characteristics, and using a few selected examples from the history of the Muslim world. Although the topics of each chapter focus on diverse matters, they have one important unifying factor – the religion of Islam. As already mentioned, the Muslim civilization is the result of the contributions of diverse cultures and many peoples, with particular legacy of the Arabs, the Persians, and the Turks.

The first chapter is devoted to the central figure of Islamic history, i.e., Muḥammad and it constitutes an overview of up-to date biographical works presenting him both as a Prophet and as a statesman. The second chapter focuses on the history of Islamic leadership, the charisma and determination of various Muslim leaders in establishing independent governments or hereditary dynasties. This chapter reflects on the political aspirations and achievements of Aḥmad Ibn Ṭūlūn, one of the Muslim leaders who in a relatively short period was capable of establishing an almost independent state and government in Egypt. The third chapter presents a scope of issues concerning the history of Islamic thought. It discusses the thought of Abū Ḥāmid Muḥammad Ibn Muḥammad al-Ghazālī, one of the greatest Muslim scholars and mystics, and it exposes the impact of his search for the truth on the relation between the "Islamic sciences" and mysticism. The fourth chapter focuses both on a discussion of the significance of the Ḥaram documents from Jerusalem for the study of Medieval Islamic history and a presentation of a detailed analysis of one particular document from the Collection. The fifth chapter is connected with the history of Islamic architecture and art. It describes the architectural evolution of the Mamlūk city of Cairo pointing to the power and creativity of Islamic architecture and to the greatness of its symbolic expression. The sixth chapter relates to the history of modern developments in Islam. It contains reflections on Muḥammad 'Alī's achievements in executing his deliberate plan to forge a new synthesis of East and West through precisely "outlined" state sponsored-reforms leading to the foundations of modern Egypt. Finally, the last chapter discusses the history of reciprocal relations between Islam and Christianity exposing both hostility and prejudice, as well as the attempts of building the bridges of mutual reconciliation and understanding.

This book is based on a wide range of sources, including primary and secondary material.

I

Muḥammad: Muslim and Western Biographies of the Prophet

As of today, about one-fifth of the world population professes a faith and a religious involvement to which they give the name "Islam."[19] Its origins are to be found in the very beginning of Islamic history. The Prophet Muḥammad employed it to signify both his own response to the Almighty Being, who had called him, and to describe that to which he was summoning his fellow Arabs. The word continues, as it has throughout some 1400 years, to be used by members of the community who relate their spiritual ancestry to the Prophet, i.e., the central figure of Islamic history.

Muḥammad Ibn ʿAbd Allāh was born into a prominent Meccan family around 570 A. D.[20] He lost his parents early and he was brought up by his uncle Abū Ṭālib. As most of his Meccan compatriots, he devoted himself to trade. It was in the town of Bostra (Syria), an important junction on the caravan route and a great centre of Christianity, where a significant incident is said to have taken place. Muḥammad accompanied his uncle Abū Ṭālib who led the caravan. In Bostra, they met a Christian monk named Baḥīrā.[21] He recognized that Muḥammad bore the signs of prophethood that the Holy Book had predicted, including "the seal of the prophethood between his shoulders."[22] Therefore, he believed that Muḥammad was the future "Envoy of

---

[19] About a little over one and half billion or about one-fifth (23.4%) of the world population are Muslims. For statistical data see: "*Executive Summary: Projections for 2010-2030*," *The Future of the Global Muslim Population*, Pew Research Center, 27 January 2011, on-line: http://www.pewforum.org/The-Future-of-the-Global-Muslim-Population.aspx, access: April 15, 2013.

[20] The precise date is unknown.

[21] In the Christian polemic concerning Islam, Baḥīrā became a heretical monk whose religious affiliation varies in different Christian sources. For a detailed discussion on related issues see: B. Roggema, *The Legend of Sergius Baḥīrā: Eastern Christian Apologetics and Apocalyptic in Response to Islam*, Leiden–Boston: Brill, 2009.

[22] Muḥammad Ibn Isḥāq, *The Life of Muḥammad: A Translation of Ibn Isḥāq's "Sīrat Rasūl Allāh,"* trans. by A. Guillaume, Oxford: Oxford University Press, 1955, p. 78-81. Also refer to: M. Rodinson, *Muhammad*, trans. by A. Carter, New York: Pantheon Books, 1980, p. 46-

Allāh."[23] As Muslim traditions says, at the age of twenty five he married a wealthy widow Khadīja, who was some fifteen years older than him. Religiously inclined, Muḥammad often retreated to a quiet place to reflect and meditate. According to Muslim historians, at the age of forty – some say forty-three – a divine commission to serve as prophet to his people was laid upon him. In 610, on a "Night of Power and Excellence," Muḥammad became the Prophet of God, receiving his first message through the Angel Gabriel.[24] Thereupon, the series of revelations collected in the Qur'ān began to come to him. This profound religious experience transformed his life and initiated a community. In other words, he assumed the, at first, highly unpopular role of religious teacher and reformer.

It is worth noting that Muḥammad did not claim to bring a new religion but to purify and restore the one true religion of Abraham. For ten years in Mecca, he preached a message of religious and social reform. The Prophet proclaimed one true God, rejecting polytheism and social injustice. The Qur'ānic message condemning the exploitation of the poor, the flaunting of wealth and ignorance, as well as forbidding corruption and fraud and prescribing strict punishments for crimes was a challenge to the prevailing socio-political as well as religious order. Muḥammad's preaching, and in particular his rejection of polytheism, seriously threatened the economic interests of the Meccans who controlled the Ka'ba, the sacred shrine for tribal idols and the site of a great annual pilgrimage and fair, which was the source of Meccan religious prestige and revenue.

After ten years of relatively limited success, some Meccan tribes remained hostile towards the Prophet and his followers. By 619, with the passing of both his wife Khadīja and his uncle Abū Ṭālib, Muḥammad had lost the pillars of his personal support and protection and the Meccan aristocracy increasingly persecuted the Prophet and his followers. As pointed out by John Esposito, they regarded Muḥammad's claim to prophecy and his reformist agenda with its explicit criticism of the political and socio-economic status quo as a serious challenge to both their economic interests and their socio-political prestige.[25] For these reasons, when the leaders of Medina invited the Prophet to serve as an arbitrator, he and his followers migrated in 622 and established there the first Muslim *'umma* (com-

-47; M. Penn, "Syriac Sources for the Study of Early Christian-Muslim Relations," *Islamochristiana*, vol. 29 (2003), p. 72-73.

[23] Some years later, as Ibn Isḥāq reports, Waraqa Ibn Naufal, the cousin of Muḥammad's first wife Khadīja Bint Khuwaylid, identified Muḥammad's experience in the cave of Hira as divine revelation. Waraqa Ibn Naufal was a *ḥanīf*, i.e., an Arab monotheist. He was familiar with both Christian and Judaic scriptures. Khadīja consulted him concerning Muḥammad's prophetic experience. Waraqa assured Muḥammad that he received a great revelation like the one sent to Mūsā (Moses) ages before (M. Ibn Isḥāq, *The Life of Muḥammad*..., p. 83, 107).

[24] The Qur'ān, S: 96, v: 1-5. See: A. Y. 'Alī, *The Meaning of the Holy Qur'ān*, Beltsville, MD: Amana Publications, 1989.

[25] J. L. Esposito, *The Islamic Threat: Myth or Reality*, New York–Oxford: Oxford University Press, 1995, p. 29.

munity). In this state, guided by divine revelation, Muḥammad united the tribes under the *Constitution of Medina*.[26] After eight years of combined diplomacy and military action, the Prophet returned in triumph to Mecca. By the time of his death in 632, most of the Arabian Peninsula had converted to Islam. Muḥammad had done what no man in previous history had ever been able to accomplish, by uniting virtually the whole of Arabia under his rule.

Muslim piety had lavished generous attention upon the Prophet. His contemporaries fastened upon his sayings and actions to collect them, remember them, and pass them on to their descendants in a living oral tradition, later to become a written one. Soon, the number of stories about the Prophet increased and reflection upon his personality became more intense. Muḥammad began to assume the characteristics of a unique person – sinless and capable of performing miracles. The tendency throughout Muslim history has been toward an always-greater idealization, even romanticization of the Prophet. This approach has culminated in the modern biographies of Muḥammad that present him not only as the great hero of all history and the most profound thinker but also as the perfect example of all virtues.[27]

As for Western scholarship on the life and activity of the Prophet, authors have often been unsympathetic in their portrayals. Some scholars have gone to the extreme of explaining Muḥammad's strange trancelike states while receiving revelations as due to epilepsy while others have outspokenly condemned him on moral grounds for his actions. One may say that Western scholarship predominantly considers Muḥammad and his teaching to be the result of historical and personality factors, rather that of divine activity. Therefore, it is rather obvious that such elements in Western writings about the Prophet either shock or offend Muslim sensibilities and are largely responsible for the defensive and apologetic tone of contemporary Muslim literature.

One of the most difficult questions in connection with Muḥammad, from a methodological point of view, arises in relation to the use of the Qur'ān as source for the Prophet's biography. It is worth noting that there is no serious doubt, among even the most skeptically inclined Western scholars, that the Qur'ān is genuinely Muḥammadan and the weight of critical study supports the conclusion that the Qur'ān's pages offer a reliable record of the proclamations, which the Prophet attributed to a divine source. Therefore, in their opinion the Qur'ān would seem to offer especially valuable resources to the biographer:

> A characteristic feature of this unique work is that it responds constantly and often candidly to Muḥammad's changing circumstances and contains a wealth of hidden data that are relevant to the task of the quest for the historical Muḥammad, although any use

---

[26] See: J. Danecki, "Konstytucja medyneńska," *Przegląd Religioznawczy*, vol. 1/168 (1993), p. 37-46.

[27] This development testifies to the continuing significance of Muḥammad for Islamic faith. Though Muḥammad's claims are more modest than those of his biographers, Muslims continue to perceive him as a great Prophet and an example to follow.

of the Qur'ān as a historical source is clearly ancillary to its primary purpose and main functions in Muslim life.[28]

Historians and biographers, past and present have recognized and employed these resources. However, one should underline that they "have only begun to tap this rich source," because the task is difficult and requires "specialized knowledge and a variety of historical and literary critical methods in order to reach sound conclusions and plausible hypotheses."[29]

As for the methodological problem to which we refer to, it becomes apparent when it is seen that the use of the Qur'ān for biographical information on Muḥammad involves the assumption that the book is, in some sense, the product and outcome of Muḥammad's interaction with his environment. The view of history and historical causation held by most modern scholars demands such an assumption. In fact, any other stand regarding the Qur'ān would be rather unintelligible. One should point out that to the pious Muslims, this assumption is wholly unacceptable because they are convinced that the Qur'ān is an eternal book whose author is God, not Muḥammad, and it is, therefore, in no respect subject to forces of historical conditioning. In conclusion, since the personality of Muḥammad played no part in the formation of the Qur'ān, the Holy Book cannot provide a key to that personality or its development. Although the difference between Muslim and others concerning the possibility of employing the Qur'ān as a biographical source may never be resolved, it is important to note this difference, and its implications should be the cause for reflection.

Muslim biographies of the Prophet

The life of the Prophet Muḥammad, to whom the Angel Gabriel revealed the verses of the Qur'ān, has provided inspiration to Muslims for hundreds of years. The earliest sources concerning the life of Muḥammad go back to the oral tradition of his sayings and actions that sprang from the circle of his immediate companions. It is worth noting that among Arabs of pre-Islamic days, there was an established and much enjoyed custom of reciting the exploits of the past, especially the valorous deeds of great heroes. With the spread of Islam and the influence of the Muslim community and as Muḥammad gained more esteem, the tales of the Prophet gradually replaced those of dead and living heroes.

The earliest attempts to report events of Muḥammad's life are the stories of his *maghāzi* or military campaigns. In the first generation after Muḥammad's death, these stories began to be controlled, and there arose, what is known as *maghāzi*

---

[28] F. Buhl, "The Prophet's Life and Career," in: *Encyclopaedia of Islam*, New Edition, vol. 7, p. 360-361.

[29] Ibid., p. 361.

literature. However, very little of this literature has survived and only two small portions of it are available in Western languages.[30]

It is worth noting that from very early on, the *maghāzī* stories were merged with *sīra*, i.e., the works that sought to preserve stories about the Prophet, *tafsīr*, i.e., the writings that attempted to preserve traditional interpretations of the verses of the Qur'ān, and *ḥadīth*, i.e., the accounts that sought to preserve sayings of and about Muḥammad.[31]

The first systematic effort to compile a biography of Muḥammad is attributed to Ibn Isḥāq (704-767), an Arab Muslim historian and hagiographer. He was born and grew up in Medina, where he had many opportunities to collect the stories of the Prophet current among the populace. These collected oral traditions, dictated to his students are known as *Sīratu Rasūli l-Lāh* (*Life of the Messenger of God*), and formed the basis for the most important biography of Muḥammad.[32] It is worth noting that Ibn Isḥāq's work did not survive in its original form but only in reports from which two are of the greatest value.[33] The first report by Ibn Hishām (died 833) that has been translated by Alfred Guillaume is widely used.[34] The second one by Yūnus Ibn Bukayr survived only in a manuscript form.[35] There are also extensive quotations from Ibn Isḥāq's work, including the sections that Ibn Hishām and Yūnus Ibn Bukayr omitted, in historical works that cover much more than the life of the Prophet. Among them, one should consider *Ta'rikh al-rusūl wa'l-mulūk* by Al-Ṭabarī (838?-923).[36]

After Ibn Isḥāq's biography, the sources most widely used for the studies on the life of the Prophet are the *Maghāzī* by Al-Wāqidī (748-822).[37] In addition, one should also note the contribution of his prominent disciple and secretary Muḥammad Ibn Sa'd (784-845), author of *Kitāb al-Ṭabaqāt al-Kabīr*, the work describing the

---

[30] A fragment of a lost book by Mūsā Ibn 'Uqba of the third generation after Muḥammad, is translated by Alfred Guillaume in his *The Life of Muḥammad*, London: Oxford University Press, 1955, p. xliii-xlvii.

[31] F. Buhl, "The Prophet's Life..., p. 361.

[32] See: W. Raven, "Sīra and the Qur'ān – Ibn Isḥāq and his Editors," in: J. D. McAuliffe (ed.), *Encyclopaedia of the Qur'an*, vol. 5, Leiden: Brill, 2006, p. 29-51.

[33] F. Buhl, "The Prophet's Life..., p. 361.

[34] Ibn Hishām, of the generation after Ibn Isḥāq, edited the latter's text according with certain principles which explains in his Preface. Ibn Hishām's work has been translated by Alfred Guillaume in his *The Life of Muhammad...*, and the most important single early source for Muḥammad's life.

[35] For a description and summary of the contents of a manuscript which contains Yūnus Ibn Bukyr's report of lectures delivered by Ibn Isḥāq see: A. Guillaume, *New Light on the Life of Muhammad*, Series: Journal of Semitic Studies, Monograph, no. 1, Manchester: Manchester University Press, 1960.

[36] See: Al-Ṭabarī, *Muḥammad at Mecca*, vol. 6, The History of Al-Ṭabarī, SUNY Series in Near Eastern Studies, Bibliotheca Persica, W. M. Watt, M. V. McDonald (trans., eds.), Albany, NY: State University of New York Press, 1988; *The Last Years of the Prophet: The Formation of the State – A.D. 630-632*, vol. 9, The History of Al-Ṭabarī, I. K. Poonawala (trans., ed.), Albany, NY: State University of New York Press, 1990.

[37] The other example is an abridged translation of Al-Wāqidī's *maghāzī* book by Julius Wellhausen: *Muhammad in Medina*, Berlin: G. Reimer, 1882.

life of the Prophet, his companions, and his successors.[38] With regard to much later sources for the biography of Muḥammad, it is important to note that of Abū al-Fidā' Ismā'īl Ibn 'Alī (1273-1331), i.e., *Al-Mukhtaṣar fī akhbār al-bashar*,[39] which was for a long time the only one known in the West.

In the course of time, the issue of both searching for new sources and compiling new biographies of Muḥammad became neglected for a few centuries. This is not to say that there were no biographies written or that the role of the Prophet in Muslim thought or piety became any less, but only that the explicit concern to search for new sources concerning the story of his life lost its momentum. When mysticism began to develop among Muslims, its exponents were quick to find sanction for both their practice and their belief in the example of Muḥammad. The mystical trend of piety created a veritable cult of the Prophet among all Muslims and, with the time, this cult would acquire a great importance, as the Ṣūfī, or mystical versions of Muḥammad's life, began to appear.[40]

In modern times, since about 1875, Muslim interest in the biography of Muḥammad has reawakened, and there have been more biographies of the Prophet in the past century than perhaps in the entire previous span of Islamic history. One may say that the growth of self-consciousness and vitality affecting the Muslims, together with the search for a new modern identity are the major reasons for the rise of this interest. Most of these new biographies are reactions against what Muslims consider wrong in the image of the Prophet, created by Western literature and through the activity of orientalists and missionaries. Because both the purpose and tone of these biographies are avowedly apologetic and argumentative, the majority of them have little historical value. Among the best modern works are *The Spirit of Islam* by Sayyid Amīr 'Alī (1849–1928),[41] *Muḥammad "A Mercy to All Nations"* by Al-Hajj Qassim 'Ali Jairazbhoy,[42] *Muḥammad the Holy Prophet* by Hafiz Ghulam Sarwar[43] and *The Life of Muḥammad* by Muḥammad Ḥusayn Haykal (1888-1956).[44]

---

[38] The Arabic text was edited and published; see: Muḥammad Ibn Sa'd, *Kitāb al-Ṭabaqāt al-Kabīr*, edited by E. Sachau, Leiden: E. J. Brill, 1904-1940.

[39] Abū al-Fidā' Ismā'īl Ibn 'Alī, *Al-Mukhtaṣar fī akhbār al-bashar*, Baghdād: Makhtabat al-Muthanná, [1968?].

[40] An example of a mystical approach to Muḥammad available in English is the poem *Mewlid Sharif* of Sulayman Chelebi, trans. by F. Lyman MacCalum, London: John Murray Publishers Ltd., 1943.

[41] See: Sayyid Amīr 'Alī, *The Spirit of Islam*, London: Christopher's Ltd., revised ed., 1922, and many other subsequent editions.The book was first published in 1891. It covers the life of Muḥammad, and the political, cultural, literary, scientific, mystic, philosophical, and social history of Islam. According to many scholars it is one of the best books on this subject.

[42] See: Al-Hajj Qassim 'Ali Jairazbhoy, *Muhammad "A Mercy to All Nations,"* London: Luzac & Co, Ltd., 1937 (first edition).

[43] Hafiz Ghulam Sarwar, *Muḥammad the Holy Prophet*, Lahore: Ashraf, 1949 (first edition).

[44] Muḥammad Ḥusayn Haykal, *The Life of Muhammad*, trans. from the 8th edition by Ismā'īl Rājī A. al-Fārūqī, Indianapolis: North American Trust Publications, 1976. For Arabic edition see: *Ḥayāt Muḥammad*, Al-Qāhirah: Maktabat al-Nahḍah al-Miṣrīyah, 1952.

As for the recent biographies of the Prophet written by Muslims, one should mention *Muḥammad: Man and Prophet: a Complete Study of the Life of the Prophet of Islam* by Adil M. Salahi.[45] His book traces the life of the Prophet Muḥammad from his birth and childhood to the triumph of Islam and its hold on Arabia. His careful analysis of the Prophet's life is written with today's Muslim and non-Muslim readers in mind. Muslims will further reflect on their thorough understanding of their faith, and non-Muslims will come to understand the love Muslims have for their Prophet.

The Messenger: The Meaning of the Life of Muḥammad by Tariq Ramadan deserves our special attention.[46] In this book Ramadan, a leading Muslim scholar, considers the ways in which the Prophet's actions, words and teachings can guide us in the modern world. He offers a biography of the Prophet Muḥammad, highlighting the spiritual and ethical aspects of his teachings and provides both an intimate portrait of a man who was shy, kind, but determined, as well as a dramatic chronicle of a leader who launched a great religion and inspired the establishment of a vast empire. Interspersed with spiritual and philosophical meditations, this profound and stimulating biography shows how Muḥammad's message can be used to address some of today's most controversial issues – from the treatment of the poor and the role of women to the interpretation of jihād and relations with other religions. *The Messenger: The Meaning of the Life of Muḥammad* by Tariq Ramadan offers Muslims a new understanding of Muḥammad's life and introduces non-Muslims to the story of the Prophet as well as to the riches of Islam.

Western biographies of Muḥammad

In the learned Latin circles of the Middle Ages (ca. 800-1400), a remarkable amount of concrete data about the life of the Prophet Muḥammad was known and available. The information or so-called traditions of Muḥammad circulated at that time in Europe came from Oriental Christians, Byzantium, and Christians in Spain. However, as highlighted by a number of scholars, non-Muslims under Islamic domination or not, were typically not concerned with the diffusion of an objective, let alone a positive image of Muḥammad.[47] Consequently, in both the selection and the

---

[45] A. M. Salahi, *Muhammad: Man and Prophet: a Complete Study of the Life of the Prophet of Islam*, Shaftesbury, Dorset–Rockport, Mass.: Element, 1995.

[46] Tariq Ramadan (born in 1962) is a Swiss academic and a leading Muslim scholar, with a large following especially between young European and American Muslims. He is also a Professor of Contemporary Islamic Studies in the Faculty of Oriental Studies at Oxford University. Ramadan presents and advocates a new study and re-interpretation of Islamic texts, and emphasizes the heterogeneous nature of Western Muslims. *Time* magazine named him one of the 100 most important innovators of the century. See: T. Ramadan, *The Messenger: The Meaning of the Life of Muhammad*, London: Allen Lane, 2007.

[47] See: A. Noth, "Muḥammad, the Prophet of Islam: 3) The Prophet's Image in Europe and the West. A) The Image in the Latin Middle Ages," in: *Encyclopaedia of Islam*, New Edition, vol. 7, p. 378.

transmission of true elements concerning the Prophet's biography, their emphasis was distant if not polemical. The already colored in a mildly negative way, the "assertions" about the life of the Islamic Prophet reached the studies of Christian authors, who not only had a rather insufficient knowledge and understanding of Islam but also aimed at disqualifying both the religion and its Prophet. Therefore, these assertions were often used selectively and changed accordingly and, above all, were interwoven with fictitious elements in such a way that they were often divested completely of their historical value. All this suited the formation of a rather negative image of Muḥammad in Christian Europe, which became a standard for years to come. As for the attitude of Christians towards Islam and the Muslims, it remained diverse and ranged from hostility to conciliation.

With regard to Oriental Christians, who had lived under Muslim rule since the seventh century, they addressed Islam, the Prophet Muḥammad, and the Muslims in a large number of apologetic and polemical works in Arabic, Syriac or Greek, and they supported their arguments with both Biblical and Qur'ānic quotations. The main target of their criticism was the Prophet Muḥammad who was usually depicted as a heretic, an impostor, and a person of low moral values. Moreover, while discrediting the Prophet's reputation, they argued that His revelation was a false doctrine, and, at best, a mere heresy. As an example, one should note here an attack on Islam by John of Damascus (655 – 747).[48] In the section devoted to heresies from his major work *The Fount of Wisdom*, the author attempted to warn Christians about the evil of Islam by portraying it as a religion swaying away from the truth. His severe attack was primarily directed at the Prophet Muḥammad, whom he accused of immoral conduct.[49]

The earliest Christian traditions of Muḥammad that came from the Byzantine Empire were primarily negative. Their authors present unfavorable accounts of both the Prophet and the rise of Islam. One of the most influential Byzantine anti-Islamic works was the *Nicetae Byzantini Philosophi confutation falsi libri quem scripsit Mohamedes Arab*.

The most important source of information on Muḥammad, however, came from Spain. With regard to the earliest accounts of Islam and of the Prophet there are two anonymous Latin Chronicles dating from 741 and 754. They contain information about the Muslim conquest, including some references to the Prophet Muḥammad, his followers and the distinct Muslim religious tradition.[50] In addition, one should

---

[48] N. Daniel, *Islam and the West: The Making of an Image*, Oxford: Oneworld Publications, 1993, p. 13-15; R. Armour, *Islam, Christianity and the West: A Troubled History*, Maryknoll, NY: Orbis Books, 2002, p. 41-45. For a thorough discussion refer to: D. J. Sahas, *John of Damascus: The "Heresy of Ishmaelites,"* Leiden: Brill, 1972.

[49] The lack of objectivity and the quite hostile attitude of John of Damascus towards Islam and Muslims may be surprising. According to traditional sources, he could have had some knowledge of Islam because he was employed for several years in the Arab administration in Damascus. See: R. Armour, *Islam, Christianity and the West...*, p. 41.

[50] Ibid., p. 87-90.

mention *Istoria de Mahomet*, written by an unknown author before 850, that survived in its entirety, and *Liber apologeticus martyrum*, written by Eulogius sometime around 857.[51] The first presents the Prophet Muḥammad as a heretic who summoned his followers to abandon idolatry and to adore a "corporeal God" in heaven.[52] The second work, it is a severe attack on Muḥammad, portraying him as heresiarch, the Antichrist and a false prophet.[53] As for the later works, i.e., from the twelve or thirteen centuries, they were based primarily on direct Arab-Islamic sources.

As for biographies of Muḥammad presented in writings from Spain, one should say that they are dominated by a tendency to prove that "in the [sic]a way he lived and acted, could not have been a Prophet and that his alleged divine revelations consequently were man's work and that Islam at the very most is an absolute heresy of Christianity."[54]

There is no doubt that the Renaissance brought a noteworthy change in the Christian perception of Islam, described by Southern as a "moment of vision."[55] It resulted from both the quest for a thorough knowledge of Muslim religion and from an aim to present more objective accounts of the Prophet Muḥammad. This new approach was presented by Nicholas of Cusa (1400-1464) in his *De pace fidei* and *Cribratio Alkorani*.[56] However, in his second important work, i.e., *Cribratio Alkorani*, the author returned to the earlier Medieval negative standard-image of the Qur'ān, the Prophet, and Islam.

New and original studies on Muḥammad and the Muslim religion were to be developed in Europe in the late sixteenth and seventeenth centuries when the Western scholars embarked on more organized and systematic studies of the Arabic language and on the publication of Arab and Islamic sources.[57] In addition, they were also keener to acquire knowledge of the Muslim world from direct encounters with

---

[51] Ibid., p. 93.

[52] According to Wolf, *Istoria* also reveals the author's familiarity with Muslim tradition, presents Islam as a monotheistic religion, and acknowledges its missionary success among the Arabs. Ibid., p. 94.

[53] K. B. Wolf, "Christian Views of Islam in Early Medieval Spain," in: John V. Tolan (ed.), *Medieval Christian Perceptions of Islam. A Book of Essays*, Garland Medieval Case Books 10, Garland Reference Library of Humanities 1786, New York–London: Garland, 1994, p. 100.

[54] A. Noth, "Muḥammad, the Prophet of Islam: 3) The Prophet's Image in Europe and the West. A) The Image..., p. 379.

[55] R.W. Southern, *Western Views of Islam in the Middle Ages*, Cambridge, MA: Harvard University Press, 1962, p. 103.

[56] See: J. E. Biechler, H. L. Bond (eds.), *Nicholas of Cusa on Interreligious Harmony: Text, Concordance, and Translation of 'De Pace Fidei'*, Text and Studies in Religion 55, New York–Toronto: Edwin Mellen Press, 1990; J. Hopkins (ed., trans., & analysis), *Nicholas of Cusa's "De pace fidei" and "Cribratio Alcorani,"* Minneapolis: A. J. Banning Press, 1990. For a discussion of Nicholas of Cusa's philosophy refer to: J. Hopkins, *A Concise Introduction to the Philosophy of Nicholas of Cusa*, Minneapolis: University of Minnesota Press, 1978.

[57] The Chair of Arabic was established at the College de France in 1539, at the University of Leiden in 1613 and at Oxford in 1636. The earlier charge of the fourteenth century Council of

various manifestations of so-called "living Islam." From the important works of that time, one should mention *Pansebeia* by Alexander Ross (1591-1654), published in 1649 (or 1650)[58] and *An Account of the Rise and Progress of Mahometanism: With the Life of Mahomet and a Vindication of Him and His Religion from the Calumnies of the Christians* by Henry Stubbe (1632-1676).

In 1705, the Dutch scholar Adrian Reland (1676-1718) published *De religione mohammedica.* Although considered by Hans Küng as "the first reasonably objective work on Islam after Ross's *Pansebeia*,"[59] this work is characterized by its animosity against Islamic civilization and a spirit of severe criticism of the Prophet Muḥammad. A similar approach is also presented by the writings of Ludovico Maracci (1612–1700), one of the best Christian experts on the Arabic language and the Qur'ān.[60]

It is worth noting that the Enlightenment thinkers brought an entirely new perspective to religion. It was linked with the new theory of religions of humankind, which called for both a recognition that other people had religions that were neither simple and necessary heresies nor that they were aberrations of Christianity and new methods for studying other religions, including Islam.[61] *La vie de Mahomet* by Count Henri Boulainvilliers (1658-1722) is a clear example of such an approach. It is the first biography of Muḥammad that combined an endeavor towards historical accuracy with a positive appreciation of both the Prophet's personality and of the Muslim religion.[62] Boulainviliers presented the Prophet as a free thinker, the founder of a religion of reason that required no severe discipline and that was stripped of miracles and mysteries. A similar interpretation can be found in the writings of Claude Savary (1758-1788).[63]

During the Enlightenment, there was a revived interest in studying the Arabic language and in translating the Qur'ān. In 1734, George Sale (1697–1736) published a highly valued and appreciated translation of the Qur'ān.[64] In his "Preliminary Treatise," Sale presented a relatively objective picture of Muḥammad, focused on facts

Vienna to establish schools for the study of Arabic, implemented briefly during the Renaissance, was coming to life once again.

[58] There are few editions of the work. See, for example: A. Ross, *Pansebeia: or, A view of all religions in the world: with the several church-governments, from the creation, till these times. Also, a discovery of all known heresies, in all ages and places: and choice observations and reflections throughout the whole,* London: Printed for M. Gillyflower and W. Freeman, 1696.

[59] H. Küng (ed.), *Christianity and the World Religions: Paths of Dialogue with Islam, Hinduism, and Buddhism*, trans. by P. Heinegg, Garden City, NY: Doubleday, 1986, p. 20.

[60] See: M. Borrmans, "Ludovico Marracci et sa traduction latine du Coran," *Islamochristiana*, vol. 28 (2002), p. 73-86.

[61] N. Daniel, *Islam and the West...*, p. 315.

[62] Ibid., p. 315.

[63] See: M. C. E. Savary (ed.), *Le Koran, traduit de l'arabe, accompagné de notes, précédé d'un abrégé de la vie de Mahomet par Savary,* Paris: Garnier, 1951.

[64] N. Daniel used Sale's version as "best expressing in English the meaning traditionally understood in Islam" in his book *Islam and the West...*, p. 32.

derived from a wide range of Muslim sources, among them being works of Qur'ānic commentators, such as Al-Baydāwī, Al-Zamakhsharī and Al-Jalālī.[65] As for the other accounts on Muḥammad from the Enlightenment period, it is important to note the contribution of Edward Gibbon. (1737-1794). In *History of the Decline and Fall of the Roman Empire* (published in six volumes between 1776 and 1788) he presented a comprehensive, balanced picture of the Prophet and Islam, created from a variety of sources displaying both positive and negative views. It is also worth noting that Gibbon's influence on the Western perception of both the Prophet and the Muslim religion remains significant. As Daniel points out:

> From recondite and learned books, most of them in Latin and little known outside the narrow world of clerics and scholars, Gibbon was able to present a picture of the Prophet and the rise of Islam that was clear, elegant, and above all convincing. Most important of all... he saw the rise of Islam not as something separate and isolated, nor as regrettable aberration from the onward march of the Church, but as a part of human history.[66]

Despite the persisting negative views concerning Islam, the beginning of the nineteenth century brought a new dimension to the Christian perception of the Prophet, characterized by the acceptance of the fact that Muḥammad and his followers had played an important part in the history of the world.[67] However, some missionaries and scholars still insisted on repeating traditional unfavorable statements, while others were inclined to a more positive view.

The biographies of Muḥammad written in the early nineteenth century – in spite of some reservations about particular points and the still persisting inclination to spread former traditional negative views of Islam – tended to overall accept as authentic the version of the prophet's biography, presented in the available source materials. About the middle of the century the works of Ibn Sa'd (784-845), Al-Ṭabarī (838-923), and above all, those of Ibn Hishām (d. 833), became known in Europe, and the new biographies, based on examinations of this variety of sources, rapidly displaced the older ones which had drawn their information from Abū'l--Fidā'(1273-1331), who in turn depended upon the relatively late historian Ibn al-Athīr (1160-1132).

This new approach of acquiring knowledge directly from the sources is reflected in the writings of Sir William Muir (1819-1905), a British official in India and a scholar who specialized in the history of Muḥammad and the early caliphate. In the 1850s, he wrote "The Muhammadan controversy," an article that demonstrated his complete opposition to the Muslim religion.[68] Similar views, as later repeated in

---

[65] Ibid., p. 322.

[66] B. Lewis, *Islam and the West*, Oxford, NY: Oxford University Press, 1993, p. 98.

[67] A. Hourani, *Islam in European Thought*, Cambridge, NY: Cambridge University Press, 1995, p. 16.

[68] Ibid., p. 19.

his famous work *Life of Muhammad*,[69] were according to Daniel, "no more sympathetic to Islam than the work of his medieval predecessors."[70] There is a similar focus on sources found in A. Sprenger's *Das Leben und die Lehre des Mohammad.*[71] The appearance of these two writings marks the birth of serious biographical works on Muḥammad.

The arguments about the character and work of the Prophet Muḥammad, viewed in secular and humanistic terms, continued to vacillate throughout the nineteenth century. Thomas Carlyle's (1795-1881) lecture "The Hero as Prophet" caused a sensation by treating Muḥammad as a sincere and honest prophet.[72] Although in his image of the Prophet Carlyle repeated some medieval accusations and was rather cautious about the final approval of Him and His mission, he was nevertheless keen to express a number of positive remarks while defending Muḥammad's sincerity.[73]

It is worth mentioning that since the eighteenth century and throughout the nineteenth century in particular, a new science of Oriental studies had been developing. For scholars in this new area of study, the starting point was the religion of Islam. Subsequently, they embarked on the task of exploring the languages, the history, and the culture of the nations that had formed Islamic civilization. Throughout the nineteenth century and into the twentieth, the Orientalists undertook numerous projects in preparing scholarly editions of valuable Arabic texts surviving in manuscript form. These academic ventures resulted in a number of new translations of the Qur'ān as well as in new treaties shedding more light not only on the life and activities of the Prophet Muḥammad, but on various aspect of Islam. Since the Western scholars had become better acquainted with the achievements of Muslim civilization, their approach to it gradually changed, acquiring more objectivity. However, that objectivity did not embrace the attitude toward religion itself. The Catholic Church still condemned Islam, considering it a heresy and refused to acknowledge Muḥammad as a prophet.

As underlined by Hans Küng, the nineteenth and twentieth centuries "have witnessed a tremendous upsurge in Orientalism and hence in scientific studies of Islam, which set the scene for a less polemical view of Islam on the part of Christian theologians and the Church."[74] Decisive progress was made on four fronts, namely

---

[69] W. Muir, *The Life of Muhammad*, 1861; rev. ed., Edinburgh: John Grant, Ltd., 1912. The first edition had introductory chapters discussing sources and the early history of Arabia. Unfortunately, these chapters have been omitted from the second and subsequent editions.

[70] N. Daniel, *Islam and the West...*, p. 327.

[71] 3 vol. Berlin: Verlagsbuchhandlung, 1861-1865

[72] A. Hourani, *Europe and the Middle East*, Berkeley: University of California Press, 1980, p. 19. Also refer to: T. Carlyle, *The Best Known Works of Thomas Carlyle: Including Sartor Resartus; Heroes and Hero Worship; and Characteristics*, New York: Book League of America, 1942.

[73] See: N. Daniel, *Islam and the West...*, p. 313-314.

[74] See: H. Küng (ed.), *Christianity and the World Religions...*, p. 21. Also refer to: C. J. Adams, "Islam and Christianity: the Opposition and Similarities," in: A. Savory and

(1) on a historical assessment of Muḥammad, (2) on a history of the Qur'ān, (3) on comprehensive research on Islamic culture from liturgy and mysticism through law and customs to literature and art, and (4) on a historical evaluation of the image of Jesus in the Qur'ān.

As in so many other aspects of Islamic studies, the publication of Ignaz Goldziher's *Muhammadanishche Studien* and other studies on early Muslim traditional material brought a revolution in thought concerning the biography of Muḥammad.[75] Goldziher demonstrated that a large part of the early traditional sayings attributed to the Prophet or stories about him are the product of contending sects or viewpoints within the Muslim community, each one eager to claim the authority of Muḥammad for its own peculiar stand. During the early years of Islamic history, there was a large wholesale fabrication of traditions, particularly of spurious prophetic sayings, for this purpose, as Muslim collectors of tradition themselves recognize and deplore, that the entire body of traditional material falls under the shadow of doubt as regards its historical reliability. Since the attainment of Goldziher's insight, biographers of Muḥammad have been compelled to subject their source materials to a critical shifting. Some Western scholars, among them Henri Lammens,[76] have drawn from Goldziher's work a rather radical conclusion that tradition is not to be used at all.[77]

As for the biographies of Muḥammad, published in the twentieth century one should note the contribution of the Swedish scholar and Bishop Tor Andrae (1885--1947). His book *Mohammed, sein Leben und sein Glaube* (*Mohamed the Man and His Faith*), considered by a great number of scholars as one of the finest volumes available in English about Islam, is an excellent survey of origins, tenets, and substance of Islam exploring Muḥammad's influence on religion, history, politics, and society.[78] It is also important to note *Das leben Muhammeds*, a well-balanced work on Muḥammad by the Danish scholar Frants Buhl (1850-1932).[79]

There is no doubt that with regard to Western biographies of the Prophet the contribution of W. Montgomery Watt (1909-2006) deserves our special attention. Watt was one of the forefront non-Muslim interpreters of Islam in the West, an enor-

D. Agius, *Logos Islamikos: Studia Islamica in Honorem Georgii Michaelis Wickens*, Papers in Mediaeval Studies no. 6, Toronto: Pontifical Institute for Medieval Studies, 1984, p. 287-306.

[75] See: the footnote no. 7, p. 11.

[76] See: H. Lammens, "Qoran et tradition, comment fut composée la vie de Mahomet," *Recherches de Sciences Religieuse*, I (1910), p. 26-51 and "L'age de Mahomet et la chronologie de la Sīra," *Journal asiatique*, Tenth Series, XVII (1911), p. 209-250.

[77] These scholars maintain that the Qur'ān is the sole reliable biographical source on Muḥammad.

[78] T. Andrae, *Mohamed: The Man and his Faith*, trans. by T. Menzel, London: George Allen & Unwin, 1936; New York: Barnes & Noble, Inc., 1935. The original work *Mohammed, sein Leben und sein Glaube* was published in Göttingen: Vandenhoeck und Ruprecht, 1932.

[79] Translated into German by H. H. Schaeder (Heidelberg: Quelle & Meyer, 1955, second edition). The original work *Muhammed's Liv* was published in 1903 in Kopenhagen: Gyldendal. The essential views exposed in this this study are presented in shorter form in English in Buhl's article "Muḥammad" in *Shorter Encyclopedia of Islam*.

mously influential scholar in the field of Islamic studies, and a much-revered name for many Muslims all over the world. Watt's comprehensive biography of the Islamic Prophet Muḥammad, *Muhammad at Mecca* (1953)[80] and *Muhammad at Medina* (1956),[81] based on a sound Muslim sources are considered to be classics in the field. These two are also available in an abridged one-volume version, namely *Muḥammad Prophet and Statesman.*[82] Watt's writings on the Prophet are notable for meticulous care with which he has traced the alliances and tribal relationships that account for the Prophet's success in taking his control over Arabia. Furthermore, the author is known for his broadly sympathetic treatment of Muḥammad's personality, and his conviction that religious developments are accompanied by, related to, and in part determined by economic developments.[83]

Many unique problems in connection with Muḥammad have intrigued scholarly interest, and in particular, the sources of his ideas and teachings. Much of nineteenth/twentieth-century scholarship was preoccupied with tracing out the historical antecedents of movements, ideas, institutions, etc., and, obviously, Muḥammad did not escape attention from this perspective. At first, the tendency was to emphasize the Prophet's dependence on Judaism. C. C. Torrey (1863-1956) in *The Jewish Foundation of Islam* best states the case for Jewish background of Islām.[84] One should also mention here *Judaism in Islam: Biblical and Talmudic Backgrounds of the Koran and its Commentaries* by Abraham I. Katsh.[85] However, since the work of Tor Andrae, mentioned above, and his *Der Ursprung des Islams und das Christendtum,*[86] the majority of scholars have come to believe the major influence upon the Prophet to have been Syrian Christianity rather than Judaism. For example, the work of Richard Bell (1876-1952), *The Origin of Islam in its Christian Environment,*[87] examines the relationship of Muḥammad's thought to Christianity.

As for the reference of Muḥammad published in French, the reader's attention may be drawn to the short, incisive study by Régis Blachère (1900-1973), *Le problème de Mahomet.*[88] Surveying the present state of our knowledge of Muḥammad in masterly fashion, the author demonstrates that Muḥammad is not the well-known

---

80 W. M. Watt, *Muhammad at Mecca*, Oxford: Clarendon Press, 1953.

81 Idem, *Muhammad at Medina*, Oxford: Clarendon Press, 1956.

82 Idem, *Muhammad Prophet and Statesman*, London: Oxford University Press, 1961.

83 In the third of these – which, in fact, constitutes his method – he has thought it was important enough to devote an entire volume explaining, defining, and illustrating; *Islam and the Integration of Society*, London: Routledge & Kegan Paul, Ltd., 1961.

84 C. C. Torrey, *The Jewish Foundation of Islam*, The Hilda Stich Stroock Lectures… at the Jewish Institute of Religion, New York: Jewish Institute of Religion Press, 1933.

85 A. I. Katsh, *Judaism in Islam: Biblical and Talmudic Backgrounds of the Koran and its Commentaries*, New York: Bloch Pub., 1954.

86 T. Andrae, *Der Ursprung des Islams und das Christendtum*, Kyrkohistorisk Årsskrif 1923/25, Uppsala: Almqvist & Wiksell, 1926.

87 R. Bell, *The Origin of Islam in its Christian Environment: The Gunning Lectures,* Islam and the Muslim World, no. 10, Edinburgh University 1925, London: Macmillan & Co. Ltd., 1926.

88 R. Blachère, *Le problème de Mahomet*, Paris: Presses Universitaires de France, 1952.

figure he is often though to be. On the contrary, at many crucial points, our sources are entirely silent, and throughout others, their reliability and the method of their use are so much in doubt, that little can be said with certainty.

With regard to the biographies of the Prophet Muḥammad published in the last decades one should note the important contribution of Martin Lings (1909-2005), an English writer and scholar. His work *Muhammad: His Life Based on the Earliest Sources* is an internationally acclaimed, comprehensive, and authoritative account of the life of the Prophet. It is based on the eighth- and ninth-century Arabic biographical sources (the *sīra*) that recount numerous events from the Prophet's life.[89] *Muhammad: His Life Based on the Earliest Sources* is presented in a narrative style that is easily comprehensible but at the same time, scrupulous and exhaustive in its fidelity to its sources. Furthermore, the revised edition, which includes the final updates made to the text before the author's death in 2005, includes new sections discussing Muḥammad's expanding influence and his spreading of the message of Islam into Syria and its neighboring states. The book has been published in 12 languages and has received numerous awards.

[89] M. Lings, *Muhammad: His Life Based on the Earliest Sources*, Rochester, VT.: Inner Traditions, 2006. The book was first published in 1983 and still in print.

II

State and Government during the Reign of the Ṭūlūnids (868-905)

Egypt conquered by the caliphate in the year 641, was regarded economically as the most important province in the empire.[90] This province was rich in goldmines, cotton, and papyrus and had fully developed its farming and weaving. This was a substantial source of revenue for the caliphate. Obviously, because of these important economic benefits Egypt was under very strict control from the beginning. Most of the revenue from the province was either sent to the caliph's treasury or went directly to the governor's pocket. Egypt was simultaneously treated as a transit point for the caliphate's escapades to North Africa and Spain. The economic exploitation of Egypt by the 'Umayyads[91] had a negative impact on its political aspirations. When

---

[90] This chapter presents a significant period in the Egyptian history; it portrays the reign of the Ṭūlūnids (868-905), the first Muslim dynasty of an independent governors and rulers of Egypt. In my presentation of the Ṭūlūnid state and government, I applied Ibn Khaldūn's theory of power-state. According to this theory I distinguished five phases in the development Ṭūlūnid regime and I analyzed them focusing on political, economic, social and cultural aspects. See: E. I. Rosenthal, "The Theory of the Power-State: Ibn Khaldūn's Study of Civilization," in: idem, *Political Thought in Medieval Islam: An Introductory Outline*, Cambridge: University Press, 1958.

[91] The 'Umayyads (661-750) the first great Muslim dynasty, based in Damascus. They transformed the Islamic state from a theocracy to an Arab monarchy. In 661 'Alī, the last Orthodox caliph was murdered and Mu'awiya, the governor of Syria, became the first 'Umayyad caliph who provided the essential centralization for the survival and continuing expansion of the Arab Empire. At its height, the 'Umayyad rule extended from the Atlantic coast of North Africa to India and from Central Asia to the Yemen. The success of the dynasty carried within it the seeds of its own destruction. The economic and social structure of the empire was dependent on the conquest of new lands. Therefore, any setbacks or reverses caused resentment and dissatisfaction. In addition, the secular nature of the dynasty aroused opposition amongst those in favor of a more theocratic state. In 747, a revolution against the 'Umayyads began in Khurassan and by 750 their regime was defeated and replaced by the rule of the 'Abbāsids, based in Iraq. Only one branch of the 'Umayyads survived by fleeing to Spain where the dynasty continued to rule until 1051. See: H. Kennedy, *The Prophet and the Age of the Caliphates, 600-1050*, London: Longman, 1986;

'Abbāsids[92] came to power, the situation did not change for the better because "the treasury of the caliphate was much more important than the development of the province as a political body."[93]

According to Ibn Khaldūn's theory of the power-state, "the economic and political developments go hand in hand."[94] This statement proved to be appropriate in the case of the Ṭūlūnids' example.

Up until the year 868, when Aḥmad Ibn Ṭūlūn (835-884) appeared on Egypt's political stage as a man of power and influences, the province was almost completely dependent on the caliphate. However, despite the financial exploitation, it remained relatively strong and stable as economic organism. This fact helped Aḥmad Ibn Ṭūlūn to execute with precision his brave political plan, namely to build, in only four years, powerful and practically independent state and government. The Western and Eastern historians consider Ibn Ṭūlūn a leader whose appearance on the political stage of Egypt brought significant and long-lasting changes in the province. One may say that he restored the magnificence of the ancient Egypt under the new, i.e., Islamic circumstances by applying in the province his own rules and laws. His strong political leadership together with his great achievements in realizing his vision of an independent state and government remains an interesting material for discussions and assessments.

The history of the Ṭūlūnid family, who practically independently governed Egypt from the year 968 to 905, focuses on the careers of its first two prominent members, namely Aḥmad Ibn Ṭūlūn Abu-l-'Abbās born in Sāmarrā or Baghdād in

---

G. R. Hawting, *The First Dynasty of Islam: The Umayyad Caliphate, AD 661-750*, London–New York: Routledge, 2000; A. Bewley, *Mu'awiya, Restorer of the Muslim Faith*, London: Dar Al Taqwa, 2002; M. Gordon, *The Rise of Islam*, Westport, CT: Greenwood Press, 2005. Also refer to: D. Madeyska, *Historia świata arabskiego: Okres klasyczny od starożytności do końca epoki Umajjadów (750)*, Warszawa: Wydawnictwa Uniwersytetu Warszawskiego, 1999.

[92] The 'Abbāsids (750-1258), the second dynasty in Islam was founded by the descendant of the Prophet Muḥammad's youngest uncle, 'Abbās Ibn 'Abd al-Muttalib (566–653), in Kufa in 750. In 762, the 'Abbāsids moved their capital to Baghdād. Within 150 years of gaining control of Persia, the caliphs were forced to cede power to local dynastic emirs who only nominally acknowledged their authority. The 'Abbāsid historical period lasting to 1258 (Mongol conquest of Baghdād) is considered the Islamic Golden Age. During this period the Muslim world became an intellectual center for science, philosophy, medicine and education. The 'Abbāsids promoted knowledge and established the House of Wisdom in Baghdād, where both Muslim and non-Muslim scholars sought to gather and translate the available works from the entire world into Arabic and Persian. They synthesized and significantly advanced the knowledge gained from the ancient Roman, Chinese, Indian, Persian, Egyptian, North African, Greek and Byzantine civilizations. See: H. Kennedy, *The Early Abbasid Caliphate: A Political History*, London–New York: Barnes and Noble, 1981; J. Lassner, *The Shaping of 'Abbāsid Rule*, Princeton, N.J.: Princeton University Press, 1980; A. K. Bennison, *The Great Caliphs: The Golden Age of the Abbasid Empire*, London: Tauris, 2009. Also refer to: J. Hauziński, *Burzliwe dzieje Kalifatu Bagdadzkiego*, Warszawa–Kraków: Wydawnictwo Naukowe PWN, 1993.

[93] J. Danecki, "Dynastia Tulunidów," *As-Sadaka*, vol. 27 (November 1983), p. 33.

[94] E. I. Rosenthal, "The Theory of the Power-State..., p. 91.

835 and his son Khumārawayh who succeded his father in 884.[95] According to Jalāl al-Dīn al-Suyūṭī[96], Aḥmad Ibn Ṭūlūn was the son of a young Turkish slave Kassima (or Mashima).[97] Other historians, including Al-Balawī, claim that Aḥmad was not the son of Ṭūlūn[98] but according to their information, Kassima was a slave of Ṭūlūn and when Aḥmad was born Ṭūlūn decided to adopt him.[99]

Aḥmad received his military training in Sāmarrā and afterwards studied theology and law in Ṭarsūs. He attended lessons from great theologians, jurists, and philosophers. It is worth noting that Aḥmad's taste for these lessons was augmentative. He desired to study with the greatest scholars and, therefore, requested from the first minister of the caliph, permission to leave the court and devote more time for his studies.[100]

In the year 868, Ibn Ṭūlūn obtained from the governor of Egypt Bāyakbāk, his father-in-law, a position of deputy governor, i.e., the military commander. When he entered Al-Fusṭāṭ to assume the office, Ibn al-Mudabbir came to receive him surrounded by his usual escort. In order to secure his "friendship" with the new military commander, Ibn al-Mudabbir offered Aḥmad Ibn Ṭūlūn 10,000 dinars.[101] The new deputy governor refused the gold and instead asked for the one hundred slaves who followed Ibn al-Mudabbir. This was the first smart move on Ibn Ṭūlūn's path towards obtaining power and independence in Egypt.

It is worth noting that the political conditions in the province during the discussed period suited his aspirations. The governors were fearful of loosing their profitable relations with the caliphs, and they preferred the court life in Sāmarrā or Baghdād to their provincial residence. Therefore, in the absence of the governor it was much easier for Aḥmad Ibn Ṭūlūn to realize his ambitious political plan, that is, to gradually gain the uncontrolled power over the province. During this period, characterized

---

[95] See: J.-J. Marcel, *Égypte depuis la conquête des arabes jusqu'à la domination française*, Paris: Firmin Didot, 1848, p. 53-82. Also refer to: Z. M. Hasan, *Les Tulunides: étude de l'Egypte musulmane a la fin du IX siècle: 868-905*, Paris: Busson, 1933.

[96] Jalāl al-Dīn al-Suyūṭī (1445-1505), a famous Egyptian historian, philosopher, jurist and theologian, known as Ibn al-Kutub (the son of books) was also a writer, religious scholar, juristic expert and teacher whose works deal with a wide variety of issues concerning Islamic theology.

[97] According to Al-Balawī the name was Qāsim (Al-Balawī, *Sīrat Aḥmad bin Ṭūlūn*, ed. by M. Kurd ᶜAlī, Damascus, 1939, p. 33). See also Ibn Khaldūn, *Ta'rīkh*, vol. 4, p. 385, where the slave's name is Nāsim.

[98] Ṭūlūn (Tolun), was a Turkish slave from Bukhara. He was sent by the governor of Bukhara with the tribute to the caliph Al-Ma'mun.

[99] For a thorough account on the life of Aḥmad Ibn Ṭūlūn, including the history of the family, refer to: Al-Balawī, *Sīrat Aḥmad bin Ṭūlūn*. The manuscript was discovered in about 1935 by Muḥammad Kurd 'Alī. He edited it with a long introduction and useful commentary. The book was published in 1939 in Damascus. ('Abd Allāh Ibn Muḥammad al-Balawī, known as Al-Balawī was a tenth-century Egyptian historian about whom there is little information.

[100] J.-J. Marcel, *Égypte depuis la conquête...*, p. 55-56.

[101] Ibid., p. 62.

by Ibn Ṭūlūn's rising power and influence, one witnesses the first three phases of the state,s development, as described by Ibn Khaldūn's theory of the power-state:

> The first phase is that in which the new group bent on domination, gains its objective and is victorious over its enemies, seizes the reins of power and wrests it from the ruling dynasty. In this phase the ruler is the exemplary leader of his men to gain authority, acquire property, defend, and protect the newly gained territory...In the second phase he becomes sovereign and alone exercises rule without his followers...The third phase is one of quiet ease and leisure to gather the fruits of rule and domination, since human nature tends to acquire wealth and to leave behind...fame.[102]

From the year 868 and throughout the next four years, Aḥmad Ibn Ṭūlūn engaged himself in various endeavors to remove Ibn al-Mudabbir, the powerful and skilful intendant of finances, whose intolerably cunning exactions and greed had earned the hatred of the Egyptians and to obtain the control over the administration. The two men fought out mainly through the medium of their agents and "connections" at Sāmarrā, and, eventually, their struggle resulted in the removal of Ibn al-Mudabbir.[103]

In 870, after the murder of Bāyakbāk,Yārjūkh was appointed as governor of Egypt. He married off one of his daughters to Ibn Ṭūlūn and confirmed him in his post as vice-governor. Yārjūkh also invested Aḥmad Ibn Ṭūlūn with the authority to govern Alexandria and Barqa.

The government established by Aḥmad Ibn Ṭūlūn was based on a strong and highly disciplined army of Turkish and Negro slaves as well as Greek mercenaries.[104] The initial step towards the creation of the Ṭūlūnid army came in 870, with the revolt of 'Īsā Ibn Shaykh, the governor of Palestine. This revolt gave Ibn Ṭūlūn the opportunity to obtain the caliph's authorization to purchase a large number of slaves in order to subjugate the rebels. For the first time, Egypt possessed its own military force, completely independent of the caliphate. The annual cost of its upkeep amounted to 9000.000 dinars.[105] Apart from establishing a new army, Ibn Ṭūlūn also focused on strengthening the fleet by constructing new naval defenses and stations.[106]

Within a few years, Aḥmad Ibn Ṭūlūn gained almost uncontrolled power in the province and practically built "a state inside a state." He skillfully consolidated his position by regular remittances of substantial tributes, which satisfied the caliph's treasury.[107] In this way Ibn Ṭūlūn gained the favor of the 'Abbāsid courtiers. It was

---

[102] E. I. Rosenthal, "The Theory of the Power-State..., p. 87.

[103] J.-J. Marcel, *Égypte depuis la conquête...*, p. 66.

[104] According Al-Ya'qūbī, during the ceremony held in 871 Ibn Ṭūlūn had his forces swear personal allegiance to him. See: S. and N. Ronart, *Concise Encyclopedia of Arabic Civilization*, Amsterdam: Djambatan, 1959, p. 536-539.

[105] H. A. R. Gibb, "Ṭūlūnids," in: *The Encyclopaedia of Islam*, vol. IV, no. 2, p. 834; M. S. Gordon, "Ṭūlūnids," *The Encyclopaedia of Islam*, New Edition, vol. 10, p. 616-618.

[106] In order to maintain his hold in Syria, he built a naval base at 'Akkā.

[107] On at least two occasions, namely in 871 and 875-876 Ibn Ṭūlūn remitted considerable sums of revenue, along with gifts, to the 'Abbāsid central administration. See: G. M. Frantz,

to Ibn Ṭūlūn, and not to Ibn Al-Mudabbir's successor, that the caliph Al-Mu'tamid (870-892) addressed his requests for Egyptian contributions to the treasury. Furthermore, Al-Mu'tamid placed the financial administration of Egypt and the Syrian Marches under Ibn Ṭūlūn, so he could personally monitor them by keeping their total worth a secret from his brother Al-Muwaffaq.

Aḥmad Ibn Ṭūlūn's success resulted from both his intelligent and perfectly executed plan and from the political difficulties of the 'Abbāsids. Caliph Al-Mu'tamid had recognized his brother Al-Muwaffaq as heir to the throne after his own son Ja'far (later named Al-Muwaffad) and had divided the empire between the two presumptive heirs. Al-Muwaffaq received the Eastern provinces as an apanage and Al-Muwaffad the Western provinces. This decision gave Al-Muwaffaq supreme power. One should also point out that in those days the caliphate was frequently threatened in the East by various attacks and independence movements. Especially dangerous was the revolt of the Zinj in the South that required intervention of large military forces of the caliphate and, in particular, the forces of Al-Muwaffaq.[108] In addition, Al-Muwaffaq, the only man capable to stand against Ibn Ṭūlūn's growing power and influences, was troubled by several threats, such as the disorders in the administration, the internal conflicts between the caliph and himself, and by the doubtful loyalty on the part of the captains of Turkish regiments.

In order to strengthen his power in Egypt Ibn Ṭūlūn established an excellent intelligence service, providing him with valuable information on all the intrigues spun against him. It is also worth noting that Aḥmad Ibn Ṭūlūn was attentive to the needs of the common people. He paid considerable attention to assure the respect for human rights, such as the freedom of belief, individual responsibility, right to justice, protection of life, etc.[109]

Ibn Ṭūlūn's government was based on the three important offices – the governor, the vice-governor and the intendant of the finances. As for the governor, he was the figurehead because he spent most of the time at the caliph's court in Sāmarrā or Baghdād. The position of the vice-governor, i.e., the deputy was taken by Aḥmad Ibn Ṭūlūn. He was the real head of state and government in the province of Egypt. The third important office was that of the intendant of the finances, i.e., the head of the administration. This office was also controlled by Aḥmad Ibn Ṭūlūn. Taking into consideration a few important facts – that the governor was most of the time absent in Egypt, that the control over the administration practically gave Aḥmad Ibn Ṭūlūn an "independence," and that both political and economic situation in the caliphate was unstable – one may conclude that under the circumstances Ibn Ṭūlūn's power could seriously undermine the 'Abbāsid authority.

Saving and Investment, Ph.D. dissertation, Ann Arbor, MI: 1978, p. 54-58. In his research, Frantz relied extensively on the analysis of surviving papyri and cited from the research of N. Abbot and A. Grohmann.

108 J.-J. Marcel, *Égypte depuis la conquête*..., p. 69.

109 J. Danecki, "Dynastia Tulunidów..., p. 34.

As previously mentioned, according to Ibn Khaldūn, "the economic and political developments go hand in hand."[110] Therefore, the prosperity of Egypt under Ibn Ṭūlūn was due principally to his consolidated power. He was in a position to refuse sending extra financial assistance to the caliph and used to send him only the previously agreed-upon amounts of money.

The reign of Aḥmad Ibn Ṭūlūn brought progressive changes in the province. His agrarian and administrative reforms encouraged the peasants to cultivate their lands with zeal, despite the heavy charges on their production. It is also worth noting that Ibn Ṭūlūn put an end to the exaction of the taxes and other charges by the officers of the fiscal administration, who used them for their personal profit. Because of the strict control, the greater part of the province's revenue remained in Egypt. Therefore, Aḥmad Ibn Ṭūlūn had at his disposal enough money to invest in order to stimulate the administration and develop commerce and industry.[111]

As for the Ṭūlūnid administrative system in Egypt, one may notice in its development a few important features. The chancery (*diwān al-insha*) was based on the model of the chancery of the 'Abbāsids. In order to keep good relation with the local population, Aḥmad Ibn Ṭūlūn held regular public sessions for people from other religions. In addition, Jews and Christians were employed in the administration. Ibn Ṭūlūn replaced Irāqī officials with the local Egyptian bureaucracy.[112] A number of famous jurists worked on regulations concerning the law and administration for Ibn Ṭūlūn's government. *The Fihrist of Al-Nadīm* informs us that Al-Ṭaḥāwī (a famous jurist from Irāq) "worked over [sic] a book for Aḥmad Ibn Ṭūlūn about marriage of the lawfully owned, in which he made lawful for him marriage of slaves."[113]

As for the Ṭūlūnid economic and financial policies, Aḥmad relied on the powerful merchant community for both financial and diplomatic support. According to Frantz, the important evidence points to a stable and prosperous economy closely administered by the Egyptian bureaucracy and propitious levels of agricultural production blessed by consistent high flooding.[114] The strength of the Ṭūlūnid economy resulted from a complex of long-term socio-economic factors and more immediate reforms on the part of Ibn al-Mudabbir in the period prior to Ibn Ṭūlūn's appointment and the Ṭūlūnid administration itself. The measures in question included changes in the tax assessment and the collection system, an expansion in the use of tax-contracts (itself the source of an emerging land-holding élite in this period), and investment and repairs in the agricultural infrastructure. It is worth noting that the key sector

---

[110] E. I. Rosenthal, "The Theory of the Power-State..., p. 91.

[111] The historical sources confirmed a significant increase of revenue from *kharaj*. In addition to the income from *kharaj*, the treasury received the annual rent from *al-amlāk* (the royal domains), which were administrated in the name of the governor of Egypt. Ibid., p. 835.

[112] G. M. Frantz, *Saving and Investment*, Ph. D. diss., Ann Arbor, MI: 1978, p. 267.

[113] B. Dodge (ed. and trans.), *The Fihrist of Al-Nadim*, vol. 1, New York–London: Columbia University Press, 1970, p. 512.

[114] G. M. Frantz. *Saving and Investment...*, p. 280.

of production, investment, and participation in Mediterranean-wide commerce was textiles and in particular, the production of linen.[115]

Public projects initiated by Aḥmad Ibn Ṭūlūn reflected both practical and ideological concerns and were primarily focused on the development of Al-Fusṭāṭ and its environs. Ibn Ṭūlūn decided to change the architectonic plan of the city, refashion the streets and markets, and build a hospital, aqueduct, and beautiful houses.[116] On the canal, which crosses the city of Cairo today, he built the bridge, i.e., the "Bridge of Lions." There he founded the citadel, distributed the portions of lands to his army officers, and ordered them to build houses and to live there. In this new district called Al-Qaṭā'i', Ibn Ṭūlūn founded a beautiful palace in which the seat of his government was located.[117] Al-Qaṭā'i' soon became a largely inhabited and lively district, full of markets, shops, and gardens.[118] As for Ibn Ṭūlūn private residence, he lived in Al-'Askar district, in a palace with a beautiful view of the Al-Moqaṭṭam hills.

Regarding the cultural life of Egypt, the Ṭūlūnid regime introduced a number of positive changes. The ruler, who had received a liberal education, showed himself as a keen patron of learning and of the arts. He encouraged the development of education in Egypt. It is worth noting that a trace of his activities concerning the cultural matters can be found in a document related to the endowment of a mosque-school at Ushmunain.[119] Ibn Ṭūlūn, and later his son Khumārawayh, like all the enlightened rulers took care not only to pleased the people by free distribution of food or entertainment spectacles, but also by elevating their hardship and by improving their economic status. One may say that by assuring the support of the local population, the Ṭūlūnids were able to protect their interests.

When Aḥmad Ibn Ṭūlūn strengthened his position as a powerful, independent, and sovereign ruler, he even felt strong enough to organize military campaigns in order to conquer new territories and extend his rule over Syria, Palestine, and the frontier zone with Byzantium.[120] The initial steps towards rule over Syria and of the frontier zone with Byzantium included two Ibn Ṭūlūn's campaigns of, i.e., in 878 and 882, during which he secured the allegiance of the military governors in major Syrian cities, with the exception of Ṭarsūs. He proclaimed himself the governor of Damascus and left his lieutenant Lu'Lu', a former Turkish slave, in command of the city. In addition, Aḥmad Ibn Ṭūlūn gained control over a new naval base at 'Akkā which considerably increased his military and financial resources. However, it also

115 Ibid., p. 281-285.

116 See: J.-J. Marcel. *Égypte depuis la conquête…*, p. 66-68.

117 Ibid., p. 74.

118 Ibid., p. 65.

119 H. A. R. Gibb, "Ṭūlūnids…, p. 836.

120 Ahmadjur, the governor of Syria, wrote a letter to the caliph Al-Mu'tamid saying that the military forces of Aḥmad Ibn Ṭūlūn increased dangerously. After this Ibn Ṭūlūn received an order from the caliph to come to Sāmarrā immediately. Instead, he sent Aḥmad Al-Wāsiṭī there, his secretary and a key member of his inner circle. See: J.-J. Marcel, *Égypte depuis la conquête…*, p. 70.

brought Aḥmad into an open conflict with his sovereign and involved him in all the unrests and antagonisms.[121] Despite the fact that the conquest of Syria added to Ibn Ṭūlūn's army new forces, it did not result in strengthening its ties with Egypt. It is also worth noting that in 878, Aḥmad Ibn Ṭūlūn had to face another challenge which seriously threatened the stability of his position. The revolt of his son 'Abbās on the Syrian-Byzantine border resulted in defections of high-ranking officers, and in particular, that of Lu'Lu' to Al-Muwaffaq.[122]

However, despite the surfacing difficulties, Aḥmad Ibn Ṭūlūn was still strong enough to manifest his power and independent authority. After the Syrian campaign, he began to add his own name to those of the caliph and the governor on the golden coins.[123] Furthermore, in order to demonstrate his supreme power and independence, he built his mosque in a newly established quarter of Al-Qaṭā'i'. The famous tower of Aḥmad Ibn Ṭūlūn's mosque combines some features borrowed from the Sāmarrān architecture as well as from some local patterns.[124]

In 882, Ibn Ṭūlūn invited the nearly powerless Caliph Al-Mu'tamid to Egypt offering him protection against his brother Al-Muwaffaq, who had been given authority over Baghdād by Al-Mu'tamid. Unfortunately, Al-Muta'mid was intercepted *en route* to Egypt, and Ibn Ṭūlūn and Al-Muwaffaq began an endless campaign against each other.[125] Being afraid of Ibn Ṭūlūn's growing power and political aspirations, Al-Muwaffaq decided to appoint Ishak Ibn Kundadj as governor of Egypt and Syria. In response, Ibn Ṭūlūn had a group of prominent jurists declare Al-Muwaffaq an usurper. In addition, both leaders had the each other cursed during Friday prayers. Al-Muwaffaq compelled the caliph to have Aḥmad cursed in the mosques in Mesopotamia, while Aḥmad had the same measures applied to Al-Muwaffaq in the mosques of Egypt and Syria.[126] However Al-Muwaffaq, although finally victorious in his war with the Zinj, decided to employ some diplomatic steps to reach a compromising agreement with Ibn Ṭūlūn, which was to achieve what he had failed to gain by an open conflict with him. Al-Muwaffaq's first diplomatic approaches met with posi-

---

[121] J. Danecki, "Dynastia Tulunidów..., p. 34-35.

[122] M. S. Gordon, "Ṭūlūnids..., p. 617.

[123] D. Sourdel, "Aḥmad B. Ṭūlūn," in: *Encyclopaedia of Islam*, New Edition, vol. 1, p. 279. See: O. Grabar, *The Coinage of The Tulunids*, New York: American Numismatic Society, 1957.

[124] The Mosque of Aḥmad Ibn Ṭūlūn is the most probably the oldest in the city surviving in its original form.

Al-Maqrīzī lists the mosque's construction start date as 876 and the mosque's original inscription slab identifies the date of completion as 879 (Al-Maqrīzī, *Khiṭaṭ*, II, p. 265). See: J.-J. Marcel, *Égypte depuis la conquête...*, p. 71-73.

It took two years to build the mosque (875-877). The cost of the whole construction was about 120,000 dinars. In the mosque Aḥmad Ibn Ṭūlūn placed a frieze contain the verses from Qur'ān. See: D. Behrens-Abouseif, *Islamic Architecture in Cairo: An Introduction*, Cairo: American University in Cairo Press, 1989; N. Warner, *The Monuments of Historic Cairo: A Map and Descriptive Catalogue*. Cairo: American University in Cairo Press, 2005.

[125] See: J.-J. Marcel, *Égypte depuis la conquête...*, p. 79-81.

[126] J. Danecki, "Dynastia Tulunidów..., p. 34-35.

tive response from Ibn Ṭūlūn. In March of 884, the negotiations were broken off by the sudden death of Ibn Ṭūlūn.

Although Aḥmad Ibn Ṭūlūn, and later his son Khumārawayh, did not spare their efforts to gain support of the religious leaders, the difficulties encountered by their state and government were, at times, increased by a certain tension with the theologians. During the conflicts between the Ṭūlūnids and the caliphate, the religious leaders usually sided with the caliph and regarded Aḥmad and Khumārawayh as usurpers.[127]

Aḥmad Ibn Ṭūlūn was succeded by his son Khumārawayh, who continued his father's policy of and pursued the process of reforms.[128] Although the political situation remained relatively stable, Khumārawayh had to face the invasion of Syria by Al-Muwaffaq aimed at separating Syria from Egypt and, consequently inhibiting the expansion of the Ṭūlūnids. During the year 885 the 'Abbāsid army conquered Damascus. In response, Khumārawayh went with his troops to Syria and soon regained areas conquered by Al-Muwaffaq. It is worth noting that both political and military gains enabled Khumārawayh to extend Egyptian authority into the Jazīra and finally (in 890) over Ṭarsūs. As mentioned by Haarman, the two treaties negotiated with the 'Abbāsids during the discussed period, indicate the extent of the Ṭūlūnids' prominence in the near Eastern political stage.[129] The first treaty, reached with Al-Muwaffaq in 886, recognized the formal Ṭūlūnid authority over Egypt and the regions of Syria for a period of thirty years in exchange for a trifling tribute.[130] The second treaty, negotiated with the new caliph Al-Mu'taḍid in 892, confirmed the terms of the earlier accord. However, one should also note that both treaties also included provisions confirming the status of the Egyptian governor as a vassal of the 'Abbāsids.

During the first period of Khumārawayh's reign, the power of the Ṭūlūnids reached its apogee. At that time, the "fourth phase" of Ibn Khaldūn's power-state could be observed:

> the ruler is satisfied with what his predecessors have built up, lives in peace with friendly and hostile rulers of his kind and imitates his precursors...as well as he can.[131]

Aḥmad Ibn Ṭūlūn left his successor with a tremendous inheritance. According to information from Ibn Taghrībirdī,[132] the heritage included 70,000 mamlūks and

---

127 H. A. R. Gibb, "Ṭūlūnids..., p. 835.

128 See: U. Haarman, "Khumārawayh B. Aḥmad B. Ṭūlūn," in: *The Encyclopaedia of Islam*, New Edition, vol. 5, p. 49-50; Ibn Khaldūn, *Ta'rīkh*, vol. 4, p. 396.

129 Ibid., p. 49.

130 H. A. R. Gibb, "Ṭūlūnids..., p. 834.

131 E. I. Rosenthal, "The Theory of the Power-State..., p. 89.

132 Ibn Taghrībirdī (1411-1469) was a famous Egyptian historian born into a family of Turkish Mamlūk élite of the 15th century Cairo. He studied under Al-'Aynī and Al-Maqrīzī, two of the leading Cairene historians and scholars of the day. His most famous work is a multi-volume chronicle of Egypt and the Mamluk sultanate called *Nujūm al-ẓāhira fī mulūk Miṣr wa'l-Qāhira.*

24,000 other soldiers, 10 millions dinārs in gold (yearly income – one-milion dinārs in gold), and in addition, 7,000 horses and 6,000 donkeys.[133]

The financial matters were still under the control of Aḥmad Ibn Ṭūlūn's right-hand man Aḥmad al-Wāsiṭī. The administrative system, established by Ibn Ṭūlūn, functioned quite well. In the first period of his reign, Khumārawayh continued the political line of his father. He developed the province especially in the sphere of commerce, agriculture, and textile industry. Furthermore, he pursued the task of modernizing the irrigation system in Egypt, cleaning the canal of Alexandria and building wells to bring drinking water for the city population. Like his father, he paid considerable attention to the development of education and culture. It is also worth noting that Khumārawayh's profound interest in painting, music and sculpture contributed to the flourishing of local arts and crafts.[134]

During the second period of his reign, Khumārawayh focused more on his private life than on politics. The expenses for his court, the construction and decoration of the palace, and the pleasure gardens, depicted by his biographers exhausted the treasury, demoralized the civil administration and dangerously weakened the army. As an example to his extravagance, one should mention the wedding of his twelve-year-old daughter with the new caliph Mu'taḍid. The beauty of the bride and the magnificent dowry of Khumārawayh's daughter Qatr al-Nadā are still remembered in many popular tales.[135]

In this period of his reign began the fifth phase of Ibn Khaldūn's power-state:

> This fifth phase is one of extravagances and waste. In this phase, the ruler destroys what his ancestors have brought together, for the sake and pleasure. For he is generous towards his intimates and liberal at his banquets in order to win…the scum of the people, whom he entrusts with great tasks which they are unable to the noble and distinguished among his people and with the followers of his predecessors, so that they are filled with hatred against him and agree among themselves to desert him. Moreover, he loses part of his troops because he spends their pay on his pleasures and prevents them from getting to know him personally…In this phase the natural aging of the dynasty (that is, the decay) sets in; a chronic disease gets hold of it without remedy or release until it collapses.[136]

At that time, the financial administration began to deteriorate. Although the historical sources did not preserve the details, the symptoms of a downfall of the Ṭūlūnid state could be inferred from both the overall situation in the government and from the actions of Khumārawayh observed during the second period of his reign.

---

133 J. Danecki, "Dynastia Tulunidów…, p. 33.

134 H. A. R. Gibb, "Ṭūlūnids…, p. 836.

135 There is no doubt that the dowry of some 400,000 dīnars, brought by Khumārawayh's daughter Qatr al-Nadā to her wedding heavily drained the Ṭūlūnid treasury. See: G. M. Frantz, *Saving and Investment…*, p. 67.

136 E. I. Rosenthal, "The Theory of the Power-State…, p. 89.

As for the major symptoms of the Ṭūlūnids' downfall, one underline: (1) the gradual decline of discipline in the civil administration and the army, (2) the expenses exceeding the possibilities of the government, (3) the numerous intrigues at the court, including a plot to kill the ruler and (4) the easygoing attitude towards the *amīrs* in allowing them a free hand in the management of their estates. In conclusion, at the death of Khumārawayh, the state and government established by his father Aḥmad Ibn Ṭūlūn was in the process of disintegration, and the downfall of the Ṭūlūnid dynasty was only a question of time.[137]

With time, the situation was getting worse and the intrigues inside the army and between the successors and Khumārawayh's family increased. The atmosphere in the army changed and some fractions inside of it began to fight each other in order to rule and gain power.[138] Khumārawayh's son Ibn ʿAsākir Jaysh who in the year 895 succeeded his father was deposed by his brother Harūn. During the reign of Harūn Ibn Khumārawayh (896-904), the central government lost almost all control of the army dominated by the Greek mercenaries.

The disturbances and intrigues inside the army and between the successors and family of Khumārawayh constituted a threat for the survival of the dynasty. The Qarmatians, the *shī'a* sect based in Syria became strong and politically influential.[139] The actions of the Qarmatians posed a serious threat not only for the Ṭūlūnids but even also for the caliphate. The sectarians rejected all Muslim authorities. The Ṭūlūnid army attempted to eliminate this dangerous movement. However, Harūn involved in private intrigues and deserted by some of his best generals was not able to lead a successful campaign while the well-organized and determined Qarmatians spread destruction all over Syria.

In the case of the Ṭūlūnid dynasty, one may agree with the following statement of Ibn Khaldūn:

> The dynasty has a natural term of life like an individual....term of life of a dynasty does not normally exceed three generations. In the first generation there are still preserved the characteristic features of rough, uncivilized rural life (*badawa*), such as hard conditions life, courage, ferocity and partnership in authority...Therefore the strength of the*'asabiya* is maintained ...and men submit to their domination. In the second generation their condition have changed, under the influence of the rule (*mulk*)... from rural to city-life, from struggle to ease and abundance, from partnership in authority to generation that has forgotten the time of *badawa*...as if it had never existed – unlike the second generation which lives on the memory of the first – and loses the sweetness of force and *'asabiya* because they are in possession of power. Ease reaches

---

[137] J. Danecki, "Dynastia Tulunidów..., p. 35.

[138] The principal commanders in Egypt, namely, Badr, Safi and Fa'ik, each obtained control of a portion of the troops and drew on the revenues of the state for their upkeep. For example, the general Tughdj Ibn Djuff was practically independent in Damascus.

[139] The Qarmatians (Arabic: *Qarāmita* "Those Who Wrote in Small Letters") were a *shī'a* Ismā'īlī group based in eastern Arabia, where in 899, they attempted to establish an utopian republic.

its peak under them because they become used to a pleasant and abundant life...The *'asabiya* collapses completely, and they forget about defense, attack and pursuit (of the enemy).[140]

The political and economic difficulties of the Ṭūlūnids during the reign of Harūn Ibn Khumārawayh led the caliph Al-Muktafi (902-908) to organize a campaign to reconquer Egypt. The 'Abbāsid fleet attacked the Ṭūlūnid fleet on the Mediterranean Sea, and in the year 904, near Tinnis, they destroyed it completely. Two of the caliph Al-Muktafi's armies, one advancing through Iraq and Palestine and the other landing at Damietta conquered Al-Fusṭāṭ, and the fortress-residence of the Ṭūlūnids in the district of Al-Qaṭā'i' was completely destroyed. Although Harūn had managed to escape from Tinnis, his cousins who had waited to kill him in Egypt. One of the murderers, namely Shaybān, even went to Al-Fusṭāṭ to declare himself governor. However, the soldiers rejected his authority asking the 'Abbāsids for help. Twelve days later, the 'Abbāsid army entered Al-Fusṭāṭ. Shaybān was deposed in 905. The army plundered the city and the inhabitants were treated with extreme cruelty. The surviving males of the Ṭūlūnid family were carried in chains to Baghdād and kept there in secret.[141]

Ṭūlūnid's short-lived regime (868-905) holds a significant place in the history of Egypt. Since the days of Cleopatra, it was practically the first independent regime, and for the first time it extended Egyptian rule over Syria. The new Islamic government established by Aḥmad Ibn Ṭūlūn brought fundamental changes in the province concerning political and economic aspects, developed social life, and influenced culture, arts, and literature. Through his bravery, unusual organizing ability, rare spirit and personality, Aḥmad Ibn Ṭūlūn built a practically independent state and government, in a relatively short period of time. His great vision helped him achieve a success for which usually few generations have to work. Unfortunately, his successors (except Khumārawayh in the first period of his reign) were not able to carry on with his great plan, and after forty years of rule, the Ṭūlūnid dynasty had to leave. However, one may agree with Muslim and Western historians that in the history of Egypt the Ṭūlūnid period was one of marked material prosperity and progress for the local population and was later recalled as the Golden Age:

Kānat min ghurari 'l-duwali wa-ayyāmuhum min maḥāsini 'l-ayyām (They were numbered among the most brilliant of dynasties, and their days among the most beneficient of days).[142]

---

[140] E. I. Rosenthal, "The Theory of the Power-State..., p. 88.
[141] Ibn Khaldūn, *Ta'rīkh*, vol. 4, p. 402-403.
[142] H. A. R. Gibb, "Ṭūlūnids..., p. 836.

III

Between "Islamic Sciences" and Ṣūfism: Al-Ghazālī's Quest for the Truth

Islamic philosophy (*al-falsafa*) has been one of the major intellectual traditions in the Islamic world, and it has influenced and been influenced by many other intellectual perspectives including scholastic theology (*kalām*) and doctrinal Ṣūfism (*al-ma'arifa*). It developed as a result of Muslim philosophical reflection on the heritage of Greco-Alexandrian philosophy. During the period from the eight to tenth centuries in Baghdād, under the patronage of the 'Abbāsids, the more or less correct translations of philosophical treaties of Plato, Aristotle, Neo-Platonists (predominantly Plotinus) into Arabic were prepared.[143] These translations gave Muslim scholars, immersed in the teachings of the Qur'ān and living in a universe in which revelation was a central reality, the basis and the starting point to prepare original commentaries and eventually their own original philosophical systems. In contrast to the Greeks, Muslim philosophers focused on "prophetic philosophy." The Qur'ān, as well as the *ḥadīth*, served as the central source of Islamic philosophical speculation for centuries. In later Islamic philosophy the sayings of the Shī 'ī imam also played a major role. Far from being simply Greek philosophy in Arabic, Persian or Turkish, Islamic philosophy integrated certain elements of Greek philosophy into the Islamic perspective, creating new philosophical schools. One may say that Islamic philosophy became an original and productive assimilation of Greek thought created by open-minded scholars of very different cultural traditions, including Arabic, Persian, Turkish, as well as an attempt to make a "foreign," namely Greek element an integral part of Islamic tradition.

Abū Ḥāmid Muḥammad Ibn Muḥammad al-Ghazālī (1055–1111) was one of the most prominent and influential philosophers, theologians, jurists, and mystics of

---

[143] See: R. Walzer, *Greek into Arabic: Essays on Islamic Philosophy*, Cambridge: Harvard University Press, 1962.

Sunni Islam.[144] He occupies a unique position in the history of Islamic thought and his contribution to its development is tremendous. Al-Ghazālī was active at a time when Sunni theology had just passed through its consolidation and had entered a period of intense challenges from both the Shī'a Ismā'īlite theology and the Arabic tradition of Aristotelian philosophy (*falsafa*). In his worldview, he combined an extensive knowledge, a deep spirituality, a rigid fundamentalism and an extraordinary independence of mind that enabled him to become a veritable challenge to philosophies of Aristotle, Plotinus and their Muslim followers, namely Al-Fārābī and Ibn Sīnā. Al-Ghazālī understood the importance of *falsafa* and developed a complex response that rejected and condemned some elements of its teaching, while also allowing him to accept and apply part of it. Al-Ghazālī's critique of twenty points of *falsafa* in his *Incoherence of the Philosophers* (*Tahāfut al-falāsifa*) is a significant landmark in the history of philosophy, as it advances the nominal critique of Aristotelian science developed later in 14th century Europe.

Al-Ghazālī's teaching, originality and influence cannot be fully understood without knowing the story of his life in a socio-political context. He was born in the town of Ṭūs, near modern Mashhad in Eastern Iran. His life can be divided into three major periods. The first was the period of learning. Al-Ghazālī received his early education in his hometown. When he was fifteen, he went to Gorgān, a place in the south-east corner of the Caspian Sea, to continue his studies. Subsequently, at the age of nineteen, he went to Nishapur to study at the important Niẓāmīya college under 'Abd al-Malik al-Juwaynī (died 1085), known as Imām al-Ḥaramayn, one of the leading religious scholars of the period. Although Al-Ghazālī focused on jurisprudence, he was also introduced to Ash'arī theology and encouraged to read the philosophy of Al-Fārābī and Ibn Sīnā (Avicenna). Later he helped with teaching at the College and was recognized as a rising scholar. After the death of his teacher Al-Juwaynī, Niẓām al-Mulk, the powerful vizier of the Seljūq Sultans invited him to join his court.

The second period of Al-Ghazālī's life was short (1091-1095) but of major significance. It was the time of his brilliant career as the highest-ranking orthodox "doctor" in the Islamic community in Baghdād. In 1091, when Al-Ghazālī was about thirty-three, he was appointed to the main professorship at the Niẓāmīya College there. During this time, he focused on both lecturing on Islamic jurisprudence and writings aiming at the refuting heresies and responding to questions from all segments of the community. In the political confusion following the assassination of Niẓām al-Mulk and the subsequent violent death of Sultan Malikshah, Al-Ghazālī himself fell into a serious spiritual crisis and finally left Baghdād, renouncing his career and the world.[145]

---

[144] For a thorough account on Al-Ghazālī's life and work refer to: E. Ormsby, *Ghazali: The Revival of Islam*, Oxford: Oneworld, 2008. Also see: H. Algar, *Imam Abu Hamid Ghazali: An Exponent of Islam in its Totality*, Oneonta, NY: iPi, 2001, p. 3-43; M. Marmura, *Probing in Islamic Philosophy: Studies in the Philosophies of Ibn Sīnā, Al-Ghazālī, and Other Major Muslim Thinkers*, Binghamton: Global Academic Pub., Binghamton University, 2005.

[145] About Al-Ghazālī's political theology see: Y. Said, *Ghazālī's Politics in Context*, Abingdon–Oxon–New York: Routledge, 2013.

This event marks the beginning of the third period of his life, that of retirement (1095-1111), but which also included a short period of teaching at the Niẓāmīya College in Nishapur.[146] After leaving Baghdād, he wandered as a Ṣūfī in Syria and Palestine before returning to Ṭūs, where he was engaged in writing, Ṣūfī practices and teaching his disciples until his death.

The inner development leading to his conversion is explained in his autobiography, *al-Munqidh min al-ḍalāl* (1108, The Deliverer from Error), which he wrote when he was about fifty. As he explained in his book, it was his habit from an early age to search for the truth. In the process, he came to doubt the senses and even reason itself as the means of attaining truth and fell into a deep skepticism that lasted about two months. However, he was eventually delivered from this with the aid of the divine light, and thus recovered his trust in reason. Al-Ghazālī's extensive studies in Islamic law, tradition, theology, philosophy and Ṣūfism, together with his long period of self--discipline led him, using his method described as that of "courage to know and the courage to doubt," to present his position with regard to various schools of Islamic thought of his days.[147] In his quest for the truth he carefully examined various "seekers after the truth," that is theologians,[148] philosophers, authoritarians (the Ismā'īlīs whom he called the party of *ta'līm* or authoritative instruction)[149] and finally the Ṣūfīs, or mystics.[150] Because of these studies, he reached the conclusion that there was no way to ascertain knowledge except through Ṣūfism. However, in order to reach this ultimate truth of the Ṣūfīs, it is necessary to renounce the world and to devote oneself to mystical practice. Al-Ghazālī came to this realization through an agonizing process of decision, which led to a nervous breakdown and finally to his departure from Baghdād.

The first encounter, according to this scheme, was with the *mutakallimūn*, that is the Ash'arī rational theologians by whom he was trained and among whom he was reckoned. In *Iḥya' 'ulūm al-dīn* (1096/7, *The Revival of the Religious Sciences*) he criticized the scholar-jurists, including theologians. According to Watt, Al-Ghazālī simply supported "the vigorous criticism of the worldliness of the rulers of the Islamic empire and of those scholars who were prepared to take office under such rulers" expressed on many occasions by the ascetic and mystical movement in Islam.[151] However, the vehemence of his expressions could suggest that this was more likely an expression of his strong personal feelings. In the preface to *The Revival of the Religious Sciences* Al-Ghazālī said:

---

[146] About the significance of learning institutions, such as college see: G. Makdisi, "Muslim Institutions of Learning in Eleventh-Century in Baghdad," *BSOAS*, vol. 24 (1961), p. 1-56: *The Rise of the Colleges*, Edinburgh, 1981.

[147] See: M.M. Sharif (ed.), *A History of Muslim Philosophy*, Karachi: Royal Book Co., 1983.

[148] A rather mild critique; he approved their conclusions but disapproved of their methods.

[149] He seriously doubted their methods.

[150] He approved their way (immediate experience) to attain the truth.

[151] W. M. Watt, *Muslim Intellectual: A Study of Al-Ghazali*, Edinburgh: Edinburgh University Press, 1963, p. 109.

> The science of the road of the world-to come, on the other hand, and the learning, wisdom, knowledge, illumination, light, guidance and direction as God calls them in scripture, by which the noble Muslims of old lived their lives, have become rejected among men and completely forgotten. Since this is a grave weakness in a religion and a black mark against it, I thought it is right to busy myself with composing this book, out of concern for the revival of the religious sciences, to show the practices to the former leaders, and to make clear the limits of the useful sciences in the eyes of the prophets and the noble Muslims of old.[152]

Throughout his book, Al-Ghazālī never allows his reader to forget his critical attitude towards the scholar-jurists of the day, including theologians, focusing on five key-points. He accuses them of (1) preoccupying themselves with worldly affairs instead of devoting their attention to the real vocation of religion, namely the preparation of man for the life of the world-to-come, (2) justifying their, at times, inappropriate conduct on religious grounds and (3) being primarily concerned with their professional qualifications as a means of gaining wealth, power, and position and thus infected by the worldliness of their rulers. Furthermore, he expresses his conviction that (4) the true scholar would have nothing to do with rulers, would not take offices from them, and instead should teach freely without any remuneration. Finally, he points out that (5) it is important not to forget that man's true destiny is the world-to-come, and in light of this, to allow the usefulness of each branch of religious knowledge to determine the extent to which it is studied.[153]

In *Al-munqidh min al-ḍalāl* (1108, *The Deliverer from Error*) Al-Ghazālī complains that the reasoning of the Ash'arī theologians is based on certain presuppositions and assumptions which they never try to justify, but which he cannot accept without some justification. In effect what happened was that he found in philosophy a way of justifying some of the bases of Ash'arī theology. This can be seen in *Al-Iqtiṣad fī al-I'tiqād* (1095, *The Golden Mean in Belief*),[154] where he introduces many philosophical arguments, including one for the existence of God. However, one should note that the theological position expressed in both *Al-Iqtiṣad fī al-I'tiqād* and his other important work, *Al-Risāla al-Qudsīya* (1097, *The Jerusalem Epistle*),[155] is Ash'arīte, and there is no fundamental difference between Al-Ghazālī and the Ash'arīte school.

From *Al-munqidh min al-ḍalāl* we may learn about his later, that is, after the period of crisis, attitude towards theology. In this book, Al-Ghazālī's views focused on two important points. First, he maintained that the aim of theologians was to defend dogma against heretical aberrations and innovations. Second, he accused them of failing to meet the logical demands of those who had studied Aristotelian logic, since their arguments were directed against those who already shared their own point of view to a considerable extent. In addition, he felt that theology contributed nothing to the

---

[152] Al-Ghazālī, *Iḥya' 'ulūm al-dīn*, cited from W. M. Watt, *Muslim Intellectual...*, p. 112.

[153] Ibid., p. 113-114.

[154] It was composed towards the end of his stay in Baghdād and after his critique of philosophy.

[155] It was composed soon afterwards in Jerusalem.

actual practice of religious life. However, it is important to point out that despite the fact that one may notice some changes resulting from the influence of philosophy and Ṣūfism, until the end of his life he seemed to have held that Ash'arī theology was true.

It is worth noting that the reflections and statements contained in *Al-munqidh min al-ḍalāl* may lead to a conclusion that Al-Ghazālī rejected theology and turned from it. Nevertheless, this should be understood in a rather limited sense. He was dissatisfied with theology because it contributed little or nothing to the attainment of that goal of the individual life which he described as "salvation" or the bliss of Paradise. However, he thought that it had a prophylactic function in the life of the community. Therefore, he continued to hold the views of the Ash'arīte school to which he always belonged. In other words, although Al-Ghazālī was rather convinced that the importance of theology had been greatly exaggerated, he continued to take up a theological position which was broadly Ash'arīte.[156]

As for Al-Ghazālī's contribution to the later development of theology, one should point out (1) the conscious-based arguments on syllogistic logic and (2) the attention to objections from a Neo-platonic standpoint. With time, according to Watt, he gradually influenced other scholars and:

> from now onwards all the rational theologians in Islam wrote in a way which assumed a philosophical outlook in pre-theological matters, and often explicitly discussed such matters.[157]

In conclusion, one may say that this new perspective introduced by Al-Ghazālī into Islamic theology became an aspect of its permanent nature.[158]

Al-Ghazālī's second encounter in his intellectual journey in search for the truth it was with Greek philosophy and, in particular, with the Muslim Neo-Platonism of Al-Fārābī[159] and Ibn Sīnā.[160] It was the second group of seekers who engaged his

---

[156] The date, which has been found for a small work called *The Restraining of the Commonalty from the Science of Theology*, marks the completion of this work only a few days before his death (W. M. Watt, *Muslim Intellectual...*, p. 119). For a thorough account on Al-Ghazālī's theological views refer to: R. Frank, *Al-Ghazālī and the Ash'arite School*, Durham, NC: Duke University Press, 1994.

[157] W. M. Watt, *Muslim Intellectual...*, p. 123.

[158] See: F. Griffel, *Al-Ghazālī's Philosophical Theology*, Oxford, NY: Oxford University Press, 2009.

[159] Abū Naṣr Muḥammad Ibn al-Farakh al-Fārābī (870-950), was a famous philosopher, scientist, cosmologist, logician, and musician of the Islamic Golden Age. Through his commentaries and treatises, he became well known among medieval Muslim intellectuals as "The Second Teacher," that is, the successor to Aristotle, "The First Teacher." For a thorough discussion on the philosophy of Al-Fārābī see: M. Fakhry, *Al-Fārābī, Founder of Islamic Neoplatonism: His Life, Works and Influence*, Oxford: Oneworld, 2002; M. S. Mahdi, *Alfarabi and the Foundation of Islamic Political Philosophy*, with a foreword by C. E. Butterworth, Chicago: University of Chicago Press, 2001.

[160] Abū 'Alī al-Ḥusayn Ibn 'Abd Allāh Ibn Sīnā (980-1037), known as Ibn Sīnā or by his Latinized name Avicenna, was a Persian philosopher, medical doctor, and scientist. His most famous

polemic attention the most and his criticism had an impact on the further development of the *kalām* and perhaps even (?) destruction of the neo-Platonic philosophy in the East.

Al-Ghazālī began philosophical studies in his early years in Nishapur, where he had probably been introduced to the subject by Al-Juwaynī, but he focused on such studies during his professorship in Baghdād which is evidenced by his treaties on logic and *Maqāṣid al-falāsifa*. Al-Ghazālī was the first Muslim theologian who undertook serious polemics with the philosophers and who realized that in order to refute the system, one should acquire a deep knowledge of it or else would act blindly.

Al-Ghazālī presents his discussion on philosophy in *Al-munqidh min al-ḍalāl* but his main attack on philosophers and their practices came with the powerful critique *Tāhāfut al-falāsifa* (1095, *Incoherence or Authodestruction of the Philosophers*).[161] In his discussion of Muslim philosophers, he focuses on the third group, namely theists, represented by Al-Fārābī and Ibn Sīnā. Their neo-Platonism adapted to Islamic monotheism allows them to claim to be Muslims. According to Al-Ghazālī everything that they transmitted falls under three headings, namely (1) what must be counted as unbelief, (2) what must be counted as heresy and (3) what is not to be denied.

Al-Ghazālī considers six philosophical sciences, i.e., mathematics, logic, natural science, metaphysics or theology, politics and ethics.[162] As for metaphysics, he criticizes it severely: "here occur most of the errors of the philosophers." Most of the other philosophical sciences he regards as neutral in themselves. In the case of mathematics, according to Al-Ghazālī, none of its results are connected with religious matters. As for logic, nothing in this science is relevant to religion by the way of denial and affirmation.[163] With regard to natural science, similar to medicine, in the view of Al-Ghazālī, it should not be rejected, except for some points. As for politics, he believes that this discussion is taken from the Divine Scriptures. Finally, in the case of ethics, people should rather refrain from the reading of these books because they contain a"mixture" of the sayings of the prophets and mystics and the philosophers' own ideas, and, therefore, according to Al-Ghazālī, it is difficult for unprepared person to distinguish true and false aspect of it.

What are the philosophical issues and debates in the *Tāhāfut al-falāsifa*? As he states in his book, the truth of the positive facts of religion can neither be proved

---

works are *The Book of Healing*, a vast philosophical and scientific encyclopaedia, and *The Canon of Medicine*, which was a standard medical text at many medieval universities in Europe. For a thorough account on his works refer to: J. McGinnis, *Avicenna*, Great Medieval Thinkers, New York–Oxford: Oxford University Press, 2010; D. Gutas, *Avicenna and the Aristotelian Tradition: Introduction to Reading Avicenna's Philosophical Works*, Leiden–New York: E. J. Brill, 1988.

[161] See: Abū Ḥāmid al-Ghazālī, *The Incoherence of the Philosophers (Tahāfut al-falāsifa), A Parallel English-Arabic Text*, translated, introduced, and annotated by M. E. Marmura, Provo, UT: Birmingham Young University Press, 2000.

[162] Refer to: ibid., p. 161-225.

[163] It should be pointed out that Aristotelian logic impressed Al-Ghazālī, especially syllogism and he used logic in his own defense of the doctrine. He also wrote several books on logic.

nor disapproved and to do otherwise leads philosophers to take quite nonsensical positions. Al-Ghazālī attacks the philosophers because many of their particular arguments are logically false and the various positions that they take in their systems as a whole are inconsistent with one another. Furthermore, some of their assumptions are unfounded. According to Al-Ghazālī, these assumptions can be neither demonstrated logically nor are self-evident through intuition.

The philosophy of religion has to accept the facts of religion as given by religion. It is worth noting that although Al-Ghazālī's whole polemic is derived from the Ash'arite theology, his method is the philosophical one. In his critique of the philosophers, he stands firmly upon the revelation and strongly opposes the philosopher's exclusive reliance on reason.[164] The scholar is convinced that there are things beyond the grasp of intellect and they have to be accepted as they are given by revelation. The philosophical methods should not enter here.

One by one Al-Ghazālī brings the points on which the philosophers can be convinced of incoherence and shows that they are unable to give logical proofs for their metaphysics.[165]

He attacks them as concerns the twenty points, beginning with the creation and ending with the last things. On seventeen points he accuses them of being heretics. He demonstrates the weaknesses of their arguments concerning the existence of God, his unity and incorporeality, and rejection that God is a simple existent without quiddity and attributes, their conception of His knowledge and some of their assertions about the heaven and human soul. On the three remaining points, Al-Ghazālī regards the philosophers as infidels. These are the following points: (1) eternity of the world, (2) denial of God's knowledge of the particulars and (3) denial of bodily resurrection. As he pointed out in the conclusion of the *Tāhāfut al-falāsifa*, these three theories are in violent opposition to Islam and to believe in them is to "accuse the Prophet of falsehood; to this no Muslim sect would subscribe." Concerning the other points, Al-Ghazālī approximates the position of the philosophers to that of Mu'tazila.

The problem to which Al-Ghazālī gives special consideration is the eternity of the world. The orthodox could not possibly accept the philosopher's claim. There is nothing eternal, but God, and all else is created. Therefore, anything co-eternal with God means violating the strict principle of monotheism.

Al-Ghazālī's challenge to the Muslim philosophers, i.e., the serious and very critical study of their doctrines made them more defensive than before. The results of his critique became a creative element in the *kalām*. Al-Ghazālī is credited with providing Islamic theology with philosophical foundations.[166]

---

164 For a thorough discussion on the issue of reason and revelation see: A. J. Arberry, *Revelation and Reason in Islam*, London: Allen & Unwin, 1957.

165 Refer to: Abū Ḥāmid al-Ghazālī, *The Incoherence of the Philosophers*..., p. 12-160.

166 See: W. M. Watt, *Islamic Philosophy and Theology*, Edinburgh: University Press, 1962; H. A. Wolfson, *The Philosophy of the Kalam*, Cambridge, MA: Harvard University Press, 1976.

According to scholars, it is difficult to say whether he is responsible for the "death" of the philosophical studies in Islam. It is true that after his death philosophical studies rather ceased to exist in the East.[167] However, one may observe these studies in the Islamic West, where Islamic philosophy had its famous representatives, such as Ibn Bajja,[168] Ibn Ṭufayl,[169] and Ibn Rushd.[170]

It is worth noting that Al-Ghazālī significantly legitimized and popularized the study of one philosophical science, namely logic. Effectively, this made the Greek modes of thinking more accessible, as compared to the more traditional Muslim ones. His attack evoked replies and the most important, i.e., *Tāhāfut al-tāhāfut* was written in the West by Ibn Rushd. With Al-Ghazālī begins the successful introduction of Aristotelianism or rather Avicennism into Muslim theology. After a period of appropriation of the Greek sciences in the translation movement from Greek into Arabic and the writings of the *falāsifa* up to Ibn Sīnā, philosophy and the Greek sciences were "naturalized" into the discourse of *kalām* and Muslim theology. Al-Ghazālī's approach to resolving apparent contradictions between reason and revelation was accepted by almost all later Muslim theologians and had, via the works of Ibn Rushd and Jewish authors, a significant influence on Latin medieval thinking.

The third encounter was with a section of Ismā'īlīya, who held that true knowledge was to be gained from an infallible imam. It is worth noting that with regard to the Ismā'īlīs, Al-Ghazālī's views were close to that of Niẓām al-Mulk, and he shared his concerns about the growth of their influences.[171] Therefore, after the assassination of the vizier in 1092, he had no hesitation responding to the request of the young caliph Al-Mustaẓhir (1094-1118), stating he should write a book refutating of the doctrines the Ta'līmites or Bāṭinites. The book, commonly known as the *Mustaẓhirī*, was completed before Al-Ghazālī left Baghdād in November

---

[167] There was an important Persian tradition of theosophical philosophy.

[168] Abū Bakr Muḥammad Ibn Yaḥyā Ibn al-Ṣā'igh al-Tūjībī (1085-1138), known as Ibn Bajja (or Avempace in the West) was one of the most important philosophers of Muslim Spain. He was also an astronomer, logician, musician, poet, and scientist. See: M. Hemli, *La philosophie morale d'Ibn Bâjja (Avempace) à travers le Tadbîr al-mutawaḥḥid (Le régime du solitaire)*, Tunis: Impr. N. Bascone & S. Muscat, 1969.

[169] Abū Bakr Muḥammad Ibn Abd al-Malik Ibn Muḥammad Ibn Ṭufayl (1105-1185) was an Andalusian philosopher and novelist, most famous for writing the first philosophical novel, *Hayy ibn Yaqdhan*. See: Z. A. Siddiqi, *Philosophy of Ibn Tufayl*, Faculty of Arts publication series, no. 18, Aligarh: Aligarh Muslim University, 1965.

[170] Abū l-Walīd Muḥammad Ibn Aḥmad Ibn Rushd (1126-1198) commonly known as Ibn Rushd or by his Latinized name Averroës, was a Spanish Andalusian Muslim philosopher, theologian, jurist, and scientist. He was a defender of Aristotelian philosophy against Ash'ari theologians led by Al-Ghazālī, whom he attacked in his famous work *Tāhāfut al-tāhāfut*. See: M. Fakhry, *Averroës (Ibn Rushd): His Life, Works and Influence*, Oxford: Oneworld, 2001.

[171] For a thorough account on Al-Ghazālī's polemical engagement with the Ismā'īlīs see: F. Mitha, *Al-Ghazālī and the Ismailis: A Debate on Reason and Authority in Medieval Islam*, Ismaili heritage series, 5, London: I. B. Tauris, in association with the Institute of Ismaili Studies, 2001.

1095.[172] He subsequently wrote several other works directed in whole or in part against the Bāṭinites.

In the *Mustaẓhirī*, Al-Ghazālī is focused on exposing inconsistencies with the esoteric doctrine of the Bāṭinites.[173] This enabled him to not only criticize the doctrine but also to explain the need of refuting it. For example, he argues that it is practically impossible to consult the imam or his representative in every case. Furthermore, he points out that although the Bāṭinites claim to abandon reasoning, they cannot avoid surreptitiously making use of it. Furthermore, as underlined by Watt, there is a considerable difference between the *Mustaẓhirī* and *Al-munqidh min al-ḍalāl* with regard to Al-Ghazālī's attitude and "appreciation" of the Bāṭinite doctrine. The caliph commissioned the first work and, therefore, it was obvious that the author focused on rather destructive criticism. As for the second work, as Watt says, it is clear that Al-Ghazālī "had realized that part of their success was due to the fact that they satisfied, however imperfectly, the deep demand in men's heart for an embodiment of the dynamic image of the charismatic leader."[174] Therefore, while being aware of such a demand, he insisted that Muslims already had such a leader, namely the Prophet Muḥammad and "he has his living expositors (presumably the scholar-jurists are meant), just as the hidden imam has his expositors, the accredited agents."[175] Here Watt brings our attention to a very important point, namely to the issue that is "untouched" or "omitted" by Al-Ghazālī. He says:

> It is perhaps worth calling attention here to what Al-Ghazālī does not say. Though the 'Abbāsid caliphs had originally claimed to have charismata, he does not attempt to make them into imams of the Bāṭinite type... neither does he attempt to attribute any charismata to the scholar-jurists... Had he wanted he could have referred to the Tradition that the scholar-jurists were the heirs of the prophets... His later thought... tended to view that there was an elite who, could obtain an insight into divine truth comparable to that of the prophets. It is perhaps in parts of his later works apparently unconnected with contemporary problems that we find his real and effective answer to the challenge of Ismā'īlism, which, even if it had little effect on the ruling institution, enabled Islamic society to preserve its characteristic structure and manner of life.[176]

Al-Ghazālī's final encounter was with Ṣūfism. However, before entering into the core of the matter, one should mention a few words about the role of mysticism in Muslim tradition.

It is worth noting that from the life of Muḥammad onwards there were Muslims to whom the element of piety or spirituality in the Qur'ān made strong appeal. In

---

172 W. M. Watt, *Muslim Intellectual...*, p. 82.

173 Bāṭin is defined as as the interior or hidden meaning of the Qur'ān. See: M. Ghālib, *Al-Ḥarakāt al-bāṭinīyah fī al-Islām*, Bayrūt–Lubnān: Dār al-Andalus, 1982.

174 Ibid., p. 85.

175 Ibid.

176 W. M. Watt, *Muslim Intellectual...*, p. 85-86.

the earliest days, such Muslims were nearly all Arabs. With the conversion of the inhabitants of Iraq, came into Islam many people familiar with the Christian mystical tradition. It is among non-Arabs that mysticism in the strict sense developed. Among the most prominent Ṣūfīs of the early period, one should mention Ḥasan al-Baṣrī (643-728), Abū Yazīd al-Bisṭāmī (d. 874–5 or 848–9), Al-Junayd (d. 910) and Al-Ḥallāj (d. 922). There was much mysticism during the tenth and eleventh centuries. It is worth noting that in those days Ṣūfīsm was not something isolated, as some Western accounts may suggest, but had become a part of the ordinary life of the Muslim *'umma*. One of the important aspects of the early ṣūfī movement was its relation to contemporary history and to social conditions. In other words, the early ascetic trends were a reaction to the wealth and luxury of the leaders and a little later, the ṣūfīs began to attack the worldliness and hypocrisy of the scholar-jurists.[177] These men, "supported" by the "strong argument" taken from the standard collection of "sound Traditions" by Al-Bukhārī (d. 870) and Muslim (d. 875), formed a closed corporation and from the times of *Miḥna* or Inquisition of (833-849), with hardly any exceptions were wholly subservient to the government.

The years from about 900 to 1100 saw fresh vicissitudes. For half a century or more after 945 Baghdād was under the rule of the Shī'ite Buwayhid sultans. Although the Sunnite scholar-jurists continued to have official recognition, their power was decreasing and they became involved in court intrigues. After the turbulent years that followed the Buwayhids decline, the advent of the Seljūqs in 1055 brought a measure of peace. When their government, guided by Niẓām al-Mulk decided to support and promote Ash'arism, the dependence of the scholar-jurists on the rulers was increased. One of the results was the succumbing of the scholar-jurists to the politicians' disease of worldliness and materialism, an "epidemic to which's criticism bear witness.[178] Under the circumstances, the movement flourished. However, the sources of worldliness were so strong in political and judicial circles that it was impossible for mystics to express their spiritual aspirations in public activity. One may say that, in this situation, it seemed quite natural that the higher spiritual aspirations should seek to express themselves through the cultivation of the inner life. Thus, the adoption of the mystic life by some members of the intellectual circles did not simply mean a refusal to face difficulties, but as Watt pointed out, "the spiritual vision which had hitherto guided the development of Islam was itself pointing to a greater concentration on the inner life."[179]

After four years in Baghdād, Al-Ghazālī felt himself so involved in the worldliness of his milieu that he was in danger of going to hell. The profound inner struggle he experienced caused a psychosomatic illness in 1095. Dryness of the tongue prevented him from lecturing and even from eating, and the doctors could do nothing to alleviate the symptoms. After about six months, he decided to leave the professor-

---

[177] Ibid., p. 131.
[178] Ibid., p. 133.
[179] Ibid.

ship and adopt the life of Ṣūfī. To avoid any attempts to stop him, he let it be known that he was setting out on a pilgrimage to Mecca. In November 1095, Al-Ghazālī left Baghdād heading to Damascus and lived there for a while. Towards the end of 1096, he went to Jerusalem. During the months of November and December 1096 he was engaged in the pilgrimage to Mecca, perhaps visiting Alexandria on the way. He went back to Damascus, but no later than June 1097 did he return to Baghdād. He spent some time there, but possibly, about 1099 returned to his native town Ṭūs. There Al-Ghazālī established a *khānāqā* where some young disciples joined him in leading a communal Ṣūfī life. In 1105 or early 1106, Fakhr al-Mulk (the son of Niẓām al-Mulk) the new vizier of the Seljūq prince offered him the professorship at the Niẓāmiyya college.

It is worth noting that this was the eleven month of the Muslim year 499. The year 500, which began on September 2, marked the beginning of a new century. According to Traditions, Muḥammad was reported to have said that God would send a *"mujaddid"* (a "renewer") of his religion at the beginning of each century. Some friends assured Al-Ghazālī that he was the "renewer" for the six century. Therefore, he accepted the invitation of Fakhr al-Mulk, went to Nishapur, and there he assumed his duties in July or August of 1106. After about three or four years of working there, Al-Ghazālī returned to Ṭūs, where he died in 1111.

In his autobiography *Al-munqidh min al-ḍalāl*, Al-Ghazālī said that he had turned to the study of Ṣūfīsm only after he found no satisfaction in his study of theology, philosophy, and Bāṭinism. However, it should be pointed out that this was not his first encounter with the Muslim mystics. Al-Ghazālī was in contact with them much earlier. The guardian to whom he and his brother were entrusted to upon his father's death was a Ṣūfī.[180] While he was a student at Ṭūs, he had a spiritual leader who was also a Ṣūfī. In Nishapur, Al-Juwaynī, under whom he was studying theology, was sympathetic to Ṣūfīsm. In addition, Al-Fārmadhī, the professor of jurisprudence under whom Al-Ghazālī worked there, was a recognized leader of the Ṣūfīs in Ṭūs and Nishapur.

As mentioned by Watt, in light of *Al-munqidh min al-ḍalāl*, during both his student years and the immediately following years, Al-Ghazālī was particularly concerned with the quest for the truth. His first crisis, while he was a complete skeptic, arose from his conclusion that the methods he had been employing did not give him absolute certainty. He had probably begun to study philosophy before this crisis, and he may have reached the point of seeing that in theology and metaphysics the philosophers did not follow a strict logical method. At the close of this period of skepticism, he found himself able to accept some basic principles because of a "light from God." One may say that he saw directly or had an immediate intuition, that the principles were true. In 1095, when the second crisis came upon him, he already had a steadfast faith in God, in prophethood and in the Last Day.[181] Although in

[180] Ibid.

[181] Ibid., p. 134.

Al-munqidh min al-ḍalāl Al-Ghazālī speaks about a personal search for the truth in his study of Bāṭinism, it may seem that he was rather fulfilling a duty imposed by the caliph.

The close examination of the doctrine of the Bāṭinites also did prove beneficial. However, this time Al-Ghazālī's aim was not to find an intellectual certainty but rather to achieve a satisfying life, a life – one worthy of Paradise. He had already realized that this mysticism entailed not only intellectual doctrines but also a way of life. In *Al-munqidh min al-ḍalāl* he said:

> Lastly I turned to the way of mystics. I knew that in their path there has to be both knowledge and activity...Knowledge was easier for me than activity. I began by reading their books... Then I realized that what is most distinctive of them can be attained only by personal experience (taste – *dhawq*), ecstasy and a change of character.[182]

The universally acknowledged *Iḥya' 'ulūm al-dīn* (1096/7, *The Revival of the Religious Sciences*), is considered to be Al-Ghazālī's greatest work.[183] *Iḥya' 'ulūm al-dīn* is divided into four "quarters." Each "quarter" consists of ten books. The first quarter, entitled "matters of service (sc. of God)." The first book, intended as an introduction, is divided into seven chapters and is focused on presenting which subjects of study or science, according to Al-Ghazālī, are important for a pious Muslim. The second book is devoted to the presentation of the basic principles of the creed and contains:

> (a) an elaboration of the Confession of Faith – "I bear witness that there is no god but God, Muḥammad is the messenger of God; (b) a discussion of education in matters of doctrine; (c) statement of Islamic doctrine in four sections, each with ten points; (d) a discussion of the relation between the faith and Islam, that is between being a believer and being a Muslim.[184]

The remaining eight books they deal with ritual purity (ablutions before worship, etc.), formal prayers or worship, tithing, fasting, the pilgrimage to Mecca, the recitation of the Qur'ān, private prayer and extracanonical devotions. Each practice is usually introduced by the Qur'ānic verses and the Traditions justifying it.

With regard to the second quarter entitled "customs," Al-Ghazālī discusses in it the external aspects of ordinary life outside the practice or cult. There are books about various aspects of everyday life, such as eating and drinking, marriage, earning one's living, and engaging in business, relations with relatives and friends, the life on retirement, traveling, the use of music, and about reforming the society and improving the reciprocal relations between people. Furthermore, Al-Ghazālī also discusses

---

[182] Cited from W. M. Watt, *Muslim Intellectual...*, p. 135.

[183] A small part of it, namely *Al-Risāla al-Qudsīya* (1097, *The Jerusalem Epistle*) was probably written separately during his stay in Jerusalem in 1096. (W. M. Watt, *Muslim Intellectual...*, p. 151.)

[184] Ibid., p. 152.

the issue of "lawful and unlawful," which is a sensitive issue of conscience. It is worth noting that for Muslims all the aspects of their lives are connected with the reviled law. Therefore, although in this quarter the author deals predominantly with rather secular matters, one may say that he never "looses sight of the contribution of the things he discusses to man's spiritual growth."[185]

The third and fourth quarters are devoted to matters related to man's inner life and are respectively entitled "things leading to destruction" and "things leading to salvation." the third quarter begins with an introduction on "mysteries of the heart", followed by a book discussing the matter of the improvement of the character. In his subsequent eight books, Al-Ghazālī considers the issues such as the control of appetites for food and sexual intercourse, the weakness of tongue, anger, worldliness, avarice, hypocrisy and love of fame, pride and vanity and self deception. The books of the fourth quarter are respectively on repentance, on patience and gratitude (to God), on fear and hope, on poverty and self-discipline, on asserting God's unity and trusting in him, on love (for God) and approval (of his decrees, on sincerity and purity of intention, on self-examination, on meditation, and on death and the life to come.

It is worth noting that as it is presented in *Al-munqidh min al-ḍalāl*, for Al-Ghazālī Ṣūfism signified much more that the devoted prayer and cultivation of ecstatic states. His adherence to ṣūfism absolutely convinced him and made him constantly aware of the fact that the life he lived was only a preparation for the life to come. Furthermore, since the prelude of the life to come was the Last Judgment, Al-Ghazālī was very concerned with the improvement of character. Therefore, be believed that some experience of mystical ecstasy should not be the goal but it could only support and make it easier to improve one's character and to reach the higher degree of reward in the life to come.

There is no doubt that in the history of Islamic thought Al-Ghazālī occupies a position of great importance and his contribution to its development is very significant. Based on both the review of various studies on Muslim thought and the readings of some original works by Muslim philosophers and theologians, including those of Al-Ghazālī one may assume that, despite the strong influence of Greek philosophy, Islamic thought – as it is particularly presented by Al-Ghazālī – remains "sufficiently Islamic."

There are certain reasons that allow making such a statement. First, the Islamic philosophy "borrowed" and "absorbed" the "tools from the classical Greek heritage," i.e., the principles of scientific research, methods of disputation, etc. Second, the elements and concepts that attracted Muslim philosophers to Greek thought were predominantly those that could "suit" the Muslim mind, namely those that assured the supremacy of religion and placed the emphasis on the issues related to problem of the soul, imagination, intuition, and to the prophetic illumination. Third, Islam and the fundamental Islamic questions, such as the unity of God, the prophecy, the relation between the reason and revelation, the concept of an ideal state, and the mystical

[185] Ibid., p. 153.

experience, occupy a central place in their treatises. Furthermore, it is worth noting that with regard to the issue of Islamic features in their concepts, Muslim philosophers were watched closely, at times criticized and most of all constantly stimulated by the traditionalist movement. As a result, Islamic philosophy lost its dynamism and vitality. In the East after Ibn Sīna, who died in 1037, no creative philosopher appeared. Only in the West did Islamic philosophy enjoy its Indian summer with some creative works of the already mentioned Ibn Bajja, Ibn Ṭufayl, and Ibn Rushd.

Although Islamic philosophy was to a certain extent defeated, there is no doubt that it occupies a significant place in the history of Islamic thought and that its masters assigned in their discussion a proper place to Islamic religion. Furthermore, the Muslim encounter with the Hellenistic culture brought Islamic and Greek culture together in a creative act. The classical heritage was revived and a "new life" was brought into Muslim religion, which outlined a new intellectual direction that Islam would probably not take on its own.

It has been customary to see Abū Ḥāmid al-Ghazālī as a vehement critic of philosophy, who rejected it in favor of Islamic mysticism. However, over the past few years such a view has come under increased scrutiny. Alexander Treiger, the author of the recently published study 2012), namely *Inspired Knowledge in Islamic Thought: Al-Ghazālī's Theory of Mystical Cognition and its Avicennian Foundation*, argues that Al-Ghazālī was instead, one of the greatest popularizers of philosophy in medieval Islam. The author supplies new evidence showing that Al-Ghazālī was indebted to philosophy in his theory of mystical cognition and in his eschatology. Moreover, within these two areas he even accepted those philosophical teachings which he ostensibly criticized. Arguing that despite overt criticism, Al-Ghazālī never rejected Avicennian philosophy and that his mysticism itself is grounded in Avicenna's teachings, the book offers a clear and systematic presentation of Al-Ghazālī's "philosophical mysticism."[186]

In the history of Muslim societies one may observe a constant process of creating new forms out of the existing matters. One may say that Islamic thought with its unique, specific "Islamic" features, as represented by the works of Al-Ghazālī, constitutes a fine outcome of such a process.

---

[186] A. Treiger, *Inspired Knowledge in Islamic Thought: Al-Ghazālī's Theory of Mystical Cognition and its Avicennian Foundation*, London–New York: Routledge, 2012.

IV

The Importance of the *Ḥaram* Collection for Studying the History of Jerusalem during the Mamlūks'Days

Ḥaram 102: Study of the Document

The Ḥaram documents: an overview of the collection

As it was reported in 1978 by Linda S. Northrup and Amal A. Abul-Hajj in their article, a group of documents dating from the 13th – 15th centuries were found in the Islamic Museum located in the precincts of the Dome of the Rock in Jerusalem. These files contained "approximately 354 complete documents as well as many other small fragments."[187] Apart from giving some important details about the collection as a whole, the authors also presented the summary description of fifty sample documents. These fifty documents include examples ranging from royal Mamlūk decrees to deeds for the sale of land in Jerusalem under Mamlūk regime. In their article Linda S. Northrup and Amal A. Abul-Hajj also added that "the existence of still other documents has become known," and pointed out that what had been found was one from the largest and potentially "most important caches of medieval Islamic documents as far discovered."[188]

The story of the discovery of the Ḥaram documents began in September 1973 with the appointment of Amal A. Abul-Hajj as assistant director of the Islamic Museum in Jerusalem. While exploring the Museum collection, her attention focused on the locked drawers that, according to the official statements, contained rather "unimportant pieces of papers." However, Amal A. Abul-Hajj insisted on inspecting the content of these drawers and she finally succeeded. On August 19, 1974, in the

---

[187] L. S. Northrup and A. A. Abul-Hajj, "A Collection of Medieval Arabic Documents in the Islamic Museum at the Ḥaram al-Sharīf," *Arabica*, vol. 25 (1978), p. 283.

[188] Ibid., p. 284.

presence of high officials of the Jerusalem Council of Awqāf who were visiting the museum to check on repairs in progress, some drawers and cupboards were unlocked. In one of the cupboards, Amal A. Abul-Hajj found the 354 documents already mentioned. She was alone in "her excitement at the discovery of what were obviously medieval Islamic documents." Therefore, she attempted to evoke interest of both the scholars and the officials. Unfortunately, her efforts were fruitless, and, as Donald P. Little underlined in his article, "it was not until she persuaded Linda Northrup, a young Mamlūk scholar who was passing through Jerusalem from a year's study in Cairo, to help her examine the documents that work began in earnest."[189]

Abul-Hajj and Northrup began their hard work. They were able to decipher fifty of the documents before Northrup had to return to the McGill Institute of Islamic Studies in Montreal in the summer of 1975. When Professor Donald P. Little, who at that time, was Northrup's Ph.D. thesis supervisor, saw the results of Abul-Hajj's and Northrup's work he became guardedly interested in the documents. Furthermore, he spared no effort to encourage his student to pursue her endeavors of working with the documents. In 1976, a larger group of papers were discovered at the Museum in Jerusalem. Finally, a year and half later, it became known that Abul-Hajj would have to resign her post at the Islamic Museum because of her upcoming marriage to an official in the American Consular Corps and that the disposition of the documents would be in doubt after her departure.

At that point, Little decided that an effort should be made to have the documents photographed to insure their preservation. His plan was to arrange considerable financial backing needed to send a team of three, namely Donald P. Little, Linda Northrup and the photographer Martin Lyons, to Jerusalem. Eventually the Institute of Islamic Studies and the Graduate Faculty of McGill University provided the financial assistance necessary with remarkable imagination, generosity, and speed.[190] The team was ready to pursue the task.

Things in Jerusalem were working well and within a period of two weeks, permission to photograph the collection was granted by the responsible authorities and as a the result of the research team's work the photographs of the documents are kept at the Museum and the McGill Institute of Islamic Studies. Some time later Little wrote an important article, in which he gave the preliminary report-survey on the entire collection as a supplement to the first report given by Northrup and Abul-Hajj. In addition, the scholar drew tentative conclusions regarding the nature and significance of the Ḥaram documents. Here are the main points of Little's findings.[191]

The Ḥaram collection consists of 883 separately cataloged documents, and it is worth noting that almost all of them are complete and intact. The majority of these

---

[189] See: D. P. Little, "The Significance of the Ḥaram Documents for the Study of Medieval Islamic History," *Der Islam*, vol. 57 (1980), p. 189-219.

[190] Charles J. Adams, Director Islamic Studies; Walter F. Hitaschfeld, Dean and Vice Principal, Faculty of Graduate Studies and Research at McGill University provided the team with financial assistance.

[191] See: D. P. Little, "The Significance of the Ḥaram Documents..., p. 189-219.

papers contain only a single document, which is written on one side of the sheet; sometimes the text is continued, or a brief note is written on the back. However, as Little underlines, in the collection one may notice a substantial number of papers containing more than one document. In fact, the papers may include from two to even nine interrelated documents. Taking into consideration, one may say that the total number of documents in the collection is well over one thousand. It is also important to note that almost all of documents that bear dates (approximately eighty percent) come from the eighth Islamic century, equivalent to the fourteenth Christian century.

Furthermore, with only a few exceptions all of the Arabic documents are related to transactions or records of events that took place in Jerusalem under the administration of the Burjī Mamlūks.[192]

As Little points out, in order to give the idea of the nature of the documents from the collection and characterize the type of information, which can be extracted from them, one can divide them into certain categories. In addition, he proposes that hey could be classified in several ways. The suggested categorization looks as follows: (1) in terms of the source of issue that we would have deal with, the royal documents, issued by the sultan or officers of state; judicial documents, issued by a *qāḍī;* notarial documents, by notaries; and private documents, or petitions submitted by private citizens, and (2) according to to subject matter, such as real estate transactions, questions of civil status, legacies, power of attorney, homicide, assault, and battery, etc.

However, as highlighted by the scholar, the Ḥaram collection could be presented according to the form of the documents, and, in this case, one should "study Ḥaram documents in their own right."[193]

While taking into primary consideration the form of the documents, one may divide the Ḥaram documents into several types.

The most important are the decrees, namely (1) the royal Mamlūk decrees (about 55) issued to the monks of St. Catherine's and signed by the sultans from the Burjī period (about 10),[194] (2) the decrees issued by *amīrs* or officials from Mamlūk bureaucracy; all of them are the letters of appointment to the religious services and they usually specify the salary for these services and (3) the decrees written at the bottom, on the side or on the back of petitions.

---

[192] Ibid., p. 195.

[193] Ibid., p. 197.

[194] The Mamlūks (1250-1517) were a local Muslim dynasty of slave origin that ruled in Egypt and Syria. They successfully challenged the Mongol threat. As defenders of Islamic orthodoxy, the Mamlūks sponsored numerous religious buildings, including mosques, madrasas, and khānqāhs. The Baḥrī dynasty (Baḥriyya Mamlūks) was of Kipchak Turkish origin and ruled Egypt from 1250 to 1382 Their name means "of the sea," referring to the location of their original residence on Al-Rodah Island, on the Nile in Cairo at the castle of Al-Rodah. They were succeeded by the Burjī dynasty (Burjīi Mamlūks) that ruled Egypt from 1382 until 1517. Their name means "of the tower," referring to their rule from the Citadel east of Cairo. During their times the political power-plays often became important in designating a new sultan. See: D. P. Little, *History and Historiography of the Mamlūks*, London: Variorum Reprints, 1986.

There is a small but significant number of documents written in the form of petitions. However, as Little says, they "are actually reports" and range from a report to an official in Jerusalem by an official in Gaza on the movements of the sultan in Egypt to "what seem to be reports on the price of crops submitted by agents to their employers."[195]

In the Ḥaram collection there is a group of 378 documents called "dead inventories."[196] It consists of (1) 333 documents in the first line of the text containing the clause "*ḥaṣala l-wuqūf 'alā*," which means in this context that the objects listed in the document were seen or viewed by the witnesses who signed it;[197] (2) the thirty-four documents which contain the phrase "*waqafa 'alā*" instead of "*ḥaṣala l-wuqūf 'alā*," both of which mean the same thing; and (3) eleven documents which begin with the phrase "*ḍubiṭat ḥawā'ij fulān* (the possessions of Fulān were recorded)." According to Little the dead inventories constitute a valuable source of information with regard to social and economic history. However, they "are the dullest to work with" because they consist largely of carelessly written lists of clothing and household articles.[198]

Within the Ḥaram collection, one may also find another large and diversified group group of documents that can be loosely classified as accounts. These 124 documents are easily recognizable by their format, which is called *daftar* in the Ottoman archives.[199] All these documents are written on a standard-sized sheet of paper (approximately 19 by 28 cms.), folded vertically in the middle, so as to form a folio which could be sewed into account book (*daftar*).[200]

The largest category of documents from the Ḥaram collection after the dead inventories consists of ninety-four *iqrārs*[201] which cover almost the entire eighth century, from 705 to 799, with more than half from the year 795 (forty-eight) and 796 (seventeen). One should mention here that the *iqrār* is known from jurisprudence books and from papyri specimens.[202]

As mentioned by Little, in the Ḥaram collection there are ten documents which have a slightly different form from the *iqrār* but that seem to serve the same purpose. These documents begin with the word *yaqūl/taqūl* rather than *iqarra/ iqarrat*, which

---

[195] The petitions and reports are among the most difficult documents to decipher.

[196] Professor Little says: "Because the Arabic phrase ("*ḥaṣala l-wuqūf 'alā*") is awkward to handle as a title and because the objects listed in the documents belonged to a dead or dying person, I have decided to call this genre dead inventories, even though this term does not give a full notion of their content." See: D. P. Little, "The Significance of the Ḥaram Documents…, p. 203

[197] Nothing is known about them, prior to the Ottoman period. They are mentioned in neither the chancery nor the *shurūṭ* manuals.

[198] See: D. P. Little, "The Significance of the Ḥaram Documents…, p. 203.

[199] Ibid., p. 205.

[200] Ibid.

[201] *Iqrār* – it is an acknowledgement recorded in writing and witnessed by competent witnesses, which is thus legally binding on the person who makes the acknowledgement.

[202] D. P. Little, "The Significance of the Ḥaram Documents…, p. 208.

means he or she says or declares rather than he or she acknowledges. Therefore, these documents might be called declarations.

Also in the collection is a group of documents that are similar to the *iqrārs* in both form and content. They begin with the formula "*ashhada 'alayhi fulān*" or "*hadara ilā shuhūdihi wa-ashhada 'alā...*, both of which mean that a person appeared before legal witnesses (*shuhūd*) whom he called upon to witness a deposition which he made in the document.

The next two types of documents in the Ḥaram collection include (1) deeds of purchase and (2) leases, which are closely related in terms of both content and form. It is worth noting that these kinds of documents are also known from earlier examples, i.e., from papyri and parchment specimens.[203]

In the Ḥaram collection there are also documents referring to the personal affairs of an individual or individuals, such as (1) nine marriage contracts (*'aqd nikāḥ*), dated 770-795; (2) four *wakalās*, dated 743-781, by which an individual assigned his power of attorney to another for certain transactions and (3) twelve *waṣiyyas*, testamentary bequeath, dated 764-795.

With regard to the other types of documents, the collection includes (1) four documents containing an *istiftā'* and *futuyā*, that is so to say a request for a legal opinion in a given case, such as the possibility of evading the stipulations of a *waqf*, along with the response of a person entitled to give such an opinion – a *muftī*; all four documents are standard in form, short, and direct to the point; and (2) sixteen documents classified as miscellaneous.[204]

It is worth noting that apart from documents in Arabic there are also in the Ḥaram collection of twenty-seven documents in Persian. According to Little, the Persian documents are important for a few reasons. First, they are similar in form to some of the Arabic types, such as bills of sale, *iqrārs* and decrees. Second, some Arabic legal terminology seems to have been translated into its Persian equivalent. Finally, parts of the Persian documents are written in Arabic, most notably the headings, which designate the content of some of the documents, and the dates, which invariably occur at the end.

Why is the discovery at the Islamic Museum, located in the precincts of the Dome of the Rock in Jerusalem that important? What are the benefits from studying these documents?

Studies on the Ḥaram documents, as underlined by Little in his article "The Significance of the Ḥaram Documents for the Study of Medieval Islamic History," would prove beneficial especially for the three fields, namely Islamic diplomatics, Islamic law and the history of Jerusalem under the Mamlūks.

With regard to Islamic diplomatic, the Ḥaram collection may enrich the known history of the Mamlūk period and together with the Sinai and Franciscan collections and European archives, would provide the largest and most varied set of Islamic

[203] Ibid., p. 211.
[204] Ibid., p. 214.

documents for any medieval state before the Ottomans. In addition, taking into account the fact that contemporary available literary sources for the study of such documents are rich, one may agree with Little that:

> Given the rudimentary state of prior research, it is no exaggeration to say that these new materials make it possible to advance our knowledge of this branch of historiography to a higher level. This is true both for those types of documents about which we already have some knowledge, such as petitions and decrees, and even more so for those specimens in the Ḥaram about which we know little or nothing.[205]

The importance of the discussed collection for the studies related to Islamic diplomatics also lies in the fact that their analysis, would allow comparisons with similar documents from earlier periods, such as those from the papyri collection and those from the later, mainly Ottoman period. All in all, such studies would definitely shed more light on the history of the development of Muslim diplomatics and thus contribute to the increasing awareness within the field.

Pertaining to Islamic law, the analysis of the Ḥaram collection would prove beneficial because the documents contain a wealth of information on the duties and practices of judges, notaries and legal witnesses. All this may increase our knowledge of the operation of Muslim judicial institutions.[206] Furthermore, as Little stresses:

> Formerly dependent for such information on chronicles and biographical dictionaries, fiqh, and chancery manuals, and adab books, we can now correlate these literary works with documentary evidence of how these officials functioned in fourteenth century Jerusalem.[207]

Finally, the last main field for which the studies of the Ḥaram collection would prove particularly important is the history of Jerusalem under the Mamlūks.[208] According to Little, because the city was not central to Mamlūk concerns, the period of Palestinian history between the Crusades and the Ottoman occupation seems to be rather dim. The references to Jerusalem in Mamlūk chronicles are few and they mostly relate to religious matters. It is worth noting that the most important history of Mamlūk Jerusalem is the *Kitāb al-uns al-jalīl bi-ta'rīkh al-Quds wal-Khalīl* by Mujīr al-Dīn al-'Ulaymī al-Ḥanbalī (died in 928). This two-volume work contains

---

[205] Ibid., p. 216.

[206] See: D. P. Little, "Two Fourteenth-Century Court Records from Jerusalem Concerning the Disposition of Slaves by Minors," *Arabica*, vol. 29 (1982), p. 16-49; idem, "The Judicial Documents from al-Ḥaram al Sharīf as Sources for the History of Palestine Under the Mamlūks," *The Third International Conference on Bilād al-Shām: Palestine (19-24 April, 1980)*, vol. I: *Jerusalem*, Amman: University of Jordan–Yarmouk University, 1983, p. 117-125; idem, "Ḥaram Documents Related to the Jews of the Late Fourteenth-Century," *Journal of Semitic Studies*, vol. 30 (1985), p. 227-269.

[207] D. P. Little, "The Significance of the Ḥaram Documents..., p. 217.

[208] For examples of the history of art and architecture, see: D. P. Little, "The Ḥaram Documents as Sources for the Arts and Architecture of the Mamlūk Period," *Muqarnas*, vol. 2 (1984), p. 62-73.

an outline of the reigns of the Mamlūk viceroys in Jerusalem, short biographies of the *'ulamā'* who lived there and valuable information concerning public building. As Little points out, the work "furnishes only a skeleton for the history of Jerusalem."[209] It could be filled and gradually completed with the results of a thorough analysis of the Ḥaram collection. One may say that the book by Huda Lutfi, *Al-Quds al-Mamlūkiyya: A History of Mamlūk Jerusalem Based on the Ḥaram Documents*,[210] is a valuable attempt at undertaking this important task.

There is no doubt that the Ḥaram documents are important for the study of Islamic institutions, for both specific ones, such as the Khānqāh, Madrasa, and Māristān known as al-Ṣalāḥiyya (there is about twenty documents about it), as well as institutions concerning endowments in general (there are dozens documents about it).[211] It is also worth noting that the Ḥaram collection gives a rare opportunity to study the lives of individuals. As Little mentions in his article, "The Significance of the Ḥaram Documents for the Study of Medieval Islamic History," there are for example about forty documents concerning the Ṣūfī and *'ālim* Burhān al-Dīn Ibrāhīm al-Nāṣirī and his family:

> including data on his means of livelihood, his salaries from various jobs, his wife and his children, his house, even a list of his books and the prices that were paid for them after his death, as well as the allowance paid to his wife and surviving children. From these documents emerges a clear portrait of an enterprising, hard-working scholar-Ṣūfī who managed, apparently, to make a decent if undistinguished life for himself by his learning and piety.[212]

Furthermore, the studies on the Ḥaram documents give an extraordinary and unique opportunity to learn about the life of the medieval common Muslim man and, and what is of great importance, the medieval Muslim woman. It is a fact, as Little underlines, that individual women "do not recur with the same frequency in the documents as men."[213]Nevertheless, from the available documents related to women, we are able to learn a great deal about their situation concerning a number of matters, such as their material status, their relationship to men, and their legal rights and duties.

The following is my analysis of the document from the Ḥaram collection, namely the *Ḥaram 102*[214] concerning Fāṭima bint Fakhr al-Dīn. This analysis, together with a presented comparison of the documents analyzed and discussed by Huda

---

[209] D. P. Little, "The Significance of the Ḥaram Documents..., p. 218.

[210] H. Lutfi, *Al-Quds al-Mamlūkiyya: A History of Mamlūk Jerusalem Based on the Ḥaram Documents*, Berlin: Klaus Schwarz Verlag, 1985.

[211] D. P. Little, "The Significance of the Ḥaram Documents..., p. 219.

[212] Ibid., p. 218.

[213] Ibid., p. 219.

[214] In the 1980s, while pursuing my Ph. D. program at the Institute of Islamic Studies at McGill University in Montreal I passed with an A mark a graduate Seminar "Arabic Historiography," conducted by Professor Donald P. Little (1985-1986 Fall Session). During this Seminar

Lutfi in her article "A Study of the Fourteenth Century *Iqrārs* from al-Quds Relating to Muslim Women,"[215] may shed a clearer light on the related issues.

Study of the document: Ḥaram 102

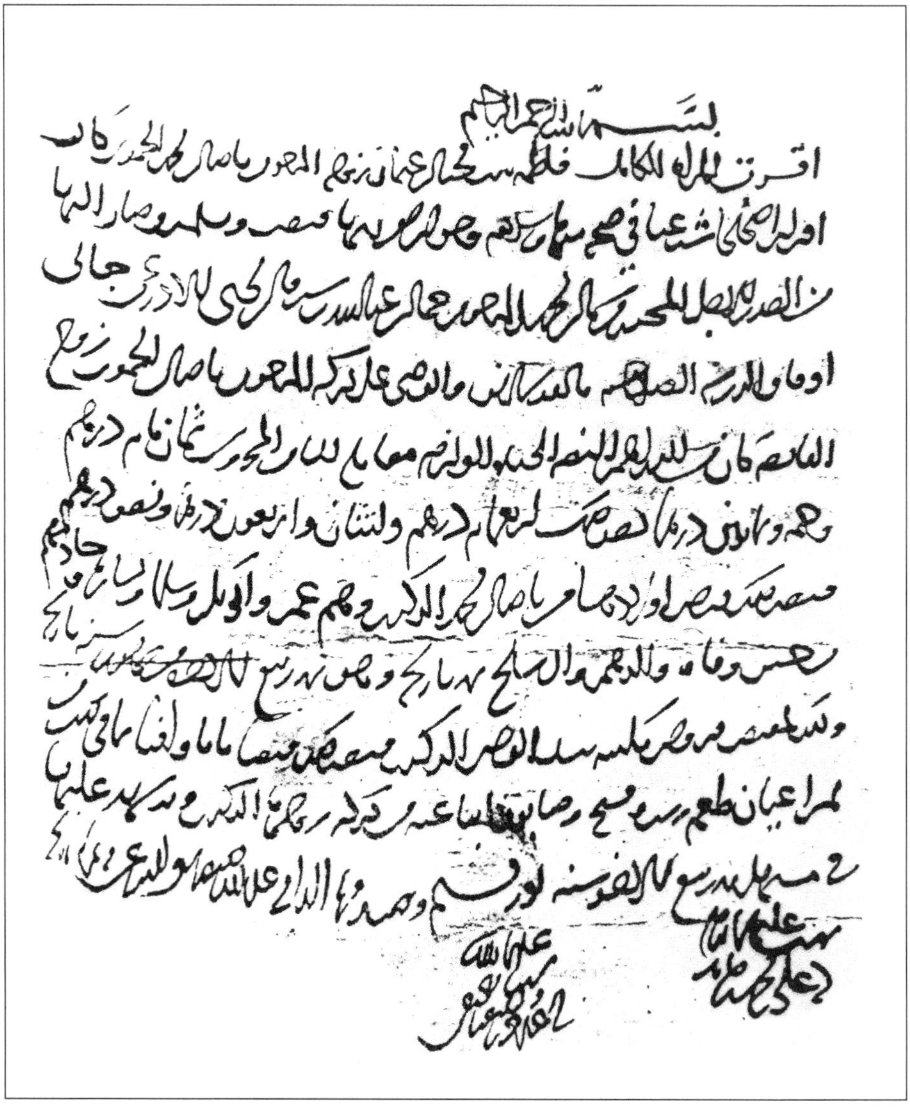
بسم الله الرحمن الرحيم

I could learn a great deal about the Ḥaram collection. As a requirement to pass the Seminar, I specifically analyzed the *Ḥaram 102.*

[215] H. Lutfi, "A Study of the Fourteenth Century *Iqrārs* from al-Quds Relating to Muslim Women," *Journal of the Economic and Social History of the Orient*, vol. 26, no. 3, (1983), p. 246-294.

Ḥaram 102: content

١) بسم الله الرحمان الرحيم
٢) أقرت المرأة الكامل فاطمة بنت فخر الدين عثمان المرحوم ناصر الدين محمد الحموي كان
٣) إقرارا صحيحا شرعيا في صحة منها وسلامة وجواز أمر انها قبضت وتسلمت وصار إليها
٤) من الصدر الاجل المحترم شمس الدين محمد بن المرحوم جمال الدين عبد الله بن شرف الدين يحي الادرعي جابر
٥) اوقاف المدرسة الصلاحية بالقدس الشريف والوصى على تركة المرحوم ناصر الدين الحموي زوج
٦) القابضة كان من الدراهم الفضة الجيدة الوازنة معاملة الشام المحروس ثمانيمائة درهم
٧) وخمسة وثمانين درهما نصف ذلك اربعمائة درهم واثنان واربعين درهما ونصف درهم
٨) قبضت ذلك فرض اولادها من ناصر الدين محمد المذكور وهم عمر وابو بكر وسلما وسارة وخادمهم
٩) من حين وفات والدهم والى سلخ شهر تاريخه وهو شهر ربيع الاخرة من شهور سنة تاريخيه
١٠) ذلك بمقتضى فروض مكتبة بيد الوصي المذكور قبضت ذلك قبضا تاما وافيا بما في ذلك من
١١) ثمن اعيان طعم زيت وملح وصابون ابتاعته من تركة زوجها المذكور وبه شهد عليهما
١٢) في مستهل شهر ربيع الاخرة سنة تسع وثمانين وسبعمائة (؟) وصدقها الدافع على ذلك التصديق الشرعي به (...) بتاريخه
١٣) شهدت عليهما بتاريخه كتبه على بن محمد بن حامد

شهدت عليهما بذلك
كتبه
جمال الدين عبد الرحمان الحنفي

ḤARAM 102: translation

Ḥaram 102 – Recto only

Date: 1 Rabī ʻ II 789 (or 787)/ 21 April 1389 (or 1387)

1- In the name of God, the compassionate, the Merciful
2- She acknowledged – the adult woman Fāṭima the daughter of Fakhr al-Dīn ʻUthmān, the wife of the late Nāṣir al-Dīn Muḥammad al-Ḥamawī, who is dead,
3- in a valid and legal iqrār manner, while she was in a state of sound body and mind and legally capable of conducting her affairs that she received and obtained possesion
4- from the most Eminent and Respected Chief Shams al-Dīn Muḥammad the son of the late Jamāl al-Dīn ʻAbd Allāh the son of Sharaf al-Dīn Yaḥyā al-Adraʻī, the rent collector
5- of the waqf of the madrasa al-Ṣalāḥiyya in Jerusalem the Noble and the executor of the estate of the late Nāṣir al-Dīn Muḥammad al-Ḥamawī, the husband

6- of the recipient. Eight hundred and eighty was of full-weight good silver dirhams in current use in Damascus the Protected,
7- half of which is four hundred and forty two and half dirhams.
8- She received this lawful share allotted to her children from the mentioned Nāṣir al-Dīn Muḥammad, namely ʻUmar, Abū Bakr, Salmā, Sāra and their servant
9- from the time of the death of their father until the end of the month of its (document's) date, i.e., the end of the month of Rabīʻ the Second from months of the year of its document's date,
10- This is in accordance with the lawful shares written by the hand of the executor mentioned above. She received this in its entirety and completely including
11- the price of food, oil, salt and soap which she bought from estate of her husband mentioned above. In regard to this, they were borne witness to
12- on the first of the month of Rabīʻ the Second of the year seven hundred eighty nine (or seven). The payer corroborated her in conformity with the law (…) on its (document's) date.
13- It was witness to them in regard to this

Written by

ʻAbd al-Raḥmān
Al-Ḥanafī

It was witness to them on its (document's) date

Written by

ʻAlī Ibn Muḥammad
Ibn Ḥāmid

Notes to *Ḥaram 102* – Recto only

Line 1: This is commonly used formula of the *basmala* in Arabic documents. In the chapter of legal acknowledgements Al-Asyūṭī states that all documents should begin with pietistic formulas of *al-basmala, al-ḥamdala* and *al-taṣliyya* for the Prophet and his family; see; Al-Asyūṭī, *Jawāhir*, I, 25. In spite of the difficult handwriting the *basmala* is the simplest to decipher in a document. Al-Asyūṭī describes in detail how this formula should be written; the notary should write each word separately, the writing of the *basmala* in the document should be similar to the writing of this formula in the Holy Book. For more details see: Al-Asyūṭī, *Jawāhir*, I, 14.

Line 2: The text begins with the verb *aqarrat* which expresses the written intention of the person initiating the legal obligation. In the Ḥaram documents *aqarra/aqarrat* is the standard with the exception of one document (no 53) is the word *iʻtarafa* is used. For the discussion of the *iqrār's* (legal acknowledgement's) form see: D.P. Little, *A Catalogue*, 189; Al-Asyūṭī, *Jawāhir*, I, 17-53. Following the verb expressing the intention *(al-niyya)* comes the identification clause *(al-tarjama)* which identifies the woman *(al-muqirra)* who makes the legal acknowledgement. Here the name of the woman is specified by the name of her husband. The identification clause is missing the name of grandfather. The name of the husband is followed by the verb *kāna* (he was) which refers to the fact that he is dead. For the identification clause see: Al-Asyūṭī, *Jawāhir*, I, 24.

Line 3: The line begins with the phrase *iqrāran shar'iyyan* which is a standard in legal documents (see: Al-Asyūṭī, *Jawāhir*, I, 25) and refers to the fact that the woman is legally permitted to make such acknowledgement and that this has been testified by two wualified witnesses. The phrase *iqrāran shar'iyyan* occurs in all six documents from *Ḥaram* collection discussed by Huda Lutfi in her article: " A Study of Six Fourteen Century *Iqrārs* from Al-Quds Relating to Muslim Woman." For the conditions required to make an *iqrār* see: Al-Asyūṭī, *Jawāhir*, I, 18; for the qualifications of witnesses and validity of document see: E. Tyan, *Le notariat,* 72-93. The following clause: *fī ṣiḥḥā minhā wa salāma wa jawāz 'amr* indicate s the legal competence of the woman (see: Al-Asyūṭī, *Jawāhir*, I, 25). This clause is also standard in the legal acknowledgements. The rest of the line indicates that the woman *(al-muqirra)* received and obtained certain possession: *qabaḍat wa tasallamat wa ṣāra ilayhā.* This clause occurs in the following documents from the *Ḥaram* collection: *108, 184, 205, 287* discussed by Lutfi in her article mentioned previously.

Line 4-5: These line specify the identification clause of the executor of the estate of the dead husband *(al-muqarr lahu).* The person identified by the name of his father and grandfather. The honorific titles *al-Ṣadr al-Ajall al-Muḥtaram* indicate that person is of little, if any distinction. Al-Asyūṭī gives a detailed discussion on the honorific titles. According to him the notary should give these titles based on his knowledge of the person and concerning the profession, activity, morality, etc. For more details see: Al-Asyūṭī, *Jawāhir*, I, 14-16, II, 582-599. The identification clause is completed by the explanation of the profession. *Jābir awqāf* refers to the office of the rent collector and accountant of the *waqf* (see: Al-Asyūṭī, *Jawāhir*, I, 337). *Waqf al-madrasa al-Ṣalāḥiyya* was instituted by Ṣalāḥ al-Dīn al-Ayyubī in 588 A.H. The building of the school-church was transformed by Ṣalāḥ al-Dīn into a *waqf* and Shāfi 'ī school. For more information about the location of *al-madrasa* and its activity until the twentieth century see: 'Ārif al-'Ārif, *al-Mufaṣṣal,* 179-160, 237-238.

Line 6: This line begins with the word *al-qābiḍa* (the recipient) which belongs to the previous clause.

Line 6-7: Here the payment clause is indicated. The phrase *al-darāhim al-fiḍḍa* refers to the currency used in the document. The added attributes *al-jayyīda al-wāzina* may indicate that the coins were carefully and precisely examined by the notary and he accepted the currency. According to Al-Asyūṭī the currency should be clearly specified; whether it is gold or silver, the weight of it, the thickness and the province in which it in use, should be mentioned. For more details see: Al-Asyūṭī, *Jawāhir*, I, 25. The phrase *mu'āmalat al-shām* refers to the province (Damascus) in which the coin specified in our document was in use. In all the Ḥaram documents almost without exception the currency of Damascus is mentioned. See: D. P. Little, "Purchase Deeds for Slaves," 307-308.

Line 8: Here the object of the acknowledgement *al-muqarr bihi* is indicated, *farḍ al-awlādihā* (the lawful share alloted to her children). As Al-Asyūṭī points out in his *Kitāb al-nafaqāt* in the case of divorce or the death of the husband the child is protected by *farḍ al-walad* . According to the scholar this *farḍ* should secure all the necessities of the child, that is: flat, food, clothes, etc. For more details see Al-Asyūṭī, *Jawāhir*, II, 222. Unially the executor of the estate of the husband, requests from the widow to make a legal acknowledgement in order to use it as a record that he paid her the fixed lawful share for keeping custody of the children. The names of the children are indicated.

Line 9-10: In the case of object of acknowledgement, it should be detailed in full and in a clear manner. The term of payment *(al-ajal)* is the very important element (see: Al-Asyūṭī, *Jawāhir*, I, 28.). In our document the payment term is specified clearly, that is from the death of the husband until the end of the month of the document's date. Then it is indicated that the widow received the lawful shares (for her children), written by the hand of the executor of her husband in its entirety and completely: *qabaḍat dhālika farḍ tāmman wāfiyan*. The phrase *tāmman wāfiyan* is standard in the Ḥaram documents (see: *Ḥaram 184* and *205* in H. Lutfi article mentioned previously).

Line 11: This line contains the list of the things which the widow Fāṭima received for her children from the estate of her dead husband, that is: *thaman a'yān ṭa'am* price of the item of food which she bought, *zayt* (oil), *malaḥ* (salt) and *ṣābūn* (soap) and from his estate: which refers to the dead Nāṣir al-Dīn. The formula *bihi shuhida* refers to an important legal element in any written document, that is to the testimony of witnesses to the content of the document.

Line 12: Here the date of the document is mentioned. The dating formula contains: the the day, month and year. In our document it is the first of Rabī' the second 789 (or 787). For more details about the dating formula see: J. A.Wakin, *The Function of Documents*, 47-49. The clause *ṣaddaqahā (...) al-taṣdīq al-shar'ī* refers to the fact that the executor of the estate of the dead husband authenticated what the widow acknowledged in legal manner, that is before two qualified witnesses and on the date of this document *(bi-ta'rīkhihi)*. For more detail see: Al-Asyūṭī, *Jawāhir*, I, 28.

Line 13: The conclusion of the legal acknowledgement (*iqrār)* is followed by the deposition of the cause of the testimony *(rasm shahāda).* Here the witness testify not only what the widow Fāṭima bint Fakhr al-Dīn acknowledged but also to the fact that the executor of the estate of her dead husband authenticated what she acknowledged. In our document clauses of testimony are not identical. The first testimony from right to left is: *shahidtu ʻalayhimā bi-taʼrīkhihi*, the second one: *shahidtu ʻalayhimā bi-dhālik*. The signatures of the witnesses are difficult to decipher. In spite of the fact that the *shurūṭ* scholars recommended the clear and good handwriting, from the study of this particular document and other Arabic documents (Arabic papyrus, other documents from the *Ḥaram* collection) we can see that the notaries did not follow this advice. Concerning the signature of witnesses the situation is even worse. In many cases the signature cannot be deciphered because of the cursiveness and carelessness of the script. In the case of our document the signature of the second witness (from right to left) is not deciphered completely. For details about the importance of clearly written signatures see: Al-Asyūṭī, *Jawāhir*, I, 28.

Commentary on *Ḥaram 102* – Recto only

The document *Ḥaram 102* transcribed, translated and analyzed here generally follows the rules of the wording of the legal acknowledgements stated by Al-Asyūṭī in the chapter "Kitāb al-iqrār" from his book *Jawāhir al-ʻuqūd wa muʻīn al-qudāt wa lʼshuhūd.* The analysis of each particular line indicates that the document contains all the necessary formulas and phrases. However, it should be pointed out that certain elements are not clearly enough specified and written. The identification clause of the woman Fāṭima (*al-muqirra)* is missing an important element, which is the name of her grandfather. The date of the document is not written clearly: the year can be deciphered as 889 or 887. Furthermore, the last words of line 12 as well as the signature of the second witness (from right to left) are difficult to decipher.

The study of our document (*Ḥaram 102)* and its comparison with two others (*Ḥaram 184, 287)* discussed by Huda Lutfi in her article: "A Study of the Fourteenth Century *Iqrārs* from al-Quds Relating to Muslim Women" suggests that *Ḥaram 102* refers to the same person Fāṭima as *Ḥaram 184* and *287*. The comparison of the names of the woman, her husband and their children and the dates of the documents (see table 1) supports this thesis. However, there are certain elements which might weaken our statement, first, the name of Fāṭima in *Ḥaram 102* is not fully specified (by the name of her grandfather) and secondly, the names of the children are identical within *Ḥaram 102* and *184* in three cases, that is ʻUmar, Salmā and Sāra. Concerning the fourth name in *Ḥaram 102* it is clearly written as Abū Bakr and in *Ḥaram 184* it was deciphered by Lutfi as Aḥmad. However, the writing of the fourth name in *Ḥaram 184* looks different. In the line 7 the name may be deciphered as Abū Bakr but in the line 8 could be deciphered as Aḥmad.

Unclear script concerning the fourth name in *Ḥaram 184*, might suggest the possibility of an error made by the notary.[216]

The dates of these three documents may also support our thesis.[217] These documents can be placed in the following chronological order: (1) *Ḥaram 287:* 22 Ṣafar 787 (content: bride, price and the loan from the husband), (2) *Ḥaram 102*: 1 Rabī ' II 789 or 787 (content: 885 dirhams and other specified things for maintenance of the four children from the estate of the dead husband), (3) *Ḥaram 184:* 2 Ramaḍān 789 (content: family allowance for three months for four children from *waqf* revenues).

As Lutfi stated in her article mentioned previously[218] Fāṭima bint Fakhr al-Dīn came from the middle-class income group. From *Ḥaram 287* we know that she was married to a merchant. When her husband died it seems (from the content of *Ḥaram 184*) that she did not have enough income. What happened to Fāṭima during these two years? Perhaps *Ḥaram 102* can be considered as a part of the answer.

Ḥaram	**Date**	**Woman**	**Husband**	**Children**
287	22 Safar 787	Fāṭima bint Fakhr al-Dīn ibn Zayn al-Dīn 'Umar al-Ḥamawiyya	Nāṣir al-Dīn ibn Muḥammad 'Alā' al-Dīn ibn Nāṣir al-Dīn Muḥammad al-Ḥamawī	
102	1 Rabī ' II 789 or 787	Fāṭima bint Fakhr al-Dīn 'Uthmān (nisba is not mentioned)	Nāṣir al-Dīn Muḥammad al-Ḥamawī	'Umar Abū Bakr Salmā Sāra
184	2 Ramaḍān 789	Fāṭima bint Fakhr al-Dīn 'Uthmān ibn Zayn al-Dīn 'Umar al-Ḥamawiyya	Nāṣir al-Dīn Muḥammad al-Ḥamawī	'Umar Abū Bakr Salmā Sāra

[216] According to Professor Little it is *li'Umar* and he corrected H. Lutfi in the following article: H. Lutfi and D. P. Little, "Iqrars from Al-Quds: Emendations," *Journal of the Economic and Social History of the Orient*, vol. 28 (1985), p. 326-330.

[217] I consulted Professor Little concerning the problem and he confirmed my assumption that the Fāṭimas in *Ḥaram 102* and in 184 and 287 are the same.

[218] See: Commentary on *Ḥaram 184*.

V

The Architecture of the Mamlūk City of Cairo

During the long history of Cairo, various dynasties contributed to the architectural development of the city. The Mamlūks, the dynasty of slave origins that ruled Egypt from 1250 to 1517, played a significant role in this process of evolution and their magnificent art changed the outlook of Cairo.

Present day Cairo was preceded by three different Islamic cities built almost on the same territory. The oldest one, al-Fusṭāṭ (641), remains as part of the Old City[219]; the second one, al-'Askar (750), was destroyed after the fall of the 'Umayyads (661--750); while the third, al-Qaṭā'i' (873), was ruined after the fall of the Ṭūlūnids (868--905). In 969, Jawhar al-Sikkīlī from the Fāṭimid dynasty (909-1171) established a new city and named it al-Qāhira. Since that time, Cairo has been the political and cultural center of Egypt. After the fall of the Fāṭimids, Cairo was governed by the Ayyūbids (1171-1250) and from 1250 until 1517 remained the capital of the Mamlūk state. The Islamic art of Cairo is preceded by ancient Egypt and Hellenized art that about the fourth or fifth century merged into the Coptic art, i.e., the art of Christian inhabitants of Egypt.[220] The Coptic art lasted until the seventh century. The art of the next few centuries constitutes an amalgam of Byzantine, Sassanid and Syrian influences which all fused together to form a new art called Islamic.[221]

For quite a long period, i.e., 1250-1517, Cairo was the domain of the Mamlūk dynasty. There are many valuable sources concerning the topography and history of the Mamlūk city. However, as Victoria Meinecke-Berg pointed out in her article on this subject,[222] the sources emphasize information concerning the administrative side

---

[219] See: W. B. Kubiak, *Al-Fustat: It's Early Foundation and Early Urban Development*, Cairo: American University of Cairo Press, 1987.

[220] For a detailed discussion see: D. Russel, *Medieval Cairo*, London: Weindenfeld and Nicholson, 1962, p. 43-58. Also refer to: K. A. C. Creswell, *The Muslim Architecture of Egypt*, New York: Hacker Art Books, 1978; R. Yeomans, *The Art and Architecture of Islamic Cairo*, New York: New York University Press, 2000.

[221] See: D. T. Rice, *Islamic Art*, Toledo: Thames and Hudson, 1975.

[222] V. Meinecke-Berg, "Quellen zu Topographie und Baugeschichte in Kairo unter Sulṭān an-Nāṣir Muḥammad b. Qalā' ūn," *Deutscher Orientalistentag*, vol. 19 (1977), p. 538.

of architectural projects, i.e., the founder, architect, cost, duration of time, etc. Only in the case of large projects can we find information about the materials, which were used, methods of work and some descriptive comments. The majority of the monuments, i.e., mosques, *madrasas*, *khānqās* and mausolea which are preserved until today, were founded by the Mamlūk sultans; the sources estimate their number as approximately two hundred thirty.[223]

Until the expedition of Napoleon in 1798, Cairo remained as during the Mamlūks' reign. Later on the city began to develop in the western direction. However, the "heart" of the Mamlūk city has retained its old shape until our days.

The city that the Mamlūks inherited from their predecessors contained the Fāṭimid walled city, the southern area that was developing between Bāb Zuwayla and the new royal city built by Ṣalāḥ al-Dīn.[224] The south part of al-Fusṭāṭ had been burned by the Fāṭimids in 1168 and until the Mamlūk era, only the part near 'Amr Ibn al-'Āṣ Mosque called Old Miṣr had been preserved. On the island of Rawda (opposite Old Miṣr) the Ayyūbids had the *baḥrī* (river) citadel, where the Baḥrī Mamlūks were stationed during Ṣāliḥ Ayyūb's reign. Before the Mamlūk era, the city was developing toward the south-west. The first sultan Baybars (1260-1277) extended the development of Cairo to the north of the Fāṭimid city. This new suburb which surrounded the mosque of Baybars was called Ḥusayniyya.

The most extensive growth of Mamlūk Cairo occurred, as I mentioned previously during the third reign of Al-Nāṣir (1310-1341). There are certain factors, which contributed to this development: (1) the reign of Al-Nāṣir was long in comparison to that of the other sultans, (2) during these thirty years Egypt enjoyed internal and external peace and political stability, (3) stability of the Nile waters led to the development of the areas which were earlier under water or subject to damage. Al-Nāṣir established a special office under the amīrs with control by Āqsunqur al-Rūmī.[225]

During the reign of Al-Nāṣir the expansion of the city continued mainly outside the Fāṭimid walls, i.e., south of Bāb Zuwayla. The south-western slopes of the Citadel, which had remained unfortified in the Ayyūbid period, were walled by Al-Nāṣir. Along with the creation of the new suburb, the new royal markets were established there. The area south of Bāb Zuwayla was principally occupied by Sultan's palace, houses for the high amīrs and important merchants. A number of new mosques appeared there, amongst them Ālmās (or Yilmāz 1329-30), Qūṣūn (1329-30), Bashtāk (1335), Alṭunbunghā al-Māridānī (1339). During the reign of Al-Nāṣir the expansion to the north, initiated by Bāybars (his mosque was built there) did not continue.

---

[223] Ibid.

[224] J. A. Williams, "Urbanization and Monument Construction in Mamlūk Cairo," *Muqarnas*, vol. 2 (1984), p. 35.

[225] This office conducted all the administrative work of Al-Nāṣir's new projects. The budget of the office remains unknown until today. V. Meinecke-Berg, "Quellen zu Topographie..., p. 541.

Sketch map of the Mamlūk Cairo

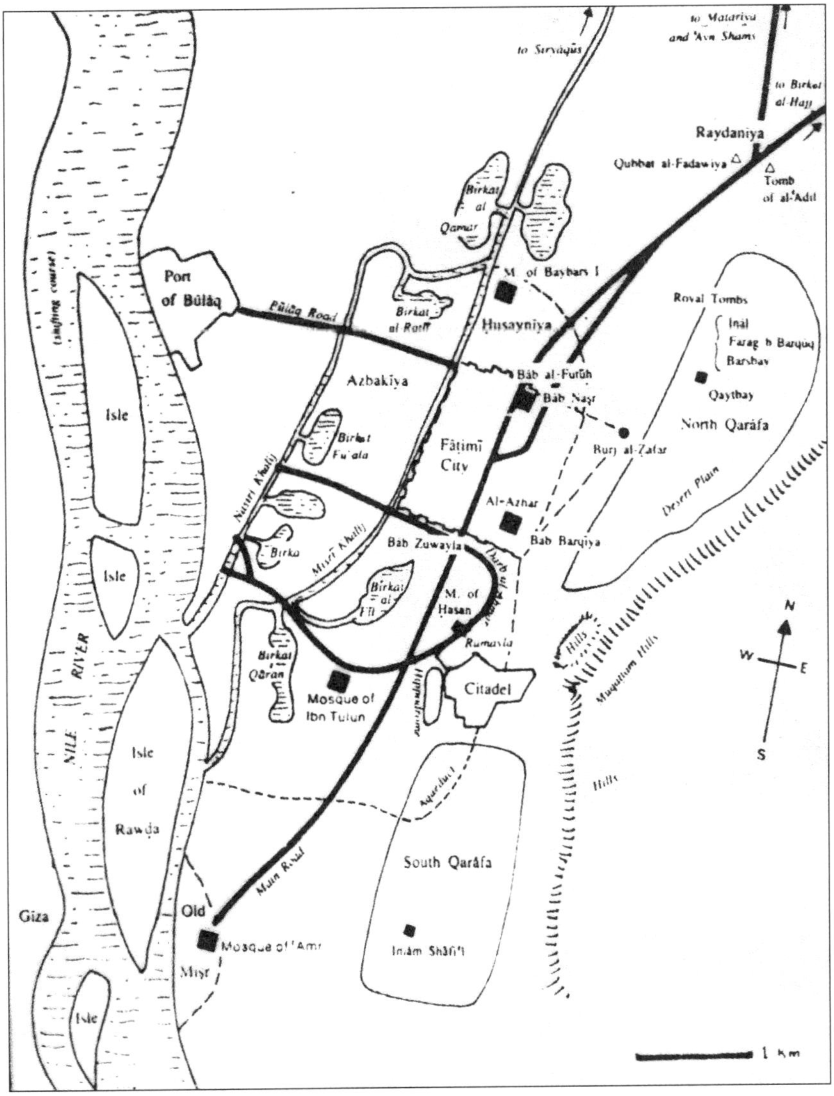

Along with the urbanization south-west of Bāb Zuwayla the creation of thoroughfares was conducted,[226] namely the street Darb al-Aḥmar leading from the citadel to Bāb Zuwayla, the Shāri' al-Ṣalība, leading from the Citadel towards the mosque of Ibn Ṭūlūn and the Khalīj originally a canal (now the Shāri' Port Sa'īd.

Within the period 1310-1325, the main urbanization projects were completed or reached advanced stages.[227] In 1325, Al-Nāṣir completed the construction of a new

[226] M. Rogers, "Al-Ḳāhira, in: "*Encyclopaedia of Islam*, New Edition, vol. 4, p. 424.

[227] V. Meinecke-Berg, "Quellen zu Topographie…, p. 542.

canal al-Khalīj al-Nāṣirī[228] to the west of the city, in order to drain the new land that had been created by the eastward shift on the riverbank, bringing water from the Nile as far as the Birkat al-Ratlī. Then al-Khalīj joined the older canal al-Khalīj al-Misrī to provide water chanel for water transport all the way north to the Sultan's new country seat in Siryāqūs. The project was realized with the help of the amīrs who built several bridges there, streets, two squares for playing polo, namely Maydān al-Nāṣirī and Maydān al-Mahara. The amīrs supplied the project with financial resources and conducted supervisory and administrative work. This "expensive enterprise" of the Sultan led to the growth of orchards, gardens and beautiful houses in the area between al-Khalīj al-Miṣrī an al- Khalīj al-Nāṣirī.

Another important project of Al-Nāṣir was the development of the riverbank area between Miṣr and Bulaq.[229] North of Miṣr he constructed al-Jāmi' al-Jādīd (1311--1312). In the area called Zarībat al-Sulṭān he erected a royal commercial warehouse (*dār wikāla*) and two large lodging complexes *(rab's*). There were also other foundations such as mosques, *madrasas*, lodging complexes and mills overlooking the Nile as well as gardens and markets all along the riverside as far north as Bulaq. However, by the early fifteenth century almost all these new foundation had been abandoned and destroyed.

During his reign, Al-Nāṣir also took upon the task to restore the Citadel, as is indicated in inscriptions found there.[230] His project was to build a southern enceinte to construct a new aqueduct connecting the Citadel with the Nile and incorporating into it part of the wall of Ṣalāḥ al-Dīn.[231] In 1312 he started to build four sāqiyas on the Nile and in 1341 incorporated into the remains of Ṣalāḥ al-Dīn's wall. This construction was later restored and lenghtened. On the Citadel Al-Nāṣir built a mosque (1318) and famous palace, Qaṣr al-Ablaq (1313-15)[232] which was destroyed in 1824. On the foot of the Citadel he established Maydān taḥt al-Qal'a, a square for military training and for playing polo.

From this brief description, we can see that during Al-Nāṣir's days al-Qāhira stretched from Ḥusayniyya in the north along the Canal al-Nāṣirī in the west, to approximately the line of the Sultan's aqueduct in the south, where it joined the Southern Qarāfa (cemetery)

In the cemeteries, dwellings for the living were side by side with tombs for the dead. In the southern area of Cairo, the separate city of Miṣr still flourished as satellite center of learning and crafts. Later on Miṣr was devastated by the plague and cut off from the prosperity by the development of then northern river port of Bulaq.

Despite the remarkable growth of Cairo's suburbs and satellites and the Sultan's encouragement of the amīrs to build monuments and mansions there, the area of the

228 Ibid., p. 541.

229 J. A. Williams, "Urbanization and Monument..., p. 37.

230 M. Rogers, "Al-Ḳāhira..., p. 430.

231 Ibid., p. 424.

232 V. Meinecke-Berg, "Quellen zu Topographie..., p. 541.

walled Fāṭimid city in general and the main street Qaṣaba in particular (from Bāb Zuwayla to Bāb al-Futūḥ) remained the desirable location for palaces and residences.

The third reign of Al-Nāṣir was a peaceful time. Therefore, the Sultan could not prove his superiority in the field of battle. According to David Ayalon,[233] the only outlet to Al-Nāṣir's dictatorial character was to embark on extravagant projects, into which great sections of population of Cairo were swept. As Victoria Meinecke-Berg mentions the Sultan was a "fanatic" of building and this fanaticism in construction extended even beyond that, which took place in Europe during the Renaissance and Baroque time.[234] Furthermore, he destroyed some palaces and foundations of his predecessors. The historians Al-Yūsufī and Al-Maqrīzī try to explain this act by certain features of Al-Nāṣir's, namely his unnatural feeling of superiority, envy and jealousy. Although the Sultan actively subsidized the public constructions, people suffered from his taxation and extortion system. When an amīr lost his favors, Al-Nāṣir would take his property, i.e., palace, mosque or madrasa from him (this happened for example with amīr Ulmās al-Khājib).

In his architectural projects, Al-Nāṣir's aim was perfection.[235] Therefore, he decided to change the shape and decoration of some of his monuments. During the time of Al-Nāṣir a number of important architectonic innovations occurred.[236] The most characteristic feature of his architecture was the evolution of the religious centers, i.e., complexes that included a *jāmi'*, *madrasa, khānqāh, zāwiya* and mausoleum.

Sultan Al-Nāṣir, the skilled politician was able to maintain a balance of power amongst the great amīrs. From the time of his death (1341) until the end of the Baḥrī period (1382) they plotted against each other. Despite the lack of stability in the government, the Mamlūk city continued to flourish and the sulṭāns continued to build new monuments in the areas developed by Al-Nāṣir until the Black Death and after.

During the time of Black Death (1347-1349) between a fourth and third of the population of Cairo died (Cairo historians credit the town with the population of from 500,000 to 600, 000 inhabitants under the reign of Al-Nāṣir).[237] Soon afterwards, when the disease abated (February 1349) the Mamlūk city of Cairo began to "recover" rapidly. However, the plague occurred again in 1403-1404, 1410-1411, 1429--1430, 1437, 1448, 1459-1460 and 1476.[238] The quarters were depopulated; soon they were ruined and devastated. The houses were plundered of their wooden beams, doors and shutters.

---

[233] D. Ayalon, "The Expansion and Decline of Cairo under the Mamlūks and its Background," in: Y. Herromet (ed.), *XXIX Congrès international des orientalistes. Résumés des communications*, Section 4, Paris 1974, p. 64-65.

[234] V. Meinecke-Berg, "Quellen zu Topographie..., p. 540.

[235] J. A.Williams, "Urbanization and Monument..., p. 40.

[236] D. Ayalon, "The Expansion and Decline..., p. 65.

[237] A. Raymond, "Cairo's Area and Population in the Early Fifteenth Century," *Muqarnas*, vol. 2 (1984), p. 22.

[238] J. A.Williams, "Urbanization and Monument..., p. 40.

In spite of all these misfortunes caused by the Black Death and more complicated set of factors, which led to the decline of the Mamlūk economy,[239] al-Qāhira continued to rebuild. In the southern zone new mosques, *madrasas, khānqās*, palaces for great amīrs and other monuments were founded. During the period 1356-1362 the new mosque of Sultan Ḥasan, considered by historians from Al-Maqrīzī to Wiet as the highest achievement of Mamlūk architecture was built.[240] At the same time, the northern Qarāfa became a royal cemeterry. In this area the following monuments were founded: *khānqāh-madrasa-zāwiya* of Sultan Barsbāy (1425); the tomb-*khānqāh-ribāt* of Sultan Ināl (1451-1456); and the mausoleum-*madrasa* of Sultan Qā'it Bāy (1472-1474).

Around the year 1400, during the reign of Al-Nāṣir al-Dīn al-Faraj the Mamlūk city experienced new misfortunes, i.e., the occurrence of low Nile floods, famine and a return of the Black Death. In addition, internal conflicts in the state arouse (1400--1422). As Al-Maqrīzī states during that time "more than half of Cairo, its estates and environs were ruined; two third of the population died of famine and plague, and innumerable others were killed in insurrections in this reign."[241] The population of the city was estimated as low as 150,000-2000,000.[242] The city continued to be rebuilt.

During the time between the reign of Al-Mu'ayyad (1412-1421) and Qā'it Bāy (1468-1496) a number of new monuments were founded, amongst them a complex which included a *madrasa, jāmi', khānqāh* and *madrasa* for Ṣūfis (this complex was built by Al-Mu'ayyad on Qaṣāba, just inside Bāb Zuwayla) and another one which contained a mausoleum, *khānqāh*, *madrasa* and *jāmi'* with residence for the Sultan, apartments for sheikhs, kitchens, *riwāq* (a living unit) and two *zāwiyas* for Ṣūfis (this complex was built by Barsbāy in the northern Qarāfa).

The new fertile days of splendor and glory for al-Qāhira came during the reign of Sultan Qā'it Bāy (1468-1496). Not only did he encourage his amīrs to take upon the task of developing and rebuilding the city, but also he himself sponsored the construction of bridges, fortresses, commercial houses and religious monuments in Cairo, Alexandria and Jerusalem[243] and also in the provincial towns of Egypt and Syria.

The new urbanization took place in the north-west area (especially to the west of the Fāṭimid city in the area called 'Azbakiyya), in Ḥusayniyya and along the road from Bāb al-Naṣr to Raydāniyya, where many palaces for amirs were built.[244] Raydāniyya became a pleasance for the Mamlūk court, many outings and processions passed that way. In this area, a hippodrome and a review stand for the occasions of the Mamlūk parades through the Qaṣada were founded. There were two

---

[239] D. Ayalon, "The Expansion and Decline..., p. 65.

[240] J. A. Williams, "Urbanization and Monument..., p. 41.

[241] Ibid.

[242] A. Raymond, "Cairo's Area..., p. 30.

[243] For a detailed discussion of the significance of the Ḥaram documents for the history of Jerusalem under the Mamlūks see: D. P. Little, "The Ḥaram Documents as Sources for the Arts and Architecture of the Mamlūk Period," *Muqarnas*, vol. 2 (1984), p. 62-73.

[244] J. A. Williams, "Urbanization and Monument..., p. 43.

roads from Raydāniyya, one led eastward to Birkat al-Ḥajj, the first stage on the pilgrim journey and the other led northward to the village of Maṭariyya with its spring and tree associated with the Virgin and Christ Child. In the area of Maṭariyya, the powerful amīr of Qā'it Bāy built two palaces, one south of Raydāniyya, i.e., complex palace-muntaza (pleasance) with *khānqāh-madrasa* (until today only a part of it, i.e., the qubba-pleasure dome remains) and another in Raydāniyya with a bigger pleasure dome known as the Qubbat al-Fadāwiyya.

Although Qā'it Bāy and his great amirs continued on with the luxurious constructions on a grand scale, it is known from historical sources that the Mamlūk economy of that time was not in a very good state (there were problems with the Indian Ocean trade and the decline of agricultural productivity). Some historians suggest that the money for all these enterprises might have come from high taxes on commerce with Europeans, from *muṣādarāt* (confiscations and extortions) and taxes from all strata of society.

The successors of Qā'it Bāy attempted to continue his way of developing the city; they founded a few monuments such as a complex containing a *madrasa, jāmi'*, mausoleum and *khānqāh* of Sultan Qānṣūh al-Ghawrī (1510-1516). However, as Wiet says, these constructions were tasteless and only the "poor imitations" of the magnificent buildings from the Qā'it Bāy's days.[245]

This brief survey of the development and evolution of the Mamlūk city al-Qāhira does not provide us with a complete picture of its architectural style. This survey has to be completed by the discussion of the most characteristic features of Mamlūk style as well as that of its expressive intent, i.e., the meaning that was given to the monuments by architects and their patrons.

There are certain characteristics of the Mamlūk state that should be taken into account, namely its military character, the emphasis on Sunni Islam as the state's religion and the Mamlūk patronage of Ṣūfī institutions. Accordingly, one must expect that the ideology of architecture incorporated in the magnificent monuments in Cairo would be that of sulṭāns and amīrs, the military élite that effectively monopolized power in Egypt.[246] The great domes, the towering high minarets, the monumental portals, ornamented facades and curved stone decorations; all this was intended to impress the onlooker with power and glory of the Sunnī Mamlūks. The development of foundations such as the *khānqāh, zāwiya* and *ribāt* gives another outlook to the Mamlūk city, indicating a strong patronage to Ṣūfī institutions. Obviously, in Mamlūk Cairo the architect would rather play a technical and supervisory role, while the "creator" was the sultan or the amir.

Although at the beginning the Mamlūks followed the architectural tradition of the Fāṭīmids, Zangids and Ayyūbids, in a relatively short period of time (about thirty

[245] Ibid.

[246] For a detailed discussion about the expressive intent of the Mamlūk architecture of Cairo see: S. R. Humphreys, "The Expressive Intent of the Mamlūk Architecture of Cairo: A Preliminary Essay," *Studia Islamica*, vol. 35 (1972), p. 69-119.

years) they developed their own architectural style.[247] As Humpreys pointed out,[248] the Mamlūks were in no sense "innovators" and added no essential new monumental types to "repertoire" which they had inherited from Zangid and Ayyūbid times. However, their structures were not only larger and more richly decorated but also more concerned with an impressive and meaningful outlook. Scholars consider Mamlūk time as a unified period in the history of art with a unique and single style. The main reason for considering Mamlūk architecture as a unity is its goal that may be termed "striving for the effect". This "effect" emerges from the most obvious and persistent elements of the Mamlūk style.

First, the objects and buildings represent a high level of material civilization. Secondly, the Mamlūk architecture attempts to give the appearance of height by the use of vertical elements, i.e., ribbed domes set on circulated drums, a series of flat-backed vertical niches running almost the entire height of the exterior facades and tall minarets with their square, octagonal and circle shafts. Thirdly, the facades of the buildings are carefully planned, richly decorated and focused upon imposing portals. Fourthly, the Mamlūk architecture is characterized by the growing dominance of stone in all parts of the structure, to the extent that stone gradually supplanted stucco as a medium of curved decoration; the Mamlūk architecture is very decorative; the facades, external and internal walls, windows, doors, minarets and domes are almost without blank spaces. Amongst the decorative elements we can find a variety of geometrical and plant designs, curved wood and stone decoration, mosaic and stucco, different forms of stalactites (especially for the ceiling and portals), Arabic inscriptions in different forms of the *neshī* script and *ablaq*, i.e., decoration based on the use of different colored stones organized in horizontal lines which provides an effect similar to chessboard. The last of the dominant characteristics of the Mamlūk architecture is the use of color, i.e., the extensive use of *ablaq* decoration, of colored marble paneling on the entire breath of the *qibla* wall and of gilt and vividly painted and stained glass.

The features of Mamlūk architecture mentioned above may be seen on the examples of the two outstanding constructions from the Baḥrī period, namely the Qalā'ūn complex[249] which includes a *madrasa*, mosque, mausoleum and *maristān* (hospital) and the *madrasa*-mausoleum of Sultan Ḥasan.

---

[247] For a thorough discussion on the characteristic features of Islamic art and architecture see: S. Blair, *The Art and Architecture of Islam, 1250-1800*, New Haven, CT: Yale University Press, 1994; R. Ettinghausen, *The Art and Architecture of Islam*, Harmondsworth: Penguin Books, 1987; R. Hillenbrand, *Islamic Architecture: Form, Function and Meaning*, Edinburgh: Edinburgh University Press, 1994; A. M. Hamdouni, *Art and Architecture in the Islamic Tradition: Aesthetics, Politics and Desire in Early Islam*, London–New York: I. B. Tauris, 2011. Also see: G. Wiet, *Cairo, City of Art and Commerce*, trans. by S. Feiler, Norman: University of Oklahoma Press, 1964.

[248] Ibid., p. 95.

[249] For a detailed description of the Qalā'ūn complex see, for example: J. D. Hoag, *Islamic Architecture*, New York: Harry N. Abrams Inc., 1977, p. 162-199.

The Qalā'ūn complex, located on Bayn al-Qaṣrayn, was initiated by Sultan al-Manṣūr Sayf al-Dīn Qalā'ūn (1280-1290) in 1284 and completed by his son Al-Nāṣir in 1293. Today all the parts of the complex, except the *maristān*, are preserved quite well.

The facade of the mausoleum that can be seen from the street is remarkable. It is in the Fāṭimid style and has high pointed arches; the pillars separating them are massive and they rest on light columns with Corinthian capitals. A band of Arabic inscription above the first row of windows runs the whole building. A typical, high (56 meters) Mamlūk minaret (the lower part of which is square, with an octagon above it, crowned by cylindrical shaft) is situated at the northern end of the facade. The entrance portal is constructed of black and white marble (*ablaq* decoration). The entrance leads into a corridor, which separates the mausoleum on the right and *madrasa* on the left side. The corridor continues on to the *maristān*.

Mausoleum (1) and Madrasa (2) of Sultan Qalā'ūn

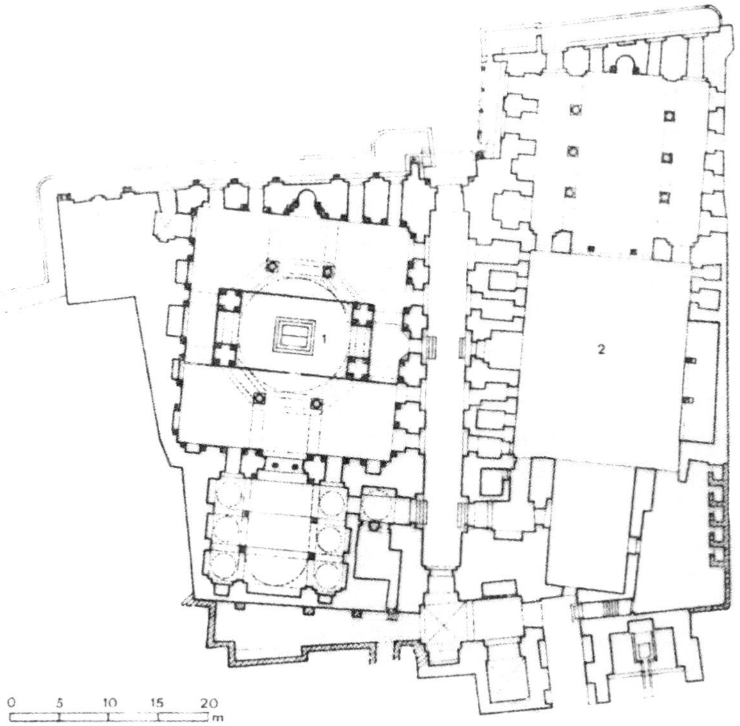

The main *īwān* of the *madrasa* is divided into three naves by porphyry columns. There are gilded mosaics in the dome and in the corners. The *madrasa* has been greatly damaged. In addition to the two principal *īwān*, it must have originally had two smaller ones. The *qibla īwān* has the form of the triptite basilica. The nave arcades are decked with bands of curved plaster interlacing around. The *qibla* wall is richly decorated.

The mausoleum is preceded by small court. The entrance facade is in the form of wooden *mashrabiyya* (4 meters wide) with the door in the centre, surrounded by friezes and stucco ornamentation with a variety of motifs. The mausoleum itself measures 21x23 meters and it is almost a square chamber. The dome of the mausoleum, which imitates that of the mosque of ‘Umar in Jerusalem, collapsed and was reconstructed in 1903. It is now supported by four square pillars and granite columns and there are eight pointed arches. Eight other arches link the centre of the dome to the walls of the room and thus form a rectangular or pentagonal wooden ceiling decorated with artistic designs. The walls of the room are covered with marble and mother-of pearl. The *miḥrāb* is ornamented by three pairs of red porphyry columns with Persian capitals, a band of polychrome inscription, marble mosaics in a shell pattern and several kinds of arches. The sarcophagus is surrounded by a curved and decorated wooden grill.

The *madrasa*-mausoleum of Sultan Ḥasan[250] was built during his reign between 1356 and 1363 by Syrian architect. It is easily recognized by its two minarets on the east side. One of them is 81,6 metres high and it is the highest of Cairo’s numerous minarets.

The main entrance (A) on the north side has an arch of stalactite formation set into the wall, decorated with inlays of green marble. The original gates now in the mosque of Al-Mu’ayyad; they are made of wood and covered with bronze plates. On this north side the exterior facade is so high that is almost resembles a rampart wall. It has eight rows of windows and is crowned with projecting cornice and pinacles.

The intricate plan of the construction (an irregular pantagon of 7,906 square metres in area) provides a separable distinct *madrasa* complex for the four orthodox schools of Islam. Each is entered individually from the *ṣaḥn* (court), has its own modest court and vaulted *īwān*.

The entrance hall, which has a cruciform corridor in the form of miniature mosque (B), leads on through several corridors to the north room of the court (C). This is also cruciform and open to the sky in the square centre and has arches around the four sides. In the middle of the *ṣaḥn* is an octagonal *ḥanafiyya* (fountain), supported by columns and surrounded by a domed roof (D). Arches and high vaulting support the ceiling of the four prayer rooms. The eastern room is very beautiful; its walls are decorated with marble and Coranic inscription in the Kufic script on a background of arabesques. From the ceiling formerly hung enamelled lamps on metal chains, most of these lamps are now in the museum of Islamic Art in Cairo. The *miḥrāb* (E) is richly decorated in Syrian style with grape and trellis motifs. The *minbar* (throne) (F) and the *dikka* (pulpit) (G) are made of white marble. The door is decorated with gold and silver.

---

[250] For a detailed description of the complex of Sulṭān Ḥasan see, for example: ibid., p. 169-174.

Through two doors, set in the wall with the *miḥrāb* is the way to the mausoleum of the Sultan (H); in its centre lays the sarcophagus beneath a dome with the stalactite decoration. Round the lower part of the mausoleum is a beautiful inscribed, polychrome frieze. Sultan Ḥasan is not buried in the mausoleum; in 1386, his son Aḥmad was buried there.

The mausoleum and *madrasa* of Sultan Ḥasan

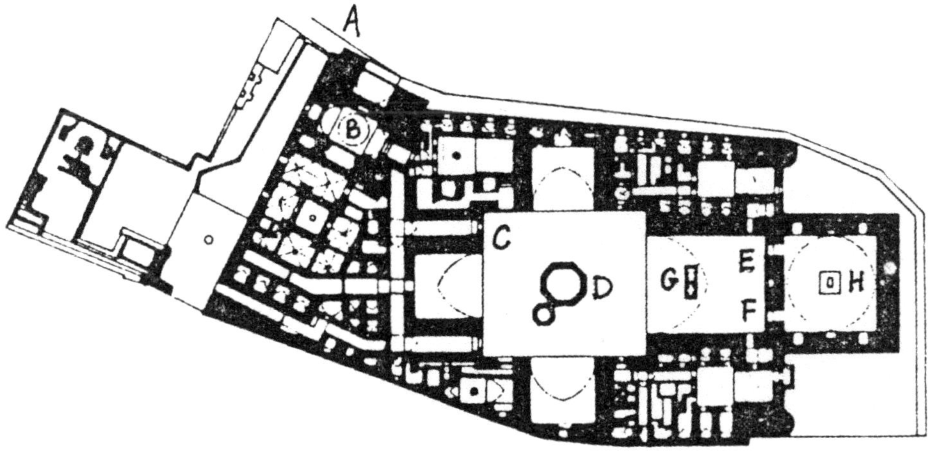

By the fourteenth century, Islamic civilization, shaken to its roots by the destructive invasion of the Mongols, was experiencing a general renaissance from Spain to Central Asia and India. According to Ibn Khaldūn Cairo was the "city" of the age:

> Today no city has more abudant sedentary learning than Cairo; she is the Mother of the World, the īwān of Islam, the wellspring of learning and the crafts.[251]

The Mamlūks, the rulers of Cairo, were a self-perpetuating corporation of military slaves. They set their "stamp" on everything they touched, i.e., the government, the arts, crafts and architecture. In spite of many misfortunes, such as plague and famine, which occurred in Egypt during the Mamlūk time, the rulers extensively developed Cairo in all aspects. They took upon the task of rebuilding and modernizing the city, creating new areas and building richly decorated monuments, which symbolize their power and glory. The "heart" of the Mamlūk city that is preserved until today testifies the high level of civilization represented by its "creators".

---

[251] Cited from J. A. Williams, "Urbanization and Monument..., p. 33.

VI

Forging a New Synthesis of East and West: The State-Sponsored Reforms of Muḥammad ʻAlī

Traditionally Egypt was a society whose inhabitants possessed the stability of an agrarian order and were rather reluctant to changes in their minds and values. At the same time, however, something about Egypt drove its rulers to entertain ambitions that end up breaking the back of their society. This was true in the case of Muḥammad ʻAlī, also known as Muḥammad ʻAlī Pasha, Ottoman governor-general (*wālī*) of Egypt from 1805 to 1849, who from one perspective can be viewed as another traditional warlord seeking to establish at the expense of the weakened Ottoman state an independent, hereditary dynasty.[252] Yet, for all the customary features of absolutism that characterized Muḥammad ʻAlī's days in Egypt, his regime also represented the first sustained program in the Middle East of state-sponsored Europeanization of the military and of the institutions that supported it, and, without any doubt led to the foundations of a modern society.

Muḥammad ʻAlī was an ethnic Albanian, born and raised in the Greek coastal city of Kawalla in Macedonia in 1769. According to family tradition, his ancestors were Turks from Arapkir in Anatolia who later settled in Konya. From there his grandfather emigrated to Kawalla. Muḥammad ʻAlī was one of seventeen children of Ibrāhīm Agha, the chief of the local town watchmen. Historians say that he was the rare combination of a soldier and political lider of genius.[253] Although almost

---

[252] For a comprehensive survey on Muḥammad ʻAlī's rule in Egypt see: E. R. Toledano, "Muḥammad ʻAlī Pasha," in: *Encyclopaedia of Islam*, New Edition, vol. 7, p. 423-431, and for a broad discussion: A. L. Sayyid-Marsot, *Egypt in the Reign of Muhammad ʻAli*, Cambridge–New York: Cambridge University Press, 1984; F. Lawson, *The Social Origins of Egyptian Expansionism during the Muhammad Ali Period*, New York: Columbia University Press, 1992; Kh. Fahmy, *All the Pasha's Men: Mehmed Ali, His Army, and the Making of Modern Egypt*, Cambridge–New York: Cambridge University Press, 1997.

[253] See: P. Mansfield, "Muhammad ʻAli's Egypt: Ottoman Rival," in: idem, *A History of the Middle East*, London: Penguin Books, 1992, p. 46-63.

illiterate,[254] he was no narrowly minded bigot. Having worked as a tobacco merchant in his youth, he was accustomed to dealing with non–Muslims and Europeans. His sharp mind was quick in absorbing new facts and analyzing their importance. Ruthless, fiercely ambitious, and capable of harsh cruelty he could also charm foreign visitors, however exalted, who would quail at his piercing gaze before continuing to admire.

Struggling for power and autonomy

When in 1798 Bonaparte landed in Egypt with his French army,[255] Muḥammad 'Alī accompanied a contingent of Macedonians and Albanians that was sent with an Ottoman expeditionary force,[256] to resist the invaders. It was at this time that Muḥammad 'Alī began his famous military career. In 1800, he was one of the two chiefs of the Albanian troops in the Turkish service who were left behind in Egypt. This secured him an influential military position, when after the final departure of the French in 1801, the Ottomans began to recover their authority over Egypt. The Napoleonic episode had a minimal direct effect on Egypt. However, through the defeat of the Mamlūk beys and the weakening of their hold on the province, it had an important indirect influence. When the French departed the beys came out of hiding and attempted, once again, to impose their authority. At the same time, Sultan Selim III tried to oust them and restore direct control from Istanbul. Eventually he failed, as the British who still occupied Alexandria sided with the beys. When the British departed in 1803 they left a situation which neither the Ottoman governor nor the beys were strong enough to prevail through, and in two years of chaos and civil war ensued. Easily grasping the complex power-game in Egypt at that time, Muḥammad 'Alī skillfully manipulated the various parties to promote his own interests. The main vehicle that served the aspiring officer was the Ottoman-Albanian unit, whose leadership he obtained in mid-1803 as the first stepping stone to power. The other competitors came from various factions of Mamlūk beys, the Ottoman governor-general regiments and the urban notables. The nature of the game consisted in striking the right balance, forming a durable coalition, playing opposition factions against each other, assessing the relative strength and vital interests of all parties, and possessing a fine sense of timing. In all this Muḥammad 'Alī bettered his rivals.

Crucial events leading to Muḥammad 'Alī's ascendant took place between 1803 and 1805.[257] There were two important political Mamlūk factions: the first led by 'Uthmān Bey al-Bardīsī and the other by Muḥammad Bey al-Alfī. The Ottoman

---

[254] He learned to read at the age of forty-seven.

[255] About the long-term impact of the French invasion on Egypt see, for example: A. Hourani, *Arab Thought in the Liberal Age*, Cambridge: Cambridge University Press, 1983.

[256] This army was defeated by Bonaparte at Abū Qīr on 25 July 1799.

[257] P. Mansfield, *A History of the Middle East...*, p. 46-47.

camp was also internally divided between the governor-general Khurshaw Pasha and the commander of Albanian force Ṭāhir Pasha. The cleavage within each camp for control of Egypt turned into a complex struggle between *ad hoc* coalitions of subgroups. In April 1803, the Ottoman–Albanians mutinied in Cairo over pay demands, and Khurshaw Pasha fled to Damietta. At that point, Muḥammad ʻAlī renewed the alliance with the Mamlūks, defeated Khurshaw Pasha and brought him to Cairo as prisoner. With Muḥammad Alfī in England to rally support for his camp, the coalition depended on the political ties between Al-Bardīsī and Muḥammad ʻAlī. Therefore the new governor-general, sent from Istanbul was eventually eliminated by that coalition early in 1804. Upon his return to Egypt Al-Alfī was ultimately forced to escape to Upper Egypt and was eliminated from the game. Al-Bardīsī then became the next target. When he imposed a new tax on the population bringing the situation on the verge of the revolt, it was Muḥammad ʻAlī who saved the inhabitants of Cairo. He abrogated the tax and drove Al-Bardīsī out of the city. By helping the population Muḥammad ʻAlī laid the foundations of his alliance with the important groups of Cairo society. Then on 13 May 1805 the *ʻulamāʼ* (Muslim scholars)[258], leading merchants and other notables who were regarded by the people of Cairo as their representatives, asked Muḥammad ʻAlī to become their governor-general.

Understandably, Selim III was suspicious of Muḥammad ʻAlī's intensions and in attempt to remove him from Egypt, appointed him *wālī* of Jeddah in Arabia. However, the Cairo notables, with the backing of the people, continued supporting Muḥammad ʻAlī. After a few month of chaos, Sultan Selim III had no choice but to confirm Muḥammad ʻAlī as the governor-general of Egypt. In consolidating his personal power and the relative autonomy of Egypt, Muḥammad ʻAlī was helped by the empire's weakening central authority. Selim III had to confront the rebellious Jannisaries[259] who were opposed to his program of reforms and of European innovations.

Having the support of the Ottoman government and having succeeded in winning the favor of inhabitants of Cairo and their spiritual leaders,[260] the *Wālī* directed his attention to the Mamlūks and to other challengers, namely the British who posed a serious threat to his political plans. Still intending to assist the Mamlūks' government take-over in Egypt and hoping to pre-empt yet another French takeover, British forces landed in Alexandria in March of 1807. As they failed to occupy Rosetta, the British troops were contained by Muḥammad ʻAlī's forces and trapped in Alexandria. They were later evacuated by the agreement. When the reforming and vigorous

---

[258] During the political crisis of 1804-1805 the *ʻulamāʼ* led by ʻUmar Mukarram allied with Muḥammad ʻAlī. Upon assuming the power, he moved to curtail their influences and place them under state control.

[259] W. L. Cleveland, *A History of the Modern Middle East*, Boulder–San Francisco–Oxford: Westview Press, 1994, p. 61-63.

[260] Many Ṣūfī orders that existed in Egypt at that time proclaimed their support for Muḥammad ʻAlī.

Sultan Selim III was deposed by the rebellious Jannisaries, the Ottoman government plunged into a long period of internal difficulties that same year, followed by reconstruction during the times of Maḥmūd II.[261] All these developments allowed Muḥammad 'Alī a much needed respite from both the Ottoman interference and the British intervention.

Soon after the departure of the British army, Muḥammad 'Alī began administrative and economic reforms which would restore Egypt's economy and assure for himself a more powerful position than any other Ottoman governor. In the meantime, the Mamlūks, who still had a strong influence in Egypt, were trying to prevent Muḥammad 'Alī's ambitious plans. In 1809, he persuaded many of the Mamlūks to settle in and around Cairo, where he was able to closely follow their movements. However, a few of the Mamlūks refused to settle there and were potentially dangerous for him. At this stage Muḥammad 'Alī prepared for the complete destruction of his last enemies in the province. In March of 1811, about seventy-four leading Mamlūks were invited to the Cairo citadel for a ceremony of investiture of Muḥammad 'Alī's son Ṭusun, who was to lead the Egyptian army against the Wahhābī rebels in Arabia. In effect, it was only a trap to gather the Mamlūks and massacre them as they were leaving the banquet.[262] At last, Muḥammad 'Alī destroyed all the forces that might interrupt his omnipotent power in Egypt.

During this period, Muḥammad 'Alī was able to not only resist interference from Istanbul but also to make the new Sultan Maḥmūd II dependent on him for keeping the empire together. In 1807 and then in 1811 the troops of Muḥammad 'Alī led by his sons Ṭusun and Ibrāhīm successfully fought the Wahhābī rebels in Arabia and recovered Islamic holy places for the Empire. The Pasha himself took part in an expedition to Yemen.[263] The successful campaign against Wahhābīs strongly increased Muḥammad 'Alī's authority in Arabia and in the entire Near East. His military achievements, growing independence and attempts to modernize the province led the European powers to consider the political importance of Egypt for the first time.

In the early 1820s Muḥammad 'Alī's focused his attention on Sudan. In 1821 he sent an army there, commanded by his son Ismā'īl, followed the next year by two more under Ibrāhīm and his son–in–law, Muḥammad. The armies included Muslim teachers from the famous Islamic University of Al-Azhar in Cairo, who urged local peoples to accept the new rulers as representatives of the great sultan-caliph of Islam[264]. The armies conquered an area half the size of Europe, nominally on behalf of the Ottoman sultan, but in reality to add to the *Wālī's* Egyptian domains. The oc-

---

[261] W. L. Cleveland, *A History of the Modern…*, p. 76-78.

[262] J. H. Kramers, "Muḥammad 'Alī 'Pasha," in: *Encyclopaedia of Islam*, vol. 3, p. 682.

[263] Muḥammad 'Alī came back to his residence before the end of the war because his position as governor seemed to be in danger.

[264] J. L. Esposito and J. O. Voll, *Islam and Democracy*, New York: Oxford University Press, 1996, p. 79.

cupation of Nubia, Sennar, and Kordofan was motivated by military concerns and economic reasons. In addition to the benefit of employing the troops away from the seat of power and wiping out the last remaining Mamlūk enclave in Dangola, the Pasha hoped to control the trade of Sudan and tap into its alleged gold deposits. However, the most important goal for him was to recruit a slave army. Muḥammad ʻAlī planned to create a modern European-style armed force, commanded by Ottoman-Egyptian officers, to replace the old-style contingents. All in all, through this invasion, Egyptian power was established in Sudan and the conquest laid the foundations of the modern Sudanese state. During this time Muḥammad ʻAlī's power also extended towards Red Sea.

Muḥammad ʻAlī's participation in the Greek revolt interrupted the campaign in Sudan.[265] In 1821, Sultan Maḥmūd II invited the Egyptian governor-general to help to put down the uprising of his Greek subjects, who were demanding independence. Muḥammad ʻAlī's well-organized and disciplined forces led by Ibrāhīm proved capable of dealing with the rebels. The intervention lasted a few years, and in 1827 Athens was captured. At this point, the European powers decided to intervene. Following the Treaty of London of 6 July 1827, Britain, Russia, and France began mediation between the Ottoman government and the Greek patriots in order to bring about an armistice that would lead to the establishment of Greek autonomy under the Sultan's suzerainty. An additional purpose was to make Muḥammad ʻAlī's troops unnecessary and bring about their withdrawal. When the Sultan refused to "cooperate" the Russian and French fleets joined the British fleet at Navarino, and on 20 October blew the combined Turkish and Egyptian fleets out of the water. According to the agreement which had been concluded between Muḥammad ʻAlī and the British admiral Cordington, Egyptian troops evacuated the peninsula, and Crete remained under Egyptian administration (until 1841).[266]

Muḥammad ʻAlī's forces suffered severe losses, and the financial strain on Egypt was heavy. However, the disaster of Navarino had not dampened the ambitions of the *Wālī* or his son Ibrāhīm. During the late twenties, the Muḥammad ʻAlī's political interests were directed toward Syria.[267] At the same time, he started to fight with the Ottoman government, which had promised him governorship over Syria as a reward for the participation in the Greek war, but never fulfilled its promise. Muḥammad ʻAlī s claim to be the governor of ʻAkkā brought him into a large conflict with the central government. On 27 May 1832 ʻAkkā was taken by Muḥammad ʻAlī's son Ibrāhīm; on 21 December the Sultan's army was defeated near Konya. Then, the Egyptian army continued its offensive against Istanbul. Only as a result from the intervention of the European powers, in particular Russia, that sided with the Ottoman government were Muḥammad ʻAlī's expansive tendencies curbed. Finally, according

---

265 P. Mansfield, *A History of the Middle East...*, p. 57.

266 J. H. Kramers, "Muḥammad ʻAlī ʻPasha..., p. 682.

267 See: F. Lawson, "Economic and Social Foundations of Egyptian Expansionism: The Invasion of Syria in 1831," *International History Review*, vol. 10 (1988), p. 71-89.

to the peaceful agreement from 6 April 1833 Muḥammad ʻAlī was granted the governorship of Syria and Adana.

Muḥammad ʻAlī placed his son Ibrāhīm in charge of the new Syrian possessions. Although Ibrāhīm had a powerful army under his command, his task of imposing a strongly centralized and modernizing administration was not easy. The various sects in Syria, namely Sunni and Shīʻa Muslims, Druze, and Maronites had become accustomed to a high degree of autonomy,[268] whether under local dynasties, such as the Azms in Damascus, the Shihabs in Lebanon, or under Ottoman *wālīs*, who remained there too briefly to establish their authority. Therefore, Ibrāhīm was confronted by a variety of economic and political interests and faced various acts of rebellion which he suppressed with his customary ruthlessness. Nevertheless, the achievements during the decade of his governorship (1831-1840) were considerable. He streamlined the administration, reformed the tax system and began the process of expanding and improving education. Ibrāhīm's aims in Syria paralelled those of his father in Egypt, who guided and directed his actions and laid the foundations of a strong state with a self-sustaining economy.

During the following seven years (1834-1840), Muḥammad ʻAlī's power reached its apogee.[269] He occupied the Najd, Hijaz and Yemen; he pushed into Iraq and almost took Baghdād. Furthermore, the *Wālī* brought the coastal chieftains in the Persian Gulf under his obedience and secured the alliance of the Sultan of Musqat and the Sheikh of Bahrain. By the end of 1839, he was virtually master of Arabia, and, aiming at the political consolidation of his military success, he entered into negotiations with Persia.

Concurrently, Muḥammad ʻAlī was implementing his program of reforms in Egypt.[270] He modernized public administration, judicature, and taxation and improved the postal services and communications. The *Wālī* also placed considerable effort on education. It became apparent to the Ottoman government that Muḥammad ʻAlī wanted to govern Egypt as an independent ruler, directing the province towards a path of European modernization.[271] Obviously, this kind of ambitious policy was dangerous for the European powers, and they waited for an opportunity to crush the most powerful vassal of the Ottomans.

Britain was the first to put an end to Muḥammad ʻAlī's plans when it had become seriously alarmed by the spread of his power along the entire eastern coast of the Red Sea from Bāb al-Mandab to Mecca.[272] The powerful Egyptian *Wālī* had even seized

---

[268] A. Hourani, *Historia Arabów*, trans. by J. Danecki, Gdańsk: Marabut, 1995, p. 228-229.

[269] S. and N. Ronard, "Muhammad ʻAli," in: *Concise Encyclopaedia of Arabic Civilization*, Amsterdam: Djambatan, 1959, p. 386.

[270] ʻAbd al-Rahman Rafiʼi, *ʻAsr Muḥammad ʻAli*, Cairo: Maktabat al-Nahda al-Misriyya, 1951, p. 615-625.

[271] In mid-1838 Muḥammad ʻAlī informed the European powers of his intention to declare independence. Although the international reaction was quite negative, he nevertheless did not withdraw his statement of intent.

[272] P. Mansfield, *A History of the Middle East…*, p. 57-58.

the Tihama coast of Yemen, bought the city of Taez from its corrupt governor, and gained control over its valuable coffee trade. The vital route to India seemed to be threatened at a time when the importance of the Arabian coast had been increased by the arrival of steamships and by the need of secure coaling stations.

The opportunity to challenge Muḥammad ʻAlī arose in January of 1839 when the Bombay Marine landed with a small force and seized the port of Aden establishing there the British rule for the next 130 years. A *de facto* alliance between Palmerston and Maḥmūd II was now in existence. In the summer of 1939, the Sultan declared war on the ambitious Egyptian *Wālī* and sent an army across the Euphrates into Northen Syria. In spite of the new training of the Ottoman forces by the German military instructors, at the battle of Nazib[273] they were once again soundly defeated by Ibrāhīm. At the same time, the admiral of the Ottoman navy decided to sail the entire fleet to Alexandria and surrender to Muḥammad ʻAlī. Sultan Maḥmūd II died suddenly before the news of Nazib reached him, and he was succeeded by his 16-year-old son Abdul Mejid. The young Sultan and his government were then at Muḥammad ʻAlī's mercy. At this stage, the Ottoman authorities were saved by the intervention of the five European powers, namely France, England, Russia, Austria, and Prussia.[274]

The Egyptian question caused an international political problem. The French, who had been patronizing Muḥammad ʻAlī for a long time, sided with him. In spite of the sympathy of the French, the convention of London of 5 July1840, which was concluded by England, Russia, Austria, Prussia and the Ottoman government, determined the terms to be imposed upon Muḥammad ʻAlī. He strongly opposed but eventually the appearance of the British fleet in Alexandria forced him to compromise. According to the peaceful agreement which was concluded on 27 November, Muḥammad ʻAlī consented to the return of the Ottoman fleet and renounced his governorship of Syria, Adana, and Crete. On the other hand, he was to keep the hereditary governorship of Egypt as part of the Turkish Empire. All these terms were confirmed by the imperial *firmān* of 13 February 1841[275] and completed by another *firmān* of 23 May. Mutual relationship points of these *firmāns* were concluded as the following: the right of the succession according to the seniority in Muḥammad ʻAli's family, the payment of a tribute and the permission to maintain an Egyptian army of 18,000 men, the higher officers of which were to be appointed by the Sultan.

Muḥammad ʻAlī's last years passed peacefully. In 1846, he visited Istanbul and made an excursion to his native Kavalla where he founded a school. In 1848, he lost his son Ibrāhīm to whom so many of his military and political successes were due. Muḥammad ʻAlī died in Alexandria in August of 1849, and he was buried in the new mosque which he had erected in the citadel of Cairo.

---

[273] Ibid., p. 59

[274] J. H. Kramers, "Muḥammad ʻAlī ʻPasha..., p. 682.

[275] Ibid., p. 683.

On the path of reforms and European modernization

Historians call Muḥammad ʻAlī "the founder of modern Egypt."[276] His military and political achievements together with the economic, social, and cultural reforms, which he undertook brought about fundamental changes in the province, directing it towards modernity. According to one of his biographers, "He began by seeking only to raise the money. He ended, however mistakenly, to develop and civilize the country."[277]

At the beginning of the nineteenth century the social and economic conditions of the Turkish provinces, including Egypt, were, according to Dodwell, very difficult:

> The Porte demands supplies and nothing but supplies; and the Pasha to satisfy her must press upon the industry of his subjects. He who is well–wished of his people, who contents himself with the ordinary revenue and who lets justice preside in his councils will undoubtedly incur his sovereign's displeasure, not because he is just, but because his justice prevents him from plundering and transmitting a portion of the acquired plunder to the *divan*. To save his existence he had nothing left but silently to resign his unhappy subjects to the rod of succeeding despot or to declare himself a rebel and to contend with his rival until the Porte, convinced of the difficulty of deposing him patiently waits for a more favorable opportunity.[278]

Egypt was perhaps in the worst condition from among all the Ottoman provinces. The economic exploitation during the reign of the Mamlūks led to the fact that even the Delta region, the most fertile land in the world, lost a third of its cultivable area. The oppression of Egypt by the Mamlūks brought the province to complete economic ruin. This occurred because during their reign "the justice was a matter of bribes, the property a matter of favor, and the life a matter of luck."[279]

This was the kind of government which Muḥammad ʻAlī inherited when he came to power. Despite the fact, that he was accustomed to this type of government, he soon realized the necessity of modernization of Egypt and became convinced that only reforms in the field of agriculture and industry could raise the money needed for developing the local economy. The period of Muḥammad ʻAlī's rule produced extraordinary changes. It should be pointed out that the primary objective of Muḥammad ʻAlī's measures – in the field of administration, land policy and the industrial and commercial mobilization – was to make the Pasha Egypt's sole proprietor and administrator of wealth.

---

[276] This phrase is discussed in many works; for example by P. M. Holt, "Muhammad ʻAli Pasha," in: idem, *Egypt and the Fertile Crescent 1516-1922: A Political History*, Ithaca, NY: Cornell University Press, 1966, p. 192.

[277] H. Dodwell, The *Study of Modern Egypt: A Study of Muhammad ʻAli*, Cambridge: Cambridge University Press, 1931, p. 220.

[278] Ibid., p. 193.

[279] Ibid., p. 194.

One of his most lasting achievements, and the one that made the implementation of his other reformist schemes possible, was the reorganization of the central administration. Government was taken away from competing Mamlūk factions and centralized under Muḥammad 'Alī's absolute authority. The power was delegated through a well-organized system. At the highest level, it rested in functionally differentiated ministries. At the middle level a new group of officials emerged, trained in technical and administrative schools, and appointed on the basis of their qualifications. This new government became more bureaucratized and more predictable. To buttress the state's control over the countryside Egypt was divided into ten *mudiriyyas* (provinces). Each province was administered by a centrally appointed *mudīr* (governor) responsible for the law, order, and tax . The village was the smallest unit of administration with its head-man (*shaykh al-balad)*, representing the ruler in every capacity. The villages were grouped in subdivisions under the *ḥakīm al-khurt.* These subdivisions were formed into districts, each under a *ma'mūr,* and finally, these divisions were grouped into the seven provinces (*mudiriyyas*) mentioned previously.

In the larger cities the organization of the government was more elaborate. There were special police forces and judges who maintained public order and prevented or punished crime. The inhabitants of the cities were divided according to the trades and occupations into guilds, each under its special *shaykh* or headman. For example in Cairo, there were 164 guilds[280] guided by the same number of *shaykhs* responsible for the conduct of the members of their respective guilds.

The security system in Egypt during Muḥammad 'Alī's days worked properly. According to the opinion of the French writer Gomard, the best result of Muḥammad 'Alī's regime and the most impressive feature was the stable security.[281] The inhabitants of Egypt at that time could cross long distances from the Nile to the desert safely, without the fear of being attacked and robbed as during the Mamlūk reign. This stability enabled the people to safely establish trade between themselves.

It is worth noting that Muḥammad 'Alī did not direct his attention towards establishing a "democratic regime," or something close to the real meaning of the word "democracy."[282] This was, and still is, a sensitive target for criticism of Muḥammad 'Alī. All the institutions he founded were only *majālis tanfidiyya*[283] – the order and the highest word belonged to him.

Although it is well-known that Muḥammad 'Alī listened to advice from the Europeans, especially the French and that he valued the European institutions as examples to follow to a certain extend, it should be underlined that his government was overall organized according to the Middle Eastern methods. There were very few Europeans (mostly French and British) employed in administration, while the highest

[280] Ibid., p. 203.

[281] E. R. Toledano, "Muḥammad 'Alī Pasha..., p. 427.

[282] Ibid., p. 615-625.

[283] These institutions were founded to realize the executive functions of the government.

positions were held only by the Ottomans of heterogeneous origin. A particularly important role was played by the sons of Muḥammad ʻAlī, especially by Ibrāhīm and by his eldest grandson ʻAbbās Hilmī.[284] On the other hand, almost all the experts needed for both the civil and military establishments were, in the first place, the Europeans, particularly the French and the Italians. As for the native Egyptians, they could find their place within the new political order. However, they played a subordinate role. With time the situation changed and the Egyptians were able to obtain important posts in the local administration. By the end of 1840, almost all the *ma'mūrs* were native Egyptians.

Muḥammad ʻAlī's strong and practically independent government was based on a well-organized army. In 1818, he decided to create a new regular army, by imposing compulsory military service and introducing forced labor for the construction of fortifications. Muḥammad ʻAlī also placed considerable attention on the creation of a modern Egyptian fleet. Initially, he had ships built in France, Italy and Bombay, but soon he started to build them in Alexandria. In 1820 Muḥammad ʻAlī established an officers' training school in Aswan with European instructors.[285] In a further attempt to produce a cadre of Egyptians with an understanding of European military sciences, the *Wālī* sent several training missions to Europe, mainly to France. The students who returned to Egypt with firsthand experience of Europe and the knowledge of its languages had a considerable impact on the future direction of their country that extended far beyond the military scope. During the subsequent twenty years Muḥammad ʻAlī founded educational institutions to train the experts in the support services required by the military, namely schools of medicine, veterinary medicine, engineering and chemistry. Eventually with time, all these schools would have an influence far beyond their initial military concerns.

As Muḥammad ʻAlī set up the European style facilities for training officers, he was faced with the need to obtain large numbers of common soldiers to fill his new army. When the *Wālī* decided on invading Sudan, he aimed to recruit an effective slave army there. However, the plans did not work and eventually Muḥammad ʻAlī turned to Egypt and began conscripting native Egyptian *fellāḥīn* (peasants).[286] Although this conscription led to depopulation of the countryside, the *Wālī* managed to build a peasant army of over one hundred thousand troops that could successfully support his bid for independence[287].

Muḥammad ʻAlī realized that in order to finance his military, he would have to exploit Egypt's resources to its limits and ensure that the central treasury obtained

---

[284] P. M. Holt, "Muhammad ʻAli," in: idem, *Egypt and the Fertile Crescent…*, p. 190.

[285] B. Lewis, *The Middle East: 2000 Years of History from the Rise of Christianity to the Present Day*, London: Weidenfeld & Nicolson, 1995, p. 296-297.

[286] Like Selim III's use of Anatolian Turks in *nizam-i jedid*, this was a departure from the existing norm in the Ottoman world.

[287] N. Farag, "Usratu Muḥammad ʻAlī," in: eadem, *Yussef Idris and Modern Egyptian Drama*, Cairo: Dar al-Maʻarif bi-Misr, 1975, p. 21-24.

the maximum possible revenues from all productive sources within the economy. At the time when Muḥammad 'Alī became *wālī* of Egypt, the existing systems of land tenure and taxation allowed considerable revenue to be diverted from the state.[288] Mamlūks and individuals within the *'ulamā'* profited from their control of *iltizām,* a tax-farming system in which tax farmers remitted a fixed annual sum to the treasury and retained whatever surplus they could extort from the peasants under their control. Therefore, the destruction of the *iltizām* system became the priority. During the first ten years of his rule, Muḥammad 'Alī confiscated *iltizām* land, and instituted a tax on extensive *waqf* revenues administered by the *'ulamā'*. The policy was first implemented only in Lower Egypt, since Upper Egypt was still under Mamlūk control. With the elimination of the Mamlūks (1811-1812), a general attack on the *iltizām* system became possible.[289]

Waqf[290] was a practice, approved by the *sharī'a* – the sacred law of Islam that permitted the income from property to be set aside in perpetuity for charitable purposes such as upkeep of mosques and schools. The revenue from *waqf* endowments was not subjected to tax. By the nineteenth century, large portions of land in Egypt were devoted to *waqfs* and, therefore, were practically outside the central government's control. The *'ulamā'* acted as a trustee group for *waqfs*' endowments and assigned *waqfs'* revenues to their designated purposes.

Between 1808 and 1814 Muḥammad 'Alī appropriated most of the remaining land on the basis of neglect by the former owners. Life pensions for the former *multazims* were paid by the treasury. The *Wālī* introduced the distribution of the land to the members of his family and to his senior employees. All of the people who received the land placed it for the service of Muḥammad 'Alī's needs. The new land policy introduced by Muḥammad 'Alī brought a large part of the cultivated land of Egypt back into the state ownership, i.e. into the hands of the *Wālī*, thus serving the dual purpose of increasing the state's control over land and revenue and of reducing the wealth and prestige of the Mamlūks and the *'ulamā'*. Over the course of his reign, Muḥammad 'Alī granted land to certain trusted officials who were expected to cultivate it in exchange for tax exemption, and gave large tracts of land to his relatives. The net result of these practices was the introduction the new concept of private land ownership and the concentration of enormous holdings in the hands of new families. This confiscation injured only the small groups; in no way did it affect the peasants who continued in their age long poverty.[291]

As previously mentioned, the new class of landowners consisted of people who would be helpful, or at least innocuous, to Muḥammad 'Alī. Among the principal beneficiaries were members of his family. Even before the general resumption of the *iltizāms* some *multazims* had been expropriated and their estates transferred to

---

288 W. L. Cleveland, *A History of the Modern...*, p. 68.

289 P. M. Holt, *Egypt and the Fertile Crescent...*, p. 189.

290 See: H. Heffening, "Waqf," *Encyclopaedia of Islam*, New Edition, vol. 12, p. 1096-1103.

291 E. R. Toledano, "Muḥammad 'Alī Pasha..., p. 426.

Muḥammad ʻAlī's relatives and supporters. During the last two decades of his reign, enormous grants of land were made to Muḥammad ʻAlī's family in the form of *jifliks*,[292] which consisted mostly of abandoned and insolvent villages. However, with the time, Muḥammad ʻAlī realized that the new land owners were unable to govern these large areas and he decided to give back part of these lands to their previous owners.

Although according to Holt Muḥammad ʻAlī's agrarian changes were not "true reforms", it should be pointed out that the land acquired was put to better use.[293] Muḥammad ʻAlī claimed to have installed 38,000 water-wheels in Egypt and several more thousand in Sudan. Thousands of *fellāḥīn* rebuilt and expanded the irrigation system; that is, dredging canals and constructing barrages so that the annual Nile flood could be stored and used for a full summer growing season when the river was low. The cultivable area of Egypt was thus increased by at least 1000,000 acres.[294]

These public work projects were carried out through extensive use of the *corvée*,[295] a levy or forced peasant labor. As with the regime's large-scale conscription practices, the *corvée* caused a temporary decline in agricultural productivity in those regions most heavily affected by the levy by uprooting peasants from their lands and forcing them to serve on work gangs. Muḥammad ʻAlī did not introduce the *corvée* into the Egyptian countryside, but he did not prohibit its application.

During the first two decades of Muḥammad ʻAlī's regime, Egyptian revenues depended heavily on the agriculture and the exportation of agricultural commodities. In order to increase revenues, the *Wālī* began to grow sugar-cane and intensified cotton cultivation.[296] He persisted on making cotton the primary commodity for Egyptian wealth in the fields of industry and commerce. The most important of the new crops was a special variety of long-staple cotton known as Jumel, after the French engineer who helped to develop it.[297] Jumel cotton was favored by the European textile industry, and it quickly became Egypt's most lucrative cash crop.

Muḥammad ʻAlī did not intend for Egypt to become an exporter of raw materials and an importer of European manufactured products. Therefore, in an effort to make the province self-sufficient, he began an industrialization program with an emphasis on war-related materials and textiles for the local market[298]. By the mid-1820s, the arsenal in the Cairo citadel was producing 1600 muskets a month. In the late 1830s, the new naval complex in Alexandria employed 4000 workers for the construction of nine warships with over 100 guns each. Machinery and managers were "imported"

---

[292] Turkish: *chiftlik*, meaning, in Ottoman usage, an estate.

[293] P. M. Holt, *Egypt and the Fertile Crescent…*, p. 189.

[294] R. L. Hl., "Muhammad ʻAli," in: *The Encyclopedia Britannica*, vol. 15, p. 645.

[295] E. R. Toledano, "Muḥammad ʻAlī Pasha…, p. 426.

[296] For a thorough discussion on agricultural reforms see: H. A. B. Rivlin, *The Agricultural Policy of Muhammad ʻAli in Egypt*, Cambridge: Harvard University Press, 1961.

[297] For a broad discussion on related issues see: R. Owen, *Cotton and the Egyptian Economy 1820-1914*, Oxford: Oxford University Press, 1969.

[298] W. L. Cleveland, *A History of the Modern…*, p. 69.

from Europe and the labor force was recruited from among Egyptian peasants and artisans. It is estimated that during the late 1830s at least 30 000 to 40 000 Egyptians were employed in industrial enterprises. However, the entire program of state-sponsored industrialization was rushed, and many of the factories were abandoned in the 1840s when Muḥammad 'Alī was forced to reduce the size of his army to 18 000 men.

The *Wālī* developed trade with the West. All revenue from the export of silk, cotton, textiles, leather, rosewater, etc., was placed into his hands. Among the British commercial community Muḥammad 'Alī had a good name for straight dealing.

Muḥammad 'Alī successfully managed the Egyptian economy and controlled its revenues through the monopoly system. He forced cultivators to sell directly to him at a fixed price, and then he sold to European buyers at the considerably higher market price. The *Wālī* controlled industrial development in a similar fashion, that is, by directing capital investment and collecting revenues. Because of this domestic monopoly, European merchants had no opportunity to purchase materials from any other Egyptian supplier other than the governor. Furthermore, Muḥammad 'Alī was able to defy many of the Capitulations'[299] restrictions that were supposed to apply to all Ottoman provinces.

As already mentioned, in order to head the administration, to develop the industry, and to run the commerce, the *Wālī* required well-educated Egyptian élite. Therefore from the beginning of his rule, Muḥammad 'Alī began to modernize the educational system with the help the European instructors.[300] A number of schools providing technical instructions of various kinds appeared. The first of them was the School of Surveying, established in 1816. The medical needs for the new army led to the foundation, in 1827, of a school of medicine directed by Clot Bey, one of Muḥammad 'Alī's best-known French advisers. The translators, who rendered the French lectures of the instructors into Arabic played very important role in the new system of teaching.

The training of technicians and experts of various kinds was also fostered by the educational missions sent to Europe.[301] The earliest missions were sent to Italy in about 1813, but they became larger and more systematic in 1826. Between 1826 and 1847, nine missions, composed of 219 members, were sent, almost entirely to France. Some students also visited Britain and Austria.

The intensive program of higher education oriented towards Western subject matter that was implemented in the newly established schools, brought with it a concurrent effort to produce suitable textbooks and instruction manuals. In 1835, Muḥammad 'Alī established the School of Languages for the express purpose of training the translators and preparing Arabic textbooks for the state schools. The significance of the School was greater than its name might suggest. The curriculum

---

[299] Capitulations: commercial treaties between the Ottoman Empire and Western European states granting Europeans favorable tariffs and exterritorial privileges.

[300] N. Farag, "Usratu Muḥammad 'Alī..., p. 21-24.

[301] P. M. Holt, *Egypt and the Fertile Crescent*..., p. 191.

comprised the study of Arabic, French, Turkish and Persian, as well as Italian and English; it also included literature, history, geography, and law. The School exercised important influence on the direction of Egypt's cultural and educational life until its closure in the 1850s. A related development was the founding of a government printing press that published the translated materials, printed government decrees for distribution, and brought about the first Arabic-language newspaper *Al-Waqā'i' al-Miṣriyya* (*The Official Gazette*) in 1928.[302] Muḥammad 'Alī's wholehearted acceptance of the printing press was a break from the cautions cultural tradition of the Ottoman world[303] and was of utmost importance in promoting the spread of Western ideas to the educated elite of Egyptian society.

As for the future of Egypt, Muḥammad 'Alī believed that the students should graduate in the fields of medicine, engineering, and military studies, which he considered the most important for the development of the province. It was not Muḥammad 'Alī's wish that his students would become too influenced with the European lifestyle, read about the modern philosophy and get involved in politics.

Among the students sent by Muḥammad 'Alī to Paris was Rifā'a Badawī al-Ṭahṭāwī (1801-1873)[304] who spent five years in Paris as the *imām* of the students of the first mission there. Upon his return to Egypt he became the inspector of schools, the member of educational commissions and the editor of the first official newspaper *Al-Waqā'i' al-Miṣriyya*. In 1836 he became the director of the School of Languages, and in 1841 he took charge of a Bureau of Translation attached to the School, and he himself having translated about a score of works.

During the 1830s, a new architectural style began to appear in the Egyptian urban scenery.[305] The mixture of Greek, Italian, and Spanish elements, often seen along the Eastern Mediterranean coast, replaced the Mamlūk and Ottoman styles.[306] By the 1840s, Mamlūk wooden lattice *mashrabiyyas* (windows) were replaced by European windows with rectangular framed panes and wooden shades. In the 1820s and the 1830s, the construction projects for public use were carried out on a large scale, including barracks for the army, dockyards for the navy, office buildings for the bureaucracy, schools, hospitals, palaces for Muḥammad 'Alī's family, and mansions for élite grandees. Many urban streets, especially in Cairo were being widened to enable more convenient passage of carriages and carts and the province roads were improved to facilitate transportation.

---

[302] B. Lewis, *The Muslim Discovery of Europe*, New York: W.W. Norton & Company, 1982, p. 304-306.

[303] About the influence of Western culture on the Middle East, including Egypt see: H. A. R. Gibb, "The Reaction in the Middle East Against Western Culture," in: idem, *Studies on Civilization of Islam*, Princeton: Princeton University Press, 1982, p. 320-344.

[304] A. Hourani, *Arabic Thought…*, p. 69-83.

[305] On the development of architecture and arts during the reign of Muḥammad 'Alī refer to: G. Wiet, *Muhammad 'Ali et les beaux-arts*, Le Caire: Dar al Maaref, 1949.

[306] This new Ottoman-Mediterranean style was called, in Arabic, *Rūmī* and in European languages *Constantinopolitan*.

During his governorship Muḥammad ʻAlī undertook some important measures related to health care.[307] However in this area, the *Wālī* reacted to crises instead of planning for anticipated problems. The French physician Clot Bey was charged with organizing a military medical corps, following Muḥammad ʻAlī's growing concerns about the poor health of his soldiers and their high mortality rate. The Board of Health and the quarantine service was established as a result of the cholera pandemic of 1830-1832. In 1836, a vaccination service was set up in Upper Egypt to cater to students and to instructors. A sanitary code for Alexandria was issued in the wake of a plague outbreak in 1841. Furthermore, the hospitals were established in all places where the government factories were in operation. It should be noted however, that except for smallpox immunization the health services were intended and instituted for the benefit of a relatively small group, namely military and civilian government personnel with minimal spillover to the population at large.

Muḥammad ʻAlī's figure has been exposed to different winds of historical opinion.[308] However, few in modern Egyptian history were idealized as much as him. Fascination with strong, charismatic leaders, perceived to have changed the course of history, is not a new phenomenon. Muḥammad ʻAlī was an Ottoman officer who owing to his talents, ambition, determination, and vision, dominated the government of Egypt for more than four decades. He managed to carve out of the Sultan's domination a patrimony, which his progeny governed until 1952. Culturally, he remained an Ottoman, whose language was Turkish and whose worldview was the nineteenth century Ottoman view. In fact, he spoke neither Arabic nor French nor English. Nevertheless, he made Egypt his abode, the seat of his government and the centre of his attention. In his personality Muḥammad ʻAlī combined the gifted general with the able administrator. He invested all his energies to create both a military might and a sound economic base in order to achieve regional hegemony.

One of his most enduring legacies was the establishment of a centralized bureaucracy. However, the complexities of his government should not be overemphasized. He ran his state in the manner of an extended household, his sons were appointed to key positions, his loyal officials received grants of land and he made the major decisions himself. Muḥammad ʻAlī was a dynast, not an Egyptian, and he is reputed to have despised his subjects. The language of his administration was Ottoman Turkish, not the local Arabic, and the initial composition of his new bureaucratic and military elite showed his preference for Turks and Circassians over native Egyptians. He also exhibited the traditional Ottoman reliance on minority groups for administrative expertise. His administration contained a high proportion of local Christians, and his most trusted adviser and minister of foreign Affairs, Boghos Pasha, was an Armenian.

The phrase "the founder of modern Egypt" has become a cliché in referring to him as a person. Muḥammad ʻAlī's character and achievements have been exces-

[307] E. R. Toledano, *State and Society in Mid-nineteenth Century Egypt*, Cambridge Middle East Library (22), Cambridge: Cambridge University Press, p. 92-93.

[308] Idem, "Muhammad ʻAli Pasha..., p. 430-431.

sively lauded by writers, both foreign and Egyptian. In Egypt at various times he has been hailed as a forerunner of Arab nationalism[309] and condemned as a ruthless exploiter of the peasants.

However, it is worth noting that his activity, the reforms that he introduced, and the ability he had to adopt European models created the base for the later *naḥda*[310] (renaissance) of the national Arab culture. He was the first who pointed the direction for this movement and set the example. By introducing these reforms, Muḥammad ʻAlī was able to give Egypt a strong centralized state organization – an indispensable tool in the modern world.

The correspondence of the European countries and the United States, who were posted in Egypt during Muḥammad ʻAlī's days, provides a lively picture of the *Wālī*. The most revealing guide to his character is in the following words: "The stocky figure, inclined in old age to obesity, the commanding face, and above all, the piercing eyes"[311] .

[309] P. Mansfield, *A History of the Middle East...*, p. 61-62. Also, refer to: G. Antonious, *The Arab Awakening: The Story of the Arab National Movement*, London: Lippincott, 1939.

[310] See: J. Bielawski, *Historia literatury arabskiej*, Warszawa: Ossolineum, p. 364-369.

[311] R. L. Hl., "Mohammad ʻAli..., p. 645.

VII

Islam and Christianity: The History of Reciprocal Relations during the Classical and Medieval Period

Among all the religions that Christianity has had to confront, Islam was both misunderstood and attacked most intensely. For more than a millennium, this religion was considered a major threat to Europe and its followers were viewed as enemies of not only Christianity but also the entire Western civilization. With regard to its political aspect, this threat began with the Arab conquest of Spain at the beginning of the eighth century and ended with the siege of Vienna by the Ottoman Turks in 1683. However, "there were not only political reasons for Christian Europe's fear."[312] It should be noted that Islam is the only world religion that came into existence after Christianity. Therefore, it was unacceptable as a true religion and for centuries after the Byzantine apologetic writings, it was regarded as a mere heresy of Christianity. However, although the thirteen centuries of history between the two religions was dominated by wars of conquest and re–conquest, aversion, prejudice, hostility and bitter and often injurious polemics, there have always been voices on both sides advocating a more positive attitude and the need for dialogue and understanding.[313]

---

[312] A. Schimmel, *Islam: An Introduction*, Albany: State University of New York Press, 1992, p. 1.

[313] For an extensive discussion on Christian-Muslim relations, based on primary sources and references see the classic analysis, thoroughly revised and updated before the author's death in 1992, describing the formation of Western attitudes about Islam by tracing the development of Christian-Islamic interaction from medieval times to the present: N. Daniel, *Islam and the West: The Making of an Image*, Oxford: Oneworld Publications, 1993. Also refer to: R. Armour, *Islam, Christianity and the West*, Maryknoll, NY: Orbis Books, 2002; H. Goddard, *A History of Christian-Muslim Relations*, Edinburgh: Edinburgh University Press, 2000; C. J. Adams, "Islam and Christianity: The Opposition and Similarities," in: A. Savory and D. Agius, *Logos Islamikos: Studia Islamica in Honorem Georgii Michaelis Wickens*, Papers in Mediaeval Studies no. 6, Toronto: Pontifical Institute for Medieval Studies, 1984, p. 287-306.

While discussing the issue of the relations between Christianity and Islam in history, one should bear in mind a number of considerations. First, it is important to realize that it was not the religious identity of the Arab conquerors that initially struck the European observers. What astonished them and prompted them to reflect were both the speed and the extent of the conquest itself, which in a few decades resulted in Arab domination of the eastern, southern and western shores of the Mediterranean Sea. Second, a presentation of Christian views regarding Islam should include their religious aspects as well as the political context, i.e., the circumstances under which such views of Islam as a religion actually appeared. Third, while discussing such views and outlooks, it is also important to realize the mental categories and capabilities that the authors had at their disposal which led to formulation of their ideas and statements.[314] Finally, one should also remember the fact that that Islam features no separation between religious and non-religious matters.[315] In addition, for Muslims, their religion is not only a system of belief and worship; it embraces all aspects of the life of its followers: the rules of civil, constitutional and criminal law.

In the history of the relations between Christianity and Islam, a few different periods may be distinguished. For the purpose of our study, the historical overview of Christian-Muslim relations is focused on selected Christian views of Islam reflecting the evolution of reciprocal contact between the followers of the two religions from hostility and ignorance to attempts at building bridges of reconciliation and understanding.

The first period is highlighted by the biography of the Prophet Muḥammad and the rise of Islam that lasted until the eleventh century. It is worth noting that Muḥammad met Christians on various occasions.[316] It was in the town of Bostra (Syria), an important junction on the caravan route and a great center of Christianity, where a significant incident is said to have taken place. Muḥammad accompanied his uncle Abū Ṭālib who led the caravan. In Bostra, they met a Christian monk named Baḥīrā.[317]

[314] K. B. Wolf, "Christian Views..., p. 86.

[315] As stated by Lewis: "If the term "religion," in one sense, conveys much more to a Muslim than to a Christian, there is another sense in which it conveys much less. As a building, as a place of worship, the equivalent of the church among Muslims is the mosque. As an institution, as a power, the Church has no equivalent in Islam. Islam has no councils or synods, no prelates or hierarchies, no canon laws or canon courts. In classical Islamic history there could be no clash between pope and emperor, since the caliph, the titular head of the Islamic state and community, combined in himself both political and religious – though not spiritual – authority. There could be neither conflict nor cooperation, neither separation nor association between church and state, since the governing institution of Islam combined both functions" (*Islam and the West*, New York: Oxford University Press, 1993, p. 4).

[316] H. Goddard discusses five instances in which it is recorded that Muhammad and the early Muslim community had some kind of direct encounter with Christians, as reported by Ibn Isḥāq (d. 767) in his *Sīrat Rasūl Allāh* (*The Life of Prophet of God*); see: H. Goddard, *A History of Christian-Muslim Relations...*, p. 19-28.

[317] In the Christian polemics against Islam, Baḥīra became a heretical monk whose religious affiliations vary in different Christian sources. For a detailed discussion on related issues see:

He recognised that Muḥammad bore the signs of prophethood that the holy book had predicted, including "the seal of the prophethood between his shoulders."[318] Therefore, he believed that Muḥammad was the future "Envoy of Allāh." Some years later, as Ibn Isḥāq reports, Waraqa Ibn Naufal, the cousin of Muḥammad's first wife Khadīja Bint Khuwaylid, identified Muḥammad's experience in the cave of Hira as divine revelation.[319]

It appears as though Muḥammad was well aware of the already-existing idea of religious monotheism due to his numerous contacts with the followers of both Judaism and Christianity. As for the attitude of Muḥammad towards Christians, it may be considered ambivalent.[320] For example, as Ibn Isḥāq reported, when the Prophet received Christians from Najran, the delegation was invited to pray in the Prophet's mosque. However, when he negotiated a political treaty with them, his view concerning Christian beliefs had no room for compromise.[321]

With regard to the Qur'ānic image of Christians, one may say that in the fundamental source of Islam there is also some ambivalence in the attitude towards them. As the Qur'ān says, Muslims will find, among the People of the Book, Christians as "nearest to them in love":

> Strongest among men in enmity
> To the Believers wilt thou
> Find the Jews and Pagans;
> And nearest among them in love
> To the Believers wilt thou
> Find those who say,
> "We are Christians":
> Because amongst these are
> Men devoted to learning
> And men who have renounced
> The world, and they
> Are not arrogant.[322]

B. Roggema, *The Legend of Sergius Bahira: Eastern Christian Apologetics and Apocalyptic in Response to Islam*, Leiden–Boston: Brill, 2009.

[318] See: M. Ibn Isḥāq, *The Life of Muḥammad: A Translation of Ibn Isḥāq's "Sīrat Rasūl Allāh,"* trans. by A. Guillaume, Oxford: Oxford University Press, 1955, p. 78-81; M. Rodinson, *Muhammad*, New York: Pantheon Books, 1980, p. 46-47.

[319] Waraqa Ibn Naufal was a *ḥanīf*, i.e., an Arab monotheist. He was familiar with the scriptures of both Judaism and Christianity. Khadīja consulted him concerning Muḥammad's prophetic experience. Waraqa assured Muḥammad that he received a great revelation like the one sent to Mūsā (Moses) ages before (M. Ibn Isḥāq, *The Life of Muḥammad...*, p. 83, 107).

[320] See: B. F. Breiner and C. W. Troll, "Christianity and Islam," in: J. Esposito (ed.), *The Oxford Encyclopedia of Modern Islamic World*, New York: Oxford University Press, 1995, vol. 1, p. 280.

[321] M. Ibn Isḥāq, *The Life of Muḥammad...*, p. 270-277.

[322] The Qur'ān, S: 5, v: 82. All the quotations are from: A. Y. 'Alī, *The Meaning of the Holy Qur'ān*, Beltsville, MD: Amana Publications, 1989.

However, at the same time, the Holy Book warns Muslims not to take Christians or Jews as close friends:

> O you who believe!
> Take not the Jews
> And the Christians
> For your friends and protectors;
> They are but friends and protectors
> To each other. And he
> Amongst you that turns to them
> [For friendship] is of them.
> Verily Allah guideth not
> A people unjust.[323]

It also accuses Christians and Jews of disbelief:

> The Jews call 'Uzayr [Ezra] a son
> Of God, and the Christians
> Call Christ the Son of God.
> That is a saying from their mouth;
> [In this] they but imitate
> What the Unbelievers of old
> Used to say. Allah's curse
> Be on them: how they are deluded
> Away from the Truth![324]

On the other hand, in the Qur'ān there are important references to the acceptance of religious pluralism. According to Issa J. Boullata, religious pluralism may be considered "one of the doctrinal principles enunciated in the Qur'ān."[325] In the light of the Qur'ān, humankind was once made up of members of a single community. Then, with God's will, various human views resulted in religious pluralism. Prophets sent by God with divine revelations guided these communities in their beliefs. As the Qur'ān says: "Unto every one of you We appointed a [different] law and way of life" (S.5: 48); and similarly: "for, every community faces a direction of its own, of which He is the focal point" (S. 2:148). Both verses, says Boullata, are followed by the command "*fa-stabiqū 'l-khayrāt*," which may be translated as "Vie, then, with one another in doing good works" (S. 5:48) or "Vie, therefore, with one another in doing good works" (S. 2:148). It is possible to assert that the Qur'ān does not favor one religious community over another. However, as Boullata points out, according to the Qur'ān "God has willed the Muslims to be a community of the middle way

---

[323] The Qur'ān, S: 5, v: 51.

[324] The Qur'ān, S: 9, v: 30.

[325] I. J. Boullata, "*Fa-stabiqū 'l-khayrāt*: A Qur'ānic Principle of Interfaith Relations," in: Y. Yazbeck-Haddad, W. Z. Haddad (eds.), *Christian-Muslim Encounters*, Gainesville: University of Florida Press, 1995, p. 43-53.

so that they might bear witness before humankind (S. 2:143)."[326] Furthermore, while dealing with people of other faiths, the Qur'ān demands from Muslims that they be kind and tactful. Moreover, one should remember that, according to the Qur'ān, "*la ikrahā fī'd-dīn*" (S. 2:256) which means, "there is no coercion or compulsion concerning religion"(S. 2:256). All in all, after analyzing the related views of the famous Qur'ānic exegetes, among them Al-Ṭabarī (d. A.D. 923), Al-Zamakhsharī (d. A.D.1144), Jalāl al-Dīn al-Mahallī (d.1459), Jalāl al-Dīn al-Suyūtī (d.1505), Muḥammad 'Abduh (d.1905), Muḥammad Rashīd Riḍā (d.1935) and Sayyid Quṭb (d.1966), Boullata concludes that in the above-mentioned passages, "*fa-stabiqū 'l-khayrāt*" and "*lā ikrahā fī'd-dīn*":

> We have the basis for interfaith dialogue and cooperation, which has the potential for leading us to a better world, if only people would heed and have good will toward one another.[327]

In the earliest history of Christian-Muslim relations, it is sometimes the positive and sometimes the negative aspect that has received greater emphasis. In the case of Muslims, according to Norman Daniel, the Qur'ān itself determines the polemic area and the disputed matters are as follows: God is not three, Jesus is not Son of God, He was not crucified and the Bible has been falsified and misinterpreted.[328] The Muslims, then, considered Christianity an abrogated religion, whose followers refused to accept God's final word.[329] Therefore, under the circumstances, Christians could be tolerated if willing to submit to the authority of Muslim state.

The first Christian reaction to Islam was quite negative and Muslims were considered barbarians with whom friendly relations were rather impossible. However, a few decades later, with the expansion of the rapidly growing Islamic empire, the situation began to change. For many non-Muslim populations in Byzantine and Persian territories, Islamic rule meant only an exchange of old rulers for new ones. The non-Muslim population under Muslim rule was given three choices:

> (1) conversion to Islam and full membership in the community; (2) retention of one's faith and payment of a poll tax; or (3), if they refused Islam or "protected" status, warfare until Islamic rule was accepted.[330]

---

[326] Ibid., p. 51.

[327] Ibid., p. 52.

[328] N. Daniel, "Christian-Muslim Polemics," in: M. Eliade, C. J. Adams (eds.) [et al.], *The Encyclopedia of Religion*, New York: Macmillan, 1987, vol. 3, p. 402-404.

[329] Regarding early Muslim Christian polemics see, for example: Muḥammad Ibn Hārūn al-Warrāq, *Anti-Christian Polemics in Early Islam: Abū Īsā al-Warrāq's Against Trinity*, edited and trans. by D. Thomas, Cambridge–New York: Cambridge University Press, 1992. For a contemporary discussion on Muslim-Christian polemics refer to: G. Anawati, *Polemique, apologie et dialogue islamo-chretiens*...; J. Waardenburg, *World Religions as Seen in the Light of Islam*...; K. Zebiri, *Muslims and Christians Face to Face*, Oxford: Oneworld Publications, 1997.

[330] J. L. Esposito, *The Islamic Threat: Myth or Reality*, New York–Oxford: Oxford University Press, 1995, p. 39.

The Christians in the conquered lands belonged to *Ahl al-Kitāb* (The People of the Book), namely to one of three major "scriptural" communities, which included Christians, Jews and Zoroastrians, and as monotheists, aside from retaining their lands and possessions, they were allowed substantial religious freedom.[331] As Krzysztof Kościelniak has pointed out, despite the fact that religion was the fundament of medieval society, both Christians and Muslims surely perceived each other not only through the prism of religious differences. Other differences, such as sociological and cultural ones, were also important in stimulating the reciprocal contacts of both groups. All this influenced the status of Christians in Muslim societies, which differed considerably depending on place and historical time.[332] Sometimes the new Muslim rulers provided more local autonomy and the local population enjoyed more religious freedom, paying lower taxes than before.[333] The development of the *Dhimnī* (the protected) status gave non-Muslims, including Christians, some legal rights as subjects of Islamic government.[334] In fact, relations between Christians and Muslims (especially the Muslim authorities) were generally good during the early period. The Muslims empire originally utilized the existing bureaucracy that included Christians, especially in Egypt, Syria and Persia. In general, the Islamic pattern of tolerance definitely contributed to the relatively peaceful Muslim-Christian coexistence. During its early period, Islam inherited the learning of the Hellenistic tradition due to some important scientific projects, including translations of works of science, philosophy and medicine from Greek into Arabic. Islam became the heir to the learning of the past and reached creative heights in architecture, science, technology and philosophy. The concept of legal rights for non-Muslims became an integral principle of Islamic law. Islamic learning and Islamic legal tolerance survived the disintegration of political unity in the ninth century and became important elements of the medieval period. The Islamic ideal, according to John Esposito, "was to fashion a world in which, under Muslim rule, idolatry and paganism would be eliminated, and People of the Book could live in a society guided and protected by Muslim power."[335]

---

331 B. Lewis, *The Middle East: 2000 Years of History from the Rise of Christianity to the Present Day*, London: Weidenfeld & Nicolson, 1995, p. 56-57. Also see: M. Arkoun, "The Notion of Revelation. From *Ahl al-Kitab* to the Societies of the Book," *Die Welt des Islams*, vol. 28 (1988), p. 62-89.

332 K. Kościelniak, *Grecy i Arabowie. Historia Kościoła melkickiego (katolickiego) na ziemiach zdobytych przez muzułmanów (634-1516)*, Kraków: Wydawnictwo UNUM, 2004, p. 74-75.

333 B. Lewis, *The Middle East*..., p. 56-57.

334 See: Y. Bat, *The Dhimmi: Jews and Christians under Islam*, trans. from French by D. Maisel (author's text), P. Fenton (document section), and D. Littman, Rutherford, NJ: Fairleigh Dickinson University Press, London: Associated University Presses, 1985. For a thorough discussion about the *dhimnī* status concerning Christians, and in particular Arabs, see: K. Kościelniak, *Grecy i Arabowie*..., p. 75-86; R. Hoyland (ed.), *Muslims and Others in Early Islamic Society*, The Formation of the Classical Islamic World, vol. 18, Burlington, VT: Ashgate, 2004.

335 J. L. Esposito, *The Islamic Threat*..., p. 39.

With regard to the Christian polemic and apologetic literature from the early period of Christian-Muslim relations, it is represented by a substantial literary output including works by Oriental Christians and Christian authors from Byzantium and Muslim Spain.[336]

Oriental Christians, who had lived under Muslim rule since the seventh century, addressed Islam and its followers in a large number of apologetic and polemical works in Arabic, Syriac or Greek, such as epistles, tractates and single-theme dialogues in which the parties were identified as "Christians" and "Saracens."[337] The authors supported their arguments with both Biblical and Qur'ānic quotations. Their attitude towards Islam and Muslims was diverse and ranged from hostility to conciliation. The early Christian polemicists were lacking a deeper knowledge and understanding of Islam. The main target of their criticism was the Prophet Muḥammad. He was usually depicted as a heretic, an impostor and a person of low moral values. Moreover, while discrediting the Prophet's reputation, they argued that His revelation was a false doctrine, and, at best, a mere heresy. As an example, one should mention here the polemics, or rather an attack on Islam by John of Damascus (655--747).[338] In the section devoted to heresies from his major work *The Fount of Wisdom*, the author attempted to warn Christians about the evil of Islam, so they could save themselves from it. He saw Islam as a religion swaying away from the truth and as a preparation for the final "holocaust" heralded by the arrival of the Antichrist. His severe attack was also directed at the Prophet Muḥammad, whom he accused of immoral conduct. The lack of objectivity and the quite hostile attitude of John of Damascus towards Islam and Muslims may be surprising. According to traditional sources, he could have had some knowledge of Islam because he was employed, for several years, in the Arab administration in Damascus.[339]

The Christian polemics that came out of Byzantium were less voluminous and different with regard to the attitude they presented towards Islam. This literary heritage contains unfavorable accounts of Muḥammad and the rise of Islam, as well as letters attacking the new religion and tractates on early Christian-Muslim disputes.[340]

---

336 For a thorough discussion, based on primary sources, see: B. Z. Kedar, *Crusade and Mission: European Approaches towards the Muslims*, Princeton: Princeton University Press, 1984, p. 3-41.

337 B. Lewis explains: "For many centuries, both Eastern and Western Christendom called the followers of the Prophet *Saracens*, a world of uncertain etymology but clearly of ethnic and not religious connotation, since the term is both pre-Islamic and pre-Christian" (*Islam and the West*, New York: Oxford University Press, 1993, p. 133).

338 N. Daniel, *Islam and the West...*, p. 13-15; R. Armour, *Islam, Christianity and the West: A Troubled History*, Maryknoll, NY: Orbis Books, 2002, p. 41-45; K. Kościelniak, *Grecy i Arabowie...*, p. 116-122. For a thorough discussion refer to: D. J. Sahas, *John of Damascus: The "Heresy of Ishmaelites,"* Leiden: Brill, 1972.

339 R. Armour, *Islam, Christianity and the West...*, p. 41.

340 For Christian-Muslim polemics from Byzantium see: J. Meyendorf, "Byzantine Views of Islam," *Dumbarton Oaks Papers*, 18 (1964), p. 113-132. Also refer to two important works by A.-T. Khoury: *Polemique byzatine et l'Islam (VIIIe-XIIIe s.)*, Leiden: Brill, 1972, and *Les*

The earliest Christian reaction to Islam that came from the Byzantine Empire was primarily negative. Muslims were considered barbarians and their religion viewed as not a true one but as a kind of Aryanism, a Christian heresy. Sophronius (560-638), the patriarch of Jerusalem and an eyewitness to the Arab conquest, complained about the cruelty, hostility and strength of the Saracens. While lamenting over the destruction of churches, the Patriarch viewed the fate of Christians as a result of their own wickedness.[341]

According to Kedar, one of the most influential Byzantine anti-Islamic works was the *Nicetae Byzantini Philosophi confutation falsi libri quem scripsit Mohamedes Arabs*, written in the middle of the ninth century by Nicetas of Byzantium.[342] In his discussion of the Qur'ān, in particular a detailed account of suras 2 to 18, he accused Muslims of adhering to an idolatrous conception of God.[343] There were also Byzantine authors who displayed more conciliatory stances. In 913 or 914, Patriarch Nicholas of Constantinople sent a letter to the Caliph al-Muktadir in which he stated that both he and the caliph had "obtained the gift of [their] authorities from a common Head."[344]

During the early period of Christian-Muslim relations, an important polemical Christian piece of literature came from Spain, a place that experienced the direct impact of Muslim rule and where "the favorable capitulation's terms meant that most Spanish Christians were largely unaffected by the change of regime in 711."[345] At the beginning, the contact between Christians and Muslims[346] was limited due to some legal restrictions and social customs. However, as it turned out, with each generation born into Andalusian society the barriers that early Muslims created between themselves and the Christians began to disappear and within a century of the conquest, the sources revealed a high degree of assimilation and acculturation in both directions, especially towards Islam.[347] Many Christians became fond of the new, more refined culture. The assimilation of Christians into Islamic society was quite advantageous for them since it enabled active participation in a culturally diversified and economically prosperous environment that linked Spain with Africa, the Near East and Central Asia. Many Spanish Christians became successful merchants on both the local and international scale. Others embarked on the task of studying the Arabic

théologiens byzantins et l'Islam: Textes et auteurs (VIIIe-XIIIe s.), Louvain–Paris: Beatrice-Nauwelaerts, 1969.

341 J. C. Lamoreaux, "Early Christian Responses to Islam,"in: J. V. Tolon (ed.), *Medieval Christian Perceptions of Islam. A Book of Essays*..., p. 15.

342 B. Z. Kedar, *Crusade and Mission*..., p. 21.

343 Ibid.

344 Ibid.

345 K. B. Wolf, "Christian Views..., p. 92.

346 During the first few decades of the rise of Islam, the terms "Muslim" and "Arab" were practically synonymous. With the territorial spread of the new religion, the term "Muslim" was also applied to people of other ethnic origin.

347 K. B. Wolf, "Christian Views..., p. 92-93.

language, theology and philosophy, enjoyed Arabic poetry; with time, while acquiring mastery in the refined Arab culture, they began to forget their own language and roots.[348] This situation seriously threatened Christian religious identity. The common practice among the Christians was to retain their religious identity. However, as Kenneth Baxter Wolf says:

> More typically Christians retained their religious identity, but did all they could to melt in the dominant society by avoiding anything that might, on the one hand, draw undue attention to their inferior status, and on the other, offend the religious sensibilities of their hosts. In short, they dressed like Muslims, they spoke like Muslims and lived like Muslims. While this process of acculturation contributed to the well-being of many Christians, other looked on with suspicion.[349]

With regard to the earliest accounts on the Muslims in Spain, one should mention two anonymous Latin Chronicles dating from 741 and 754. Apart from information about the Muslim conquest, there are some references to the Prophet Muḥammad, his followers and the distinct Muslim religious tradition.[350]

As for the Christian polemical literature, the earliest Latin works lack information about either their authors or their content. Among them are *Disputation Felicis cum Saraceno*, which survived only as a title mentioned in one letter of Alcuin to Charlemagne, and *Istoria de Mahomet*, written by an unknown author sometime before 850 and survived in its entirety.[351] The latter work presents the Prophet Muḥammad as a heretic who summoned his followers to abandon idolatry and adored a "corporeal God" in heaven. However, according to Wolf, *Istoria* also reveals the author's familiarity with Muslim tradition, presents Islam as a monotheistic religion, and acknowledges its missionary success among the Arabs.[352]

The "enforced success" of the Muslim religion and culture in Spain resulted in protests and even martyrdom of some Christians. In the late spring of the year 851, a monk named Isaac publicly denounced Muḥammad in front of a Muslim *qāḍī* (judge) and proclaimed the divinity of Christ, for which he was decapitated. Soon, a few monks and priests shared his fate, thus inaugurating the so-called "Cordoban martyr movement," which generated a number of victims.[353] The monastic communities supported the movement. However, given the advanced level of Christian assimilation and acculturation, which had been going on for one hundred and forty

---

[348] See: B. Lewis, *The Arabs in History*, New York: Oxford University Press, 1993, p. 134.

[349] K. B. Wolf, "Christian Views..., p. 93.

[350] Ibid., p. 87-90.

[351] Ibid., p. 93.

[352] Ibid., p. 94.

[353] Ibid., p. 95-96; N. Daniel, *Islam and the West...*, p. 16-17. Also refer to: E. P. Colbert, *The Martyrs of Cordoba (850-859): A Study of the Sources*, Washington, D.C., 1962; A. Cutler, "The Ninth-Century Spanish Martyrs' Movement and the Origins of Western Christian Missions to Muslims," *Muslim World*, vol. 55 (1965), p. 321-339; J. Waltz, "The Significance of the Voluntary Martyrs of Ninth-Century Cordoba," *Muslim World*, vol. 60 (1970), p. 143-59.

years in forced coexistence, it was expected that the martyr movement would be rather unpopular among the Christians in Cordoba and, following pressure from Muslim authorities, some Christians repudiated Isaac and others.

Among the men who led the reaction, one should mention the priest Eulogius (who died as a martyr in 859) and Paul Alvarus, a layman.[354] Their apocalyptic writings were inspired by the idea that the hegemony of Islam was a preparation for the appearance of the Antichrist. They believed that the Christians in Spain were fighting for survival under Muslim rule. *Liber apologeticus martyrum*, written by Eulogius sometime between 857 and his death, is a severe attack on Muḥammad, portraying him as heresiarch, the Antichrist and a false prophet and presenting Islam as a misguided derivative of Christianity rather than an entirely separate and rival system.[355] There is no doubt that approaching the matter from that standpoint enabled the author to picture Isaac and other martyrs as truly virtuous defenders of the faith who deserved to be honored by their community. Paul Alvarus similarly defended the martyrs and their actions in his *Indiculus luminosus*, written in 854.[356]

It is important to emphasize that the early Christian polemics that came out of Muslim Spain, in particular from Cordoba, shed some light on the nature of Christian-Muslim relations during that time and presented two opposing views on Islam: "one as a dangerous false prophecy and the other as a monotheistic religion based on a distinct revelation" that "may have been replicated in other Spanish communities under Muslim rule in that period."[357]

It is also worth noting that the authors who could observe and experience firsthand the outcome of Islamic rule and were influential in shaping views, according to Southern, demonstrated "ignorance of [a] peculiarly complex kind":

> They were ignorant of Islam, not because they were far from it like the Carolingian scholars, but for the contrary reason that hey were in the middle of it. If they saw and understood little of what went on round them, and if they knew nothing of Islam as a religion, it was because they wished to know nothing.... Significantly they preferred to know about Mahomet from the meager Latin source which Eulogius found in Christian Navarre, rather then [sic] from the fountainhead of the Koran or the great biographical compilations of their Moslem contemporaries.[358]

This simplistic approach to Islam became a standard pattern for a few centuries to come.

It is rather hard to find anti-Islamic literature from before the twelfth century in early medieval Catholic Europe, with the exception of Spain and the effort of

---

[354] See: C. M. Sage, *Paul Albar of Cordoba: Studies on his Life and Writings*, Washington, D.C.: Catholic University od America Press, 1943. This work includes a translation of Alvar's *Life of Eulogius*, p. 190-214.

[355] K. B. Wolf, "Christian Views..., p. 100.

[356] Ibid., p. 98.

[357] Ibid., p. 102.

[358] R. W. Southern, *Western Views of Islam in the Middle Ages*, Cambridge: Harvard University Press, 1962, p. 25-26.

Charlemagne, who asked Alcuin in 799 for "the disputation of Felix with a Saracen."[359] The absence of Christian-Muslim polemics in Catholic Europe is usually wrongly explained by the fact that apart from in Spain, there was no direct contact with Muslims. In addition, it is mistakenly believed that in the early medieval times, practically no information about Muslim conquests or the beliefs or habits of Muslim people infiltrated Europe. Kedar argues with these incorrect assumptions by presenting examples of various reciprocal contacts in Italy and France and referring to works from a substantial body of Latin literature containing information about the Muslim conquests, beliefs and habits.[360]

By the middle of the eleventh century, Christian-Muslim history was approaching a new phase of its development, namely the period of the Crusades.[361] Although in the Middle East the strength of Islam was still unquestionable, the balance of power there shifted from the Arabs to the Turks. The Eastern Christian Empire, by then much reduced in size, was facing a new challenge, namely the expansion of the Seljūk Turks. Under the circumstances, the Byzantine Emperor Alexius I Comnenos realized that a stronger Europe that had been freed from barbarian invasions and that had already begun the successful military campaign against Muslim dominance in Spain, Portugal and Sicily, could offer help in recovering the Holy Land.

It all started on November 27, 1095, at the Council of Clermont in Le Puy (France), where in response to urgent appeals for help from the Byzantine emperor, Pope Urban II in his sermon called upon all Christians to march to the Holy Land and free Jerusalem. The Pontiff's plea launched a crusading effort that would endure for the next two centuries and had a tremendous impact on Western culture. For Urban II, the Crusades were an opportunity not only to strengthen his authority but also to enforce the papacy's role in legitimizing temporal rulers, and a chance to reunite the Eastern (Greek) and Western (Latin) Church. The Pope's plea mobilised Christian rulers and their subjects to unite and engage in a campaign that would present new political, military and economic advantages to stagnant Europe. Furthermore, especially for the nobles of France, it was also an opportunity to bring rowdy knights under control by directing their fighting potential to a good cause, namely the recovery of the Holy Land. The first Crusade was successful and resulted in the capture of Jerusalem (1099) and the establishment of four Latin Kingdoms. However, the success was short-lived and by the middle of the twelfth century, the Muslims mounted an effective military response. In 1187, the army led by Ṣalāḥ al-Dīn recaptured

---

[359] B. Z. Kedar, *Crusade and Mission...*, p. 25.

[360] See: ibid., p. 25-29.

[361] For a broad discussion of Christian-Muslim relations during the period of the Crusades, based on primary sources, see: ibid., p. 57-203; also refer to: J. Hoeberichts, *Francis and Islam*, Quincy: Franciscan Press, 1997; J. Riley-Smith, *The Oxford History of the Crusades*, New York: Oxford University Press, 2002; M. Bull, N. J. Housley (eds.), *The Experience of Crusading*, 1. Western Approaches, Cambridge: Cambridge University Press, 2003; K. Kościelniak, *Grecy i Arabowie...*; N. Housley, *Contesting the Crusade*, Malden, MA: Blackwell Publishing, 2006; J. Żebrowski, *Dzieje Syrii*, Warszawa: Wydawnictwo Akademickie Dialog, 2006.

Jerusalem.[362] The subsequent Crusades did not bring significant changes since they "had degenerated into intra-Christian wars, wars against enemies who papacy denounced as heretics and schismatic.[363]

There is no doubt that the period of the Crusades was a time of cruelty, hostility, vehemence and violence. Nevertheless, one may not underestimate the impact the Crusades had on the reciprocal contacts between Christians and Muslims. For the first time, Europe had the chance to get acquainted with the advancement and richness of Muslim civilisation. That experience gave the West an inspiration and motivation for change. Christian Europe came back to new life, entering a path of new developments. The Franks modernised their armies and arms, old cities were rebuilt and new ones established. Furthermore, the growth of new commercial enterprises and financial institutions stimulated economic prosperity. The Muslim East inspired a new, more sophisticated and refined lifestyle and supplied the West with "novelties," such as spices, perfume, satin, silk and various attributes of lavishness and luxury.[364]

Direct contact with Muslims, especially taking into account their spiritual life, let Christians get better acquainted with Islam and encouraged them to engage in systematic studies of that religion. The impulse to pursue such studies was stimulated by the writings of the noted abbot of Cluny monastery – Pierre Maurice de Montboissier, better known as Peter the Venerable (1092 – 1156),[365] who believed that in order to fight Muslims successfully, it was important for Christians to know the followers of Islam better.[366] During his stay in Spain, where he inspected Cluny's branch monasteries and conferred with the Spanish emperor Alfonso VII, he had the chance to observe Christians and Muslims living side by side and eventually engaging in a dialogue of life.[367] Moreover, while in Spain, he met Peter of Toledo and other skilled translators of Arabic.[368] Thus, Peter the Venerable was able to grasp and

---

[362] He was one of the most talented Muslim commanders. For a thorough study about Saladin and his achievements see: A. S. Ehrenkreutz, *Saladin*, Albany: State University of New York Press, 1972.

[363] J. L. Esposito, *The Islamic Threat...*, p. 42.

[364] B. Lewis, *Arabs in History...*, p. 138.

[365] See: J. Kritzek, *Peter the Venerable and Islam*, Princeton: Princeton University Press, 1964.

[366] A. Hourani, *Europe and the Middle East*, Berkeley: University of California Press, 1980, p. 9, 23.

[367] See: M. R. Menocal, *The Ornamant of the World: How Muslims, Jews, and Christians Created a Culture of Tolerance in Medieval Spain*, Boston: Little Brown, 2002.

[368] Under the Muslim government, Toledo, Cordoba and Seville became important scholarly centers where Muslims, Christians and Jews worked together on various translating projects. The school of Toledo specialized in translating Arabic, Syriac and Greek manuscripts, including scientific, philosophical and historical ones, into Latin. These writings from the ancient world had been lost to Western Europe during the barbarian invasions. Fortunately, they had survived in Greek in Byzantium and in Arabic and/or Syriac in Islamic centers in the Middle East, particularly in Baghdad [there worked Ḥunayn Ibn Isḥāq (809-873), known in Latin as Johannitus, a famous

recognise the essence of the opportunities that his stay in Spain might bring about and had enough courage to initiate serious studies of Islam in Europe. The abbot commissioned Peter of Toledo and some other scholars to embark on an important project, i.e., translating the *Apology* of al-Kindy,[369] the three other Arabic language tractates and the Qur'ān itself into Latin.[370] The entire project formed the Toledan Collection.[371] At the head of it, Peter of Toledo placed *A Summary of the Entire Heresy of the Saracens*, his own apologetic work based on new, more reliable sources. Although the new sources helped Peter of Toledo to write with more accuracy and credibility, his final judgement of the Prophet Muḥammad and Islam was as negative as that of his predecessors. However, his idea to collect authentic Islamic sources and to make them available to Christians was an important step in Christian-Muslim relations.

In the meantime, Christian theologians engaged in sharp polemics with Muslims. The attitude of the Church toward Islam remained negative. Christians continued to reject Islam, considering it a heresy,[372] while the Qur'ān and the Prophet Muḥammad remained the primary targets of their vicious attacks. With the Reconquest of Spain under way and the early successes of Crusaders, more and more Muslims came under Christian domination. Since the number of restrictions on reciprocal contacts implemented by Christian authorities was increasing, the dissonance between the two religions remained.

As mentioned earlier, in the middle of continuous Christian-Muslim confrontations, aside from reciprocal hostility and struggle, there were always some attempts to bridge the two separate worlds. This was the case of scholarly centers in Spain, such as Toledo and Cordoba, and in the Norman Kingdom in Sicily, where

---

scholar and translator of Greek scientific treaties into Arabic and Syriac]. Finally, these important works became available to Western Europe through Spain. As J. Kritzek pointed out "there was no intellectual center in Europe that was not touched in some way by, that did not owe some debt to, the school of Toledo" (*Peter the Venerable*..., p. 54).

[369] The book is commonly called by its Arabic name *Risalah*. It consists of two parts: *The Letter from a Saracen* (Al-Hāshimī) and *The Reply of a Christian* (Al-Kindy, also spelled Al-Kindī). Modern scholarship has not been able to reach a consensus on when the text was actually composed; estimates range from the ninth to the eleventh centuries. The translator of this famous text was Peter of Toledo, a Jew who converted to Christianity. Al-Kindy's *Apology* gained circulation and popularity among Christian scholars in the Middle Ages because it provided a model of argumentation against Islam. These attacks focused in particular on the Qur'ān, the prophethood of Muḥammad and the spreading of the faith by conquest. These themes formed the main topics of Christian scholarship on Islam in the Middle Ages (N. Daniel, *Islam and the West*..., p. 29-30; R. Armour, *Islam, Christianity and the West*..., p. 83).

[370] The first Latin translation of the Qur'ān by Robert Ketton appeared in 1143. For a thorough discussion refer to: T. E. Burman, *Reading the Qur'an in Latin Christendom, 1140-1560*, Philadelphia: University of Pennsylvania Press, 2007, p. 60-122.

[371] See: R. Armour, *Islam, Christianity and the West*..., p. 81-85.

[372] Christians totally rejected Islam because the new religion did not accept the divinity of Jesus Christ and the doctrine of Trinity, namely the fundaments of Christian theology.

Muslims, Jews and Christians discussed, debated and studied together, relatively free of the religious coercion and bitterness that followed later.[373] Fortunately, the predominantly uncompromising Christian position concerning theological matters did not affect the sphere of other sciences. Christians embarked on the task of examining Muslim scholars' achievements in astronomy, mathematics, medicine and philosophy.[374] As a result of these studies, Medieval Europe rediscovered ancient achievements which gave creative nourishment to its new quest for knowledge, learning and development.

One may say that the translation of Islamic sources, a project realized by Peter the Venerable, was an important step toward acquiring a more objective Christian view of Islam. However, the polemical activity of Christians known as Mozarabs, among them converted Jews, who lived in Spain and over the centuries of Muslim rule there became Arabicized in language and culture though maintaining their Christian belief and practice, was of much greater significance. As Thomas E. Burman points out:

> All these Spanish Christians "nurtured among Muslims," whether converted Andalusian Jews or Mozarabs had an intimacy with Islam that no other European Christian could match in the twelfth century. Known best collectively as Andalusian Christians…these Arabic–speaking Catholics had immediate and centuries' long experience of Islam, and as such they provided historians interested in Medieval-European perceptions of Islam with the opportunity to examine how Christians who knew Islam in the flesh attempted to understand and confront it intellectually.[375]

The apologetic and anti-Islamic writings of the eleventh- and twelfth-century Andalusian Christians reveal their authors' intellectual approach to Islam, namely how they studied Islam (sources and methods) while developing its image from their first-hand experience. In this regard, Burman says, practically all the Andalusian-Christian works share the tendency to draw on and interweave both material and methods from at least three crucial bodies of literature, namely "(1) the vast body of Islamic Traditional literature known usually as the Hādīth, (2) Middle-Eastern Christian theological and apologetic works written in Arabic; and (3) contemporary Latin theology."[376] All this enabled Andalusian-Christian scholars, among them Pedro de Alfonso (1062-1110), a Christian convert from Judaism, to apply both the methods and terms derived from Muslim sources in order to defend and explain Christian doctrines more convincingly. At the same time, the sources provided Christians with

---

[373] R. Armour, *Islam, Christianity and the West…*, p. 96, 99-100.

[374] See: W. M. Watt, *The Influence of Islam on Medieval Europe*, Edinburgh: Edinburgh University Press, 1972, p. 30-44, 58-71.

[375] T. E. Burman, "*Tathlīth al-waḥdanīyâh* and the Twelfth-Century Andalusian-Christian Approach to Islam," in: J. V. Tolan (ed.), *Medieval Christian Perceptions to Islam. A Book of Essays…*, p. 110. For a further discussion on related issues see: idem, *Religious Polemic and the Intellectual History of the Mozarabs, 1050-1200*. Leiden: Brill, 1994.

[376] Idem, "*Tathlīth al-waḥdanīyâh…*, p. 111.

more thorough explanations of Muslim beliefs and practices.[377] Although this new approach did not change the overall medieval Christian image of Islam, it was an attempt to exchange the fight for a sophisticated argument and a sound preparation for more positive developments to come.

It should be pointed out that despite the predominantly reluctant and intolerant attitude of the Catholic Church towards Islam in medieval times, there were also some appeals for reconciliation and understanding. In 1076, Gregory VII (1015-1085),[378] a famous medieval Pope and a great reformer, in his letter to Emir An-Nāṣīr referred to common roots in the "patriarch Abraham."[379] Furthermore, the Pope urged Christians and Muslim to enter the path of love and understanding based on the common belief in One God. In his monograph *L'Eglise catholique et Islam*, Michel Lelong points out that even the gloomy history of the Crusades is marked by some conciliatory initiatives, namely religious meetings and disputes.[380]

The results of such measures were diverse. The majority of Christians remained rather faithful to their inherited hostile attitude toward Muslims and still considered Islam to be a religion of faults and a threat. They criticised the lack of sincerity of Muslim practices and made little effort to understand Muslims' intentions. As Daniel points out, the term *heresy*, "treated as a common noun in referring to Islam, was used carelessly and casually used in this connection." All in all, Christians could view Islam only as "a corruption of Christian truth."[381] Still, differences were counted and emphasised but similarities ignored. However, there was also a flicker of hope. For a number of Christians, a direct encounter with the followers of Islam and the observance of their deep religious belief was a breakthrough and an enriching experience. Opinions even appeared that the religious attitudes and practices of Muslims could become an inspiration for Christians.[382]

The medieval time was marked by the development of the Christian missionary activity of the mendicant orders, such as Dominicans and Franciscans. They both worked for the conversion of Jews and Muslims in Spain, North Africa and the Holy Land. The Franciscans focused on mission work and direct preaching. The Dominicans' efforts were primarily directed towards training missionary

---

[377] The works presenting such a tendency, and in particular an anonymous twelfth-century treatise known as *Tathlîth al-waḥdanîyâh* (Trinitizing the Unity of God or Confessing the Three-fold Nature of the Oneness) are discussed at length by T. E. Burman: "*Tathlîth al-waḥdanîyâh*..., p. 109-128.

[378] About the attitude of Pope Gregory VII to Muslims, see: A. Hourani, *Islam in European Thought*, Cambridge–New York: Cambridge University Press, 1995, p. 9-10.

[379] See: Pope Gregory, *The Register o Pope Gregory VII 1073-1085: An English Translation*, trans. by H. E. J. Cowdrey, Oxford–New York: Oxford University Press, 2002, p. 204-205.

[380] M. Lelong, *L'Eglise catholique et L'Islam*, Paris: Maisonneuve & Larose, 1993, p. 44. For a polemic during the time of the Crusades see: R. Ebied and D. Thomas (eds.), *Muslim-Christian Polemics during the Crusades*, Leiden: Brill, 2005.

[381] N. Daniel, *Islam and the West*..., p. 213.

[382] M. Lelong, *L'Eglise catholique*..., p. 13.

monks. In order to pursue their task effectively, they established several schools for learning Arabic. Dominicans also advocated continuing the Crusades alongside preaching activities.

Among the known Dominicans one should mention William of Tripoli (1220--1273), who was "relatively well informed about the beliefs and history of the Muslims."[383] His work *De Statu Saracenorum (Tract on the Standing of the Saracens)* reveals that William's good command of Arabic enabled him to not only get acquainted with the Qur'ān and appreciate its unique style and language, but also to study the commentaries well. Therefore, in his discussions on related issues he was able to quote from different Islamic sources, well aware of their value. According to Daniel, "this careful distinction between the text, commentators and the Qur'ān provides evidence showing respect and appreciation of the text."[384] His attitude towards the Prophet Muḥammad and Muslims rather parallels the previous negative images. However, the accounts are more substantial since the author quotes from Muslim sources. Furthermore, as Rollin Armour says, Tripoli "noted instances where Christianity and Islam agreed, citing passages on Jesus and Mary from the Qur'ān and the *ḥadīth*, quoting from the Qur'ān at length and quite accurately."[385]

Another famous Dominican missionary, Ricaldo da Monte di Croce (1243-1320), known as Ricoldo of Monte Croce, is credited with important works on Islam, among them *Contra Legem Sarracenorum* and *Itinerarium*. He joined the Dominican order in 1267 and in 1280 began a long journey of about twenty years to the Middle East with two aims: to learn about Islam and to work on converting Muslims. Ricoldo of Monte Croce succeeded in the first goal but not in the second.[386] His *Itinerarium* is an account of his travels that gave him the tremendous opportunity to explore the Muslim environment. The author began by visiting the Holy Land, travelled across Syria, through Mesopotamia and into Persia and stayed for some time in Baghdād, the city that witnessed the Muslim golden age, decline under Mongols rule, and still remained an important center for Islamic learning. However, his direct experience with the Muslims, their religion and their culture did not have much impact on his image of Islam, and his arguments resembled earlier ones, namely those from the medieval canon attacks against Islam, such as that the doctrines of the Qur'ān were heresies and could not be God's law, that Muḥammad was an impostor and a forerunner of the Antichrist, etc.[387] However, it should be noted that Ricoldo of Monte Croce was among the few Christian polemicists who gained direct experience with the Muslims by living side by side with them and therefore his criticism acquired some moderation. He even praised Muslim for their "piety and morals."[388]

---

[383] B. Z. Kedar, *Crusade and Mission...*, p. 180.

[384] N. Daniel, *Islam and the West...*, p. 194.

[385] R. Armour, *Islam, Christianity and the West...*, p. 89-90.

[386] Ibid., p. 90.

[387] N. Daniel, *Islam and the West...*, p. 87-88.

[388] R. Armour, *Islam, Christianity and the West...*, p. 91.

As for the Franciscans, the missionary activity of Francis of Assisi (1181-1226) and Ramon Lull (1232-1315) deserves our special consideration.

St. Francis of Assisi's short trip to Egypt and his meeting with the Ayyūbid sultan Malik al-Kāmil in 1219 in Damietta, the Egyptian village in the Nile Delta, is considered not only one of the best-known of the Franciscan's missionary efforts but is also one of the most significant examples of the medieval encounters between the followers of Christianity and Islam.[389] As mentioned, the initial purpose of that meeting was an attempt to convert the Sultan to Christianity.[390] However, the matter went in a different direction. It happened that on his way to Damietta, St. Francis visited the camps of the Crusaders. He was astonished to find his brothers in faith overcome by vehement hostility towards Muslims. Therefore, St. Francis realized that the words of the Gospel should be addressed first to his fellow believers. Another learning moment, this time a positive astonishment, was awaiting St. Francis in Damietta. The meeting with the Sultan proved to be different than expected. St. Francis of Assisi found out, to his surprise, that Malik al-Kāmil was not a barbarian, but a simple, pious man and a sensitive intellectual whose heart was full of love to One God – Allāh and who spoke openly about the futility and harm of religious wars.[391]

As Christian Troll pointed out, the meeting in Damietta had a great impact on St. Francis of Assisi and significantly changed his view on Islam.[392] From that time, he was convinced that true faith and love for One God may be also found in the hearts of Muslims.[393] In Chapter 16 of his book *Regula non-boullata of 1221*, St. Francis advised the Christians of two ways of going "among" the Muslims.[394] The first way was to avoid quarrels and disputes and to be a subject to every human creature for God's sake (1 Peter 2:13), and in so doing bearing witness to the fact that they were Christians. The second was to proclaim the word of God openly, when they were able to see that it was God's will. According to Lelong,[395] the encounter in Damietta could have become a starting point for a dialogue with the followers of Islam. However, the vast majority of Christians were not ready yet for such a change.

---

389 B. Z. Kedar, *Crusade and Mission...*, p. 119-126.

390 The issue of St. Francis's journey to Damietta and his meeting with Malik al-Kāmil is presented by St. Bonaventure in his *Biography of St. Francis*. See: R. Prejs and Z. Kijas (eds.), *Źródła Franciszkańskie: Pisma św. Franciszka, Źródła biograficzne św. Franciszka, Pisma św. Klary i źródła biograficzne, Teksty ustalające normy dla braci i sióstr od pokuty*, Kraków: Wydawnictwo OO. Franciszkanów "Bratni Zew," 2005, p. 914-916.

391 Unknown Author, *Dzieje Błogosławionego Franciszka i jego towarzyszy*, in: *Źródła Franciszkańskie...*, p. 1197-1198.

392 C. W. Troll. "Mission and Dialogue: The Example of Islam," *Encounter*, no. 189-190, (November-December 1992), p. 12.

393 For a detailed study on St. Francis's teachings concerning the relations with Muslims, see: J. Hoeberichts, *Francis and Islam*, Quincy: Franciscan Press, 1997.

394 For an analysis of Chapter 16, both its literary context and conceptual exegesis, see: ibid., p. 43-138.

395 M. Lelong, *L'Eglise catholique...*, p. 17.

The other famous Franciscan missionary was Ramon Lull (1233-1315), a poet, philosopher, theologian and mystic from Majorca.[396] Lull grew up during the times of the Reconquista, when Christianity was gaining back its influences on the island. His worldview was shaped by exposure to Catalonian culture, characterized by pluralism and even syncretism, and influences of Christian, Jewish and Muslim philosophical and mystical traditions. During the years 1262-1265, as a result of a Christ revelation, Lull decided to reform himself.[397] From that point, his entire life was devoted to the mission of spreading the Gospel to non-Christians, and in particular, Muslims.[398] He described himself as *Christianus arabicus*, which in modern language would mean a Specialist on Islam. Lull was a precursor to a modern missionary, a man of charisma and a scholar who was familiar with not only Islamic doctrine but also with Muslim tradition, philosophy, theology and mysticism.[399] Furthermore, he believed that in order to conduct his mission correctly and effectively, he should know the Arabic language. Only by knowing people's language could he initiate and conduct with them an honest, rational and sincere dialogue. It should be mentioned that Lull was neither afraid of Islam nor of entering into any kind of discussion with Muslim theologians. In his numerous works, among them the famous *Libre del gentil e dels tres savis*,[400] he referred to Muslim doctrines and attempted to share his thorough knowledge with future generations of missionaries.[401] During the times of the Crusades, he proved that fighting Muslims by sword would not bring results and the only possible way to gain their hearts and even souls was to approach them with respect, tolerance and love. His unusual, in comparison with that of his contemporaries, attitude towards Muslims, and the originality of his mission among them, which focused not on negation of everything that was Islamic but on a sincere attempt to get to know

---

[396] See: S. M. Zwemer, *Raymund Lull: First Missionary to the Moslems*, Three Rivers: Diggory Press, 2006. This work was originally published by Funk and Wagnalls, New York, 1902.

[397] A. Sawicka, *Drogi i rozdroża kultury katalońskiej*, Kraków: Księgarnia Akademicka, 2007, p. 78-79.

[398] See: R. Lull, "Pieśń Rajmunda," in: J. S. Kafel (ed.), *Antologia mistyków franciszkańskich*, vol. 2: *Wiek XIII-XIV*, Warszawa: Akademia Teologii Katolickiej, 1986, p. 258. Also refer to: D. Urvoy, "Ramon Lull et l'Islam," *Islamochristiana*, vol. 7 (1981), p. 127-146.

[399] According to D. Urvoy, with regard to the opportunities of Christian-Muslim encounters and dialogues during the thirteenth and fourteenth centuries, sufism appeared as a possible common "field for exchanges in philosophy and theology." The author mentions Ramon Lull's spiritual dispute with Muslims ("Soufisme et dialogue islamo-chretien," *Islamochristiana*, vol. 30 (2004), p. 55-64).

[400] See: R. Llull, *Libre del gentil e dels tres savis*, Patronat Ramon Llull. Nova edicio de les obres de Ramón Llull, vol. 2, A. Bonner (ed.), Palma de Mallorca: Publicacions de I'Abadia de Montserrat, 2001. For a recent edition R. Llull's works, containing all the previous critical editions, refer to *Nova edicio de les obres de Ramon Llull*, Palma: Nabu Press, 1990.

[401] For a thorough discussion on Lull's writing related to Islamic philosophy, theology and mysticism refer to: J. Judycka, *Wiara i rozum w filozofii Rajmunda Lulla*, Lublin: Wydawnictwo KUL, 2005.

and understand Islam and its followers, could enable us to consider him the first missionary-publicist.[402]

Another important voice that could change the history of Christian-Muslim relations, if taken into consideration in the right time, came from St. Thomas Aquinas. He was one of the greatest scholars who benefited from philosophical texts translated by Muslim, Jewish and Christian famous scholarly centers, such as Toledo, Cordoba and Sicily.

As pointed out by James Waltz, the literature devoted to St. Thomas Aquinas (1225-1274) and Islam had as its primary concern the impact of Islamic philosophy on his thought and hardly explored the issue of his attitude towards Muslims.[403] Furthermore, the scholar brings clear evidence of both the possibilities that St. Thomas had to acquire quite extensive knowledge about Islam and the results of such advantages as presented in his writings. He grew up in a family engaged in the service of the Emperor Frederick II, whose army boasted Muslim soldiers and whose court supported Muslim scholars.[404] Later, at the University of Naples, St.Thomas had the opportunity to study the works of Ibn Rushd, Averroes (1126-1198), the greatest Muslim Aristotelian, whose thought inspired a new and refreshing insight into major philosophical and religious themes. Finally, in Paris, he encountered and closely followed the theological formulations of Al-Fārābī (870-950), and explored the scholarship of other Muslim thinkers.[405] It is worth noting that St. Thomas was also well aware of the main issues concerning Christian-Muslim polemics and disagreements. However, as pointed out by Waltz, "it appears rather unlikely that St.Thomas knew the disputation literature directly, although John of Damascus, whom he often cites, gave guidelines for disputations and composed a tract, *On Heresy of the Ismaelites* "which Thomas may have read and used."[406] However, Waltz argues that St. Thomas's knowledge of Islam "was yet severely limited," since:

> He could not consult the *sharī'a* or *ḥadīth* which embody Islamic law, he certainly manifests no knowledge of Islamic history, and, despite the claim that Muḥammad's

---

[402] T. Mastnak, *Crusading Peace: Christendom, the Muslim World, and Western Political Order*, Berkeley: University of California Press, 2002, p. 104.

[403] J. Waltz, "Muhammad and the Muslims in St. Thomas Aquinas," *The Muslim World*, vol. 66/2, April (1976), p. 81-95. The author mentions here an interesting study by M.-D. Chenu who proposed research on "Islam and Christendom" based on the *Summa contra Gentiles*. See: M.-D. Chenu, *Introduction à l'étude de Saint Thomas d'Aquin*, Montréal: Institut d'études médiévales de l'université de Montréal, 1950; *Toward Understanding St. Thomas*, Libratry of Living CatholicThougnt, trans. by A.-M. Landry and D. Huges, Chicago: H. Regnery, 1964, p. 295.

[404] See: Ph. Lomax, "Frederick II, His Saracens and the Papacy," in: J. V. Tolan, *Medieval Christian Perceptions to Islam: A Book of Essays*..., p. 175-197.

[405] J. Waltz, "Muhammad and the Muslims..., p. 87. For a thorough discussion on the influence of Muslim thinkers on Western Medieval thought, see: R. Hammond, *The Philosophy of Al-Farabi and its Influence on Medieval Thought*, New York: Hobson Book Press, 1947; E. A. Myers, *Arabic Thought and the Western World in the Golden Age of Islam*, New York: Ungar, 1964.

[406] J. Waltz, "Muhammad and the Muslims..., p. 86.

perversions and fabrications "can be seen by anyone who examines his law," there is no evidence that he ever read the Qur'ān, although Latin translations were available.[407]

St. Thomas Aquinas wrote about Islam in his *Summa contra Gentiles* and *De rationibus fidei contra Saracenos, Graecos et Armenos*. His attitude towards Islam, as revealed in these works, according to Waltz, seems to be far from objective or sympathetic and the arguments used against the Muslim religion are traditional Christian ones alleging violence or Muḥammad's lack of miracles. While St. Thomas acknowledged that Muḥammad taught some truth accessible to human reason, such as monotheism, he attempted to discredit his teaching by focusing on the Prophet's audience. He was convinced that Muḥammad's false doctrines could attract only brutes and nomads.[408] The major problem with Islam, as seen by Aquinas, "was its lack of authority, an authority that miracles could provide."[409] It should be pointed out that in St. Thomas's view of Islam, a new, important feature appeared which could explain the lack of positive outcomes from Christian-Muslim encounters.

In his book *Islam and the West: Making of an Image*, Norman Daniel attempts to find the reasons for the persistent, intolerant and reluctant Christian attitude towards Islam. The author quotes St. Thomas Aquinas, who in the thirteenth century had pointed out the need to search for new moral and philosophical arguments that could be acceptable for Muslims. He emphasised that in the case of the polemics with Muslims, the use of both biblical authorities and rational methods of argument had proven futile. Aquinas suggested that theological discussions with the followers of Islam should instead focus on the defense of faith rather than on its proof. Most important was establishing a common ground for a possible way of communication and eventual understanding. Aquinas was convinced that the use of force was definitely inappropriate for converting Muslims "because to believe is a matter of will."[410] It was quite possible that the history of the relations between Christianity and Islam would have taken a different path and the bridges could have been built much earlier if the words of St. Thomas Aquinas had been taken into consideration.

It is worth noting that in the thirteenth century, the universities in Paris and Salamanca introduced studies of the Arabic language. It was a clear sign that the West had embarked on the serious task of examining the achievements of Muslim civilization using primary sources.

In the course of the thirteenth century, the West systematically grew stronger and was preparing for its next military campaigns. The subsequent Crusades, however, did not bring the awaited results. With the Mongol invasion and the fall of the Abbasid caliphate in 1258, Christian hopes for victory were once again raised. However, they quickly vanished, because in Egypt power was taken by an effec-

---

[407] Ibid., p. 86-87.

[408] Ibid., p. 83-84.

[409] R. Armour, *Islam, Christianity and the West…*, p. 98.

[410] J. Waltz, "Muhammad and the Muslims…," p. 92.

tive and strong dynasty, namely the Mamlūks.[411] The Crusaders, then, were losing previously-conquered cities one after the other. In 1291, 'Akkā, the last fortress of the Crusaders, fell. In addition, a new force appeared in the Muslim West. A well-armed, well-trained and strong wave of Turkish tribes from Central Asia approached the Middle East. The Turks embraced Islam, established a dynasty[412] and with determination began to build their empire. In a relatively short period, the Ottomans became the champions and the defenders of their new faith.

During medieval times, the efforts of the Christian polemicists with Islam and missionaries engaged in contact with Muslims had two major aims: to discourage Christians from becoming Muslims and to encourage Muslims to become Christians. However, both proved to be rather idle goals, and, as Bernard Lewis concluded, "it took some centuries before they decided that the first was no longer necessary and the second was impossible."[413]

There is no doubt that during the thirteen centuries of Christian-Muslim relations, the negative attitude of Christians towards the followers of Islam underwent a gradual positive evolution. One may say that by the first decade of the twentieth century, the Church was "prepared" to introduce in its teaching profound changes concerning relations with non-Christian religions, including Islam.

---

[411] The Mamlūks (1250-1517) were a local Muslim dynasty of slave origin that ruled in Egypt and Syria. They successfully challenged the Mongol threat. As defenders of Islamic orthodoxy, the Mamlūks sponsored numerous religious buildings, including mosques, madrasas and khānqāhs. See: D. P. Little, *History and Historiography of the Mamlūks*, London: Variorum Reprints, 1986.

[412] The Ottomans (1281-1922) were a dynasty of Turkish sultans established by Osman (1258-1324) in Anatolia shortly after the Mongol's invasion. Following the conquest of Constantinople in 1453 and a successful military campaign in Asia and North Africa, they came to rule Islamic lands also threatening Europe; in the eighteenth century a gradual downfall of the Empire began. See: C. Imber, *The Ottoman Empire, 1300-1650: The Structure of Power*, New York: Palgrave, 2002; B. Tezcan, *The Second Ottoman Empire: Political and Social Transformation in the Early Modern World*, Cambridge–New York: Cambridge University Press, 2010.

[413] B. Lewis, *Islam and the West*, New York: Oxford University Press, 1993, p. 13.

Epilogue

As of today, about one-fifth of the world's population is Muslim. They come from different nationalities, ethnic and tribal groups, and cultures, speak many languages and practice distinct cultures. Islamic civilization is a blend of Arabic, Persian, Turkish, Greek, Roman, Indian, Egyptian, Chinese, and many other elements which have been acquired in the course of its historical development.

Beginning as the faith of a small community of believers in Arabia in the seventh century, Islam rapidly became one of the major world religions. After the death of the Prophet Muḥammad the world of Islam continued to expand and by the mid-eighth century, it extended from the Iberian Peninsula to the inner Asian frontiers of China. From the end of the effective power of the caliphs in the tenth century to the beginning of the sixteenth, the size of the Muslim world almost doubled. The vehicles for expansion were not conquering armies, but traveling merchants and itinerant teachers active in Saharan and sub-Saharan Africa, in Central Asia, and in the many different communities in the Indian Ocean basin. As a result from the ongoing Islamization process, by the end of the fifteenth century the Muslim world became very different from what it had been at the height of 'Abbāsid's power and it brought together people of different ethnic origins and cultures. Islam was no longer a faith identified with a particular world region; it had become more universal and cosmopolitan in its articulation and in the nature of the community of believers.

The Muslim world continued to expand in the early modern era. A number of major Islamic states emerged during the sixteenth century. The largest and the most powerful was Ottoman Empire, which had expanded from its original base as a Turkish warrior state in western Anatolia. However, by the seventeenth century it began to weaken in the face of internal strife and external threats. During the next two centuries most of the Muslim world came under direct or indirect European control. Although the cultural life was gradually dominated by European influences, there were important developments in the sphere of Islamic renewal that also had a considerable long-term significance. In the nineteenth century, European expansion and influences in the sphere of culture became an increasingly important force in Muslim societies. Napoleon's invasion of Egypt in 1798 became a symbol of the new era. The Muslim world entered the path of a wide range modern reforms. Ottoman Empire reforms enhanced the secular and more liberal aspects. In Egypt, Muḥammad

'Alī, the Ottoman governor after French withdrawal, initiated similar reforms, and by the second half of the century, Egypt was virtually independent and undergoing major socio-political transformations. However, these modern reforms did not prevent continued military losses to European powers as well as their political and economic domination.

By the end of the nineteenth century the important new development was the emergence of Islamic modernism. Muḥammad 'Abduh in Egypt and various thinkers in other parts of Islamic world argued that faith and reason were compatible and that Islam was a reason-based faith. Therefore, they were pointing out that it was necessary to create an effective synthesis of Islam and modernity.

World War I opened a new chapter in Islamic history. The Ottoman Empire was defeated and occupied, and both the caliphate and the sultanate were formally abolished as Turkish nationalism came to the forefront. Similar Westernizing reforms and the development of more secularist nationalism dominated the rest of the Muslim world. However, the period between the two world wars witnessed the emergence of some explicitly Islamic movements. With time new movements, introduced by the modern educated *élite*, not explicitly *'ulamā'* in background, began to advocate a more direct adoption of Islam in modern society.

In the second half of the twentieth century, as the era of European imperialism ended, Muslim societies became politically independent. At the end of the twentieth century, the Muslim world continued to change under the influence of a new generation of Islamically active intellectuals. In the new thinking there was still an emphasis on the importance of the Islamic message for all aspects of life, but this did not mean an adherence to older, comprehensive political programs or a demand for uniformity in acceptance of Islamic ideals. Muslim intellectuals began to accept pluralism in a global context, not just as a practical necessity but as a positive aspect of life. Furthermore, they were open to a historical, critical analysis of the foundations of the faith and the Islamic tradition.

In Muslim tradition the *'umma* – the socio-political community established by Muḥammad in Medina – has remained the model for a true Islamic state and society and the emphasis on the sole sovereignty of God has provided an important foundation for Muslim political thinking and social and cultural development throughout Islamic history. While many people commonly speak of Islam and Muslims in a broad, all-encompassing manner there are many interpretations of Islam and many different Muslims. Despite these differences, all Muslims continue to affirm the basic core of the faith in monotheism as defined by the revelation to Muḥammad and preserved in the Qur'ān.

Bibliography

Abū al-Fidā', Ismā'īl Ibn 'Alī. *Al-Mukhtaṣar fī akhbār al-bashar*. Baghdād: Makhtabat Al-Muthanná, [1968?].

Adams, Charles J. "Islam and Christianity: The Opposition and Similarities." In: Roger M. Savory and Dionisus A. Agius eds. *Logos Islamikos: Studia Islamica in Honorem Georgii Michaelis Wickens*. Papers in Mediaeval Studies no. 6. Toronto: Pontifical Institute for Medieval Studies, 1984, p. 287-306.

______________. "Islamic Religious Tradition." In: Leonard Binder ed. *The Study of the Middle East: Research and Scholarship in the Humanities and Social Sciences*. New York: Wiley, 1976, p. 29-96.

Adamson, Peter. *Al-Kindī*. "Great Medieval Thinkers" Series. Oxford–New York: Oxford University Press, 2007.

Aharoni, Re'uven. *The Pasha's Bedouin: Tribes and State in the Egypt of Mehemet Ali, 1805--1848*. London–New York: Routledge, 2007.

Al-'Ārif, 'Ārif. *Al-Mufaṣṣal fī ta'rīkh al-Quds*. Jordan: Fawzī Youssef Library, 1961.

Al-Asyūṭī, Shams al-Dīn Muḥammad Ibn Aḥmad al-Minhājī. "Kitāb al-iqrār." In: *Jawāhir al-'uqūd wa mu'īn al-qudāt wa'l-shuhūd*. Vol. I. Cairo, 1955, p. 17-54.

____. "Kitāb al-nafaqāt." In: *Jawāhir al-'uqūd wa mu 'īn al-qudāt wa'l-shuhūd*. Vol. I. Cairo, 1955, p. 210-221.

Al-Balawī. *Sīrat Aḥmad bin Ṭūlūn*. Edited by Muhammad Kurd 'Alī. Damascus, 1939.

Al-Fārābī. "The Political Regime." In: *Medieval Political Philosophy: A Sourcebook*. Edited by Ralph Lerner and Muhsin Mahdi. Translated by Fauzi Najjar. Toronto: Collier-Mc-Macmllian, 1963, p. 31-58.

Algar, Hamid. *Imam Abu Hamid Ghazali: An Exponent of Islam in its Totality*. Oneonta, NY: Islamic Publications International, 2001.

Al-Ghazālī, Abū Ḥāmid. *Al-Ghazālī on Love, Longing, Intimacy and Contentment (Kitāb al-maḥabba wa'l-shawq wa'l-uns wa'l-riḍā)*. Book XXXVI of The Revival of the Religious *sciences (Iḥyā' 'ulūm al-dīn)*. Translated by Eric L. Ormsby. Cambridge: Islamic Texts Society, 2011.

__________________. *Munqidh min al-ḍalāl (The Faith and Practice of al-Ghazālī)*. Translated and edited by William Montgomery Watt. London: G. Allen & Unwin,1953.

__________________. *The Incoherence of the Philosophers (Tahāfut al-falāsifa), A parallel English-Arabic text*. Translated and edited by Michael E. Marmura. Provo, UT: Birmingham Young University Press, 2000.

'Alī, Abdullah Yūsuf. *The Meaning of the Holy Qur'ān*. Beltsville, MD: Amana Publications, 1989.

ʿAlī Sayyid Amīr. *The Spirit of Islam: A History of the Evolution and Ideals of Islam with a Life of the Prophet.* London: Christophers, 1922.

Al-Ṭabarī, Abū. *Ta'rīkh al-rusūl wa'l-mulūk. Muḥammad at Mecca.* Vol. 6. The History of Al-Tabari. SUNY Series in Near Eastern Studies: Bibliotheca Persica (Albany, N.Y.). Translated and edited by William Montgomery Watt, Michael V. McDonald. Albany, NY: State University of New York Press, 1988.

____________. *The Last Years of the Prophet: The Formation of the State – A. D. 630-632.* Vol. 9, The History of Al-Tabari. Translated and edited by Ismail K. Poonawala. Albany, NY: State University of New York Press, 1990

Al-Wāqidī, Muḥammad Ibn ʿUmar. *Muhammed in Medina: Das ist Vākidī's Kitāb al-Maghāzī in verkürzter deutscher Wiedergabe.* Translated by Julius Wellhausen. Berlin: G. Reimer, 1882.

Al-Warrāq, Muḥammad Ibn Harūn. *Anti-Christian Polemics in Early Islam: Abū 'Īsā al--Warrāq's Against Trinity.* Translated and edited by David Thomas. Cambridge–New York: Cambridge University Press, 1992.

Anawati, Georges Ch. *Polémique, apologie et dialogue islamo-chrétien: Positions classique médiévales et positions contemporaines.* Euntes Docete, XXII, Roma: Pontificia Universita Urbaniana, 1969.

Andrae, Tor. *Der Ursprung des Islams und das Christendtum. Kyrkohistorisk Årsskrif 1923/25.* Uppsala: Almqvist & Wiksell, 1926.

__________. *Mohamed: The Man and His Faith.* Translated by Theophil Menzel. London: George Allen & Unwin, 1936, New York: Barnes & Noble, Inc., 1935.

Antonious, George. *The Arab Awakening: The Story of the Arab National Movement.* London: Lippincott, 1939.

Arberry, Arthur J. *Revelation and Reason in Islam.* London: Allen & Unwin, 1957.

Arkoun, Mohammad. "The Notion of Revelation. From Ahl al-Kitab to the Societies of the Book." *Die Welt des Islams*, vol. 28 (1988), p. 62-89.

Armour, Rollin. *Islam, Christianity and the West: A Troubled History.* Maryknoll, NY: Orbis Books, 2002.

____________. *Islam, chrześcijaństwo i Zachód. Burzliwe dzieje wzajemnych relacji.* Translated by Iwona Nowicka. Kraków: WAM, 2004.

Atil, Esin. *Renaissance of Islam: Art and Architecture of the Mamlūks.* Washington, DC: Smithsonian Institution Press, 1981.

Ayalon, David. "The Expansion and Decline of Cairo under the Mamlūks and its Background." In: *Résumès des communications*, Y. Hervouet (ed.), *XXIX Congrès international des orientalistes*, Section 4. Paris, 1974, p. 64-65.

Bat, Ye'or. *The Dhimmi: Jews and Christians under Islam.* Translated by David Maisel, Paul Fenton, David Littman. Rutherford, NJ: Fairleigh Dickinson University Press, London: Associated University Presses, 1985.

Becker, Carl Heinrich. *Christianity and Islam.* London–New York: Harper & Brothers, 1909.

Behrens-Abouseif, Doris. *Islamic Architecture in Cairo: An Introduction.* Cairo: American University in Cairo Press, 1989.

Bell, Richard. *The Origin of Islam in its Christian Environment: The Gunning Lectures.* Islam and the Muslim World, no. 10. Edinburgh University 1925. London: Macmillan & Co. Ltd., 1926.

Bennison, Amira K. *The Great Caliphs: The Golden Age of the Abbasid Empire.* London: I. B. Tauris, 2009.

Bewley, Aisha. *Mu'awiya, Restorer of the Muslim Faith*. London: Dar Al Taqwa, 2002.

Biechler, James E. and Bond, H. Lawrence eds. *Nicholas of Cusa on Interreligious Harmony: Text, Concordance, and Translation of 'De Pace Fidei'*. Text and Studies in Religion 55. New York–Toronto: Edwin Mellen Press, 1990.

Bielawski, Józef. *Historia literatury arabskiej*. Wrocław–Warszawa–Kraków: Ossolineum, 1968.

Blachère, Régis. *Le problème de Mahomet*. Paris: Presses Universitaires de France, 1952.

Blair, Sheila S. *The Art and Architecture of Islam: 1250-1800*. London–New Haven, CT: Yale University Press,1994.

Borrmans, Maurice. "Ludovico Marracci et sa traduction latine du Coran." *Islamochristiana*, vol. 28 (2002), p. 73-86.

Boullata, Issa. J. *An Anthology of Islamic Studies*. Montreal: McGill Indonesia IAIN Development Project, 1992.

___________. "*Fa-stabiqū'l-khayrāt*: A Qur'ānic Principle of Interfaith Relations." In: Yvonne Yazbeck-Haddad and Wadi Z. Haddad eds. *Christian-Muslim Encounters*. Gainesville: University of Florida Press, 1995, p. 43-53.

Breiner, Bert. F. and Troll, Christian W. "Christianity and Islam." In: John L. Esposito ed. *The Oxford Encyclopedia of Modern Islamic World*. Vol. 1. New York: Oxford University Press,1995, p. 280-286.

Buhl, Frants. "The Prophet's Life and Career." *The Encyclopaedia of Islam*. New Edition. Vol. 7, p. 360-376.

Bull, Marcus and Housley Norman J. eds. In: *The Experience of Crusading*. 1, Western Approaches. Cambridge: Cambridge University Press, 2003.

Burman, Thomas E. *Reading the Qur'an in Latin Christendom, 1140-1560*. Philadelphia: University of Pennsylvania Press, 2007.

___________. *Religious Polemic and the Intellectual History of the Mozarabs, 1050--1200*. Brill's Studies in Intellectual History, 52. Leiden: Brill, 1994.

___________. "*Tathlīth al-waḥdanīyâh* and the Twelfth-Century Andalusian-Christian Approach to Islam." In: John V. Tolan ed. *Medieval Christian Perceptions of Islam: A Book of Essays*. Garland Medieval Case Books 10, Garland Reference Library of Humanities 1786. New York–London: Garland, 1994.

Carlyle, Thomas. *The Best Known Works of Thomas Carlyle: Including Sartor Resartus, Heroes and Hero Worship, and Characteristics*. New York: Book League of America, 1942.

Chelebi, Sulayman. *The mevlidi sherif.* The Wisdom of the East Series. Translated by F. Lyman MacCallum. London: John Murray Publishers Ltd., 1943.

Chenu, Marie-Dominique. *Introduction à l'étude de Saint Thomas d'Aquin*. Montréal: Institut d'études médiévales de l'université de Montréal, 1950.

___________. *Toward Understanding St. Thomas*. Library of Living Catholic Thought. Translated by Albert M. Landry and Dominic Huges. Chicago: H. Regnery, 1964.

Cleveland, William L. *A History of the Modern Middle East*. Oxford–Boulder, CO: Westview Press, 1994.

Colbert, Edward P. *The Martyrs of Cordoba (850-859): A Study of the Sources*. Washington, DC: Catholic University of America Press, 1962.

Corbin, Henry. *Histoire de la philosophie islamique*. Paris: Gallimard, 1986.

___________. *Historia filozofii muzułmańskiej*. Translated by Katarzyna Pachniak. Warszawa: Dialog, 2005.

Creswell, Keppel A. C. *The Muslim Architecture of Egypt*. New York: Hacker Art Books, 1978.

Curiel, Raoul and Gyselen, Rika eds. *Itinéraires d'Orient: Hommages à Claude Cahen*. Res orientales (Bures-sur-Yvette), 6. Bures-sur-Yvette–Leuven: Groupe d'études pour la civilisation du Moyent-Orient–Peeters Press, 1994.

Cutler, Allan. "The Ninth-Century Spanish Martyrs' Movement and the Origins of Western Christian Missions to the Muslims." *Muslim World*, vol. 55 (1965), p. 321-339.

Danecki, Janusz. "Dynastia Tulunidów." *As-Sadaka*, vol. 27 (XI 1983), p. 31-35.

____________. "Konstytucja medyneńska." *Przegląd Religioznawczy*, vol. 1/168 (1993), p. 37-46.

Daniel, Norman. "Christian-Muslim Polemics." In: Mircea Eliade, Charles J. Adams eds. [et al.]. *The Encyclopedia of Religion*. Vol. 3. New York: Macmillan, 1987, p. 402-404.

____________. *Islam and the West: The Making of an Image*. Oxford: Oneworld Publications, 1993.

De Bellefends, Y. L. "Iqrār." *The Encyclopaedia of Islam*. New Edition. Vol. 1, p. 1078--1081.

Dodge, Bayard. *The Fihrist of Al-Nadim. A Tenth-Century Survey of Muslim Culture*. Vol. 1. New York–London: Columbia University Press, 1970.

Dodwell, Henry. *The Founder of Modern Egypt: A Study of Muhammad 'Ali*. Cambridge: Cambridge University Press, 1931.

Ebied, Riffat Y. and Thomas, David eds. *Muslim-Christian Polemics during the Crusades: The Letter from the People of Cyprus and Ibn Abī Ṭālib al-Dimashqī's Response*. Leiden: Brill, 2005.

Ehrenkreutz, Andrew S. *Saladin*. Albany, NY: State University of New York Press, 1972.

Esposito John L. *The Islamic Threat: Myth or Reality*. New York–Oxford: Oxford University Press, 1995.

____________. and Voll, John O. *Islam and Democracy*. New York: Oxford University Press, 1996.

Ettinghausen, Richard and Grabar, Oleg. *The Art and Architecture of Islam: 650-1250*. Harmondsworth, Middlesex, England: Penguin Books, 1987.

Fahmy, Khaled. *All the Pasha's Men: Mehmed Ali, his Army, and the Making of Modern Egypt*. Cambridge–New York: Cambridge University Press,1997.

Fakhry, Majid. *Averroes (Ibn Rushd): His Life, Works and Influence*. Oxford: Oneworld, 2001.

___________. *A History of Islamic Philosophy*. New York: Columbia University Press, 1970.

___________. *Al-Fārābī, Founder of Islamic Neoplatonism: His Life, Works and Influence*. Oxford: Oneworld, 2002.

Farag, Nadia R. "Usratu Muḥammad 'Alī." In: *Yussef Idris and Modern Egyptian Drama*. Cairo: Dar al-Ma'arif bi-Misr, 1975, p. 21-24.

Frank, Richard M. *Al-Ghazali and the Ash'arite School*. Durham, NC: Duke University Press, 1994.

Frantz G. M. *Saving and Investment in Medieval Egypt*. Ph.D. dissertation. Ann Arbor, Michigan, 1978.

Frishman, Martin, and Khan, Hasan-Uddin eds. [et al.]. *The Mosque: History, Architectural Development & Regional Diversity*. New York: Thames and Hudson, 1994.

Gacek, Adam. *Arabic Manuscripts: A Vademecum for Readers*. Leiden–Boston: Brill, 2009.

Ghālib, Muṣṭafá. *Al-Ḥarakāt al-bāṭinīyah fī al-Islām*. Bayrūt, Lubnān: Dār al-Andalus, 1982.

Gibb, Hamilton A.R. "The Reaction in the Middle East Against Western Culture." In: *Studies on the Civilization of Islam*. Princeton. NJ: Princeton University Press, 1982, p. 320-344.

________________. *Studies on the Civilization of Islam*. Princeton, NJ: Princeton University Press, 1982.

________________. ed., trans. *Travels of Ibn Baṭṭūṭa*. Vol. 1. Cambridge: University Press, 1956.

________________. "Ṭūlūnids." In: *The Encyclopaedia of Islam*. Vol. 4, no. 2, p. 833-836.

Goddard, Hugh. *A History of Christian-Muslim Relations*. Edinburgh: Edinburgh University Press, 2000.

Goldziher, Ignaz. *Muhammedanische Studien*. 2 vols. Halle: M. Niemeyer, 1889-1890.

Gordon, Matthew S. *The Rise of Islam*. Westport, CT: Greenwood Press, 2005.

________________."Ṭūlūnids." In: *The Encyclopaedia of Islam*. New Edition. Vol. 10, p. 616-618.

Grabar, Oleg. *The Coinage of the Ṭūlūnids*. New York: American Numismatic Society, 1957.

__________. "Reflection on Mamlūk Art." *Muqarnas*, vol. 2 (1984), p. 1-13.

Gregory, Pope. *The Register of Pope Gregory VII 1073-1085: An English Translation*. Translated by Herbert E. J. Cowdrey. Oxford–New York: Oxford University Press, 2002, p. 204-205.

Griffel, Frank. *Al-Ghazālī's Philosophical Theology*. Oxford–New York: Oxford University Press, 2009.

Gronke, Monika. "La rédaction des actes privé dans le monde musulman médiéval: théorie et practique." *Studia Islamica*, vol. 59 (1984), p. 159-174.

Grunebaum, Gustave E. von. *Der Islam in seiner klassischen Epoche, 622-1258*. Zürich–Stuttgart: Artemis Verlag, 1966.

____________________. *Medieval Islam: A Study in Cultural Orientation*. Chicago: University of Chicago Press, 1953.

Guillaume, Alfred. *New Light on the Life of Muhammad*. Series: Journal of Semitic Studies. Monograph, no. 1. Manchester: Manchester University Press, 1960.

Gutas, Dimitri. *Avicenna and the Aristotelian Tradition: Introduction to Reading Avicenna's Philosophical Works*. Leiden–New York: Brill, 1988.

Haarmann, Ulrich, "Khumārawayh B. Aḥmad B. Ṭūlūn." In: *The Encyclopaedia of Islam*. New Edition. Vol. 5, p. 49-50.

Hamdouni, Alami M. *Art and Architecture in the Islamic Tradition: Aesthetics, Politics and Desire in Early Islam*. London–New York: I. B. Tauris, 2011.

Hammond, Robert. *The Philosophy of al-Farabi and its Influence on Medieval Thought*. New York: Hobson Book Press, 1947.

Hasan, Zaki M. *Les Tulunides: étude de l'Égypte musulmane à la fin du IXe siècle: 868-905*. Paris: Busson, 1933.

Hauziński, Jerzy. *Burzliwe dzieje Kalifatu Bagdadzkiego*. Warszawa–Kraków: Wydawnictwo Naukowe PWN, 1993.

Hawting, Gerald R. *The First Dynasty of Islam: The Umayyad Caliphate, AD 661-750*. London–New York: Routledge, 2000.

Haykal, Muhammad H. *Ḥayāt Muḥammad*. Al-Qāhirah: Maktabat al-Nahḍah al-Miṣrīyah, 1952.

__________________. *The Life of Muḥammad*. Translated by Ismail R. al Fārūqī. Indianapolis: North American Trust Publications, 1997.

Heffening, H. "Waqf." In: *The Encyclopaedia of Islam*. New Edition. Vol. 12, p. 1096-1103.

Hemli, Mongi. *La philosophie morale d'Ibn Bâjja (Avempace) à travers le Tadbîr al-mutawaḥḥid (Le régime du solitaire)*. Tunis: Impr. N. Bascone & S. Muscat, 1969.

Hillenbrand, Robert. *Islamic Architecture: Form, Function and Meaning*. Edinburgh: Edinburgh University Press, 1994.

Hoag, John D. *Islamic Architecture*. New York: H.N. Abrams Inc., 1977.

Hodgson, Marshall G. S. *The Venture of Islam: Conscience and History in a World Civilization*. Vol. 3. Chicago: University of Chicago Press, 1974.

Hoeberichts, Jan. *Francis and Islam*. Quincy, IL: Franciscan Press, 1997.

Holt, Peter M. *Egypt and the Fertile Crescent 1516-1922: A Political History*. Ithaca, NY: Cornell University Press, 1966.

Hopkins, Jasper. *A Concise Introduction to the Philosophy of Nicholas of Cusa*. Minneapolis: University of Minnesota Press, 1978.

____________ ed., trans. *Nicholas of Cusa's "De pace fidei" and "Cribratio Alcorani."* Minneapolis: A.J. Banning Press, 1990.

Hourani, Albert H. *Arabic Thought in the Liberal Age 1798-1939*. Cambridge: Cambridge University Press, 1983.

____________. *Europe and the Middle East*. Berkeley: University of California Press, 1980.

____________. *Islam in European Thought*. Cambridge–New York: Cambridge University Press, 1995.

____________. *Historia Arabów*. Translated by Janusz Danecki. Gdańsk: Marabut, 1995.

Housley, Norman. *Contesting the Crusade*. Malden, MA: Blackwell Publishing, 2006.

Hoyland, Robert G. ed. *Muslims and Others in Early Islamic Society*. The Formation of the Classical Islamic World. Vol. 18. Burlington, VT: Ashgate, 2004.

Humphreys, Stephen, R. "The Expressive Intent of the Mamlūk Architecture of Cairo: A Preliminary Essay." *Studia Islamica*, vol. 35 (1972), p. 69-119.

Ibn Bajja. "The Governance of the Solitary." In: Ralph Lerner and Muhsin Mahdi eds., trans. Fauzi Najjar. *Medieval Political Philosophy: A Sourcebook*. Toronto: Collier-McMacmillan, 1963, p. 122-134.

Ibn Hishām, ʻAbd al-Malik and Ibn Isḥāq Muḥammad. *The Life of Muḥammad: A Translation of Ibn Isḥāq's "Sīrat Rasūl Allāh."* Translated by Alfred Guillaume. London: Oxford University Press, 1955.

Ibn Rushd, Abū 'l-Walīd Muḥammad bin Aḥmad. "The Decisive Treatise." In: *Medieval Political Philosophy: A Sourcebook*. Edited by Ralph Lerner and Muhsin Mahdi. Translated by Fauzi Najjar. Toronto: Collier-McMacmillan, 1963, p. 163-188.

________________________________. *Tahāfut al-Tahāfut* (*The Incoherence of Incoherence*). 19. UNESCO Collection of Great Works. Arabic Series; "E. J. W. Gibb Memorial" Series. New Series, 19. Translated by Simon Van Den Berg. London: Luzac 1954.

Ibn Saʻd Muḥammad. *Kitāb al-Ṭabaqāt al-Kabīr*. Edited by Eduard Sachau. Leiden: Brill, 1904-1940.

Ibn Sīnā, Abū ʻAlī Ḥusayn Ibn ʻAbdallah."On the Divisions of Rational Sciences." In: *Medieval Political Philosophy: A Sourcebook*. Edited by Ralph Lerner and Muhsin Mahdi. Translated by Fauzi Najjar. Toronto: Collier-McMacmillan, 1963, p. 95-98.

_______, Abū ʻAlī Ḥusayn Ibn ʻAbdallah. "On the Proof of Prophecies and the Interpretation of Prophets Symbols and Metaphors." In: *Medieval Political Philosophy: A Sourcebook*. Edited by Ralph Lerner and Muhsin Mahdi. Translated by Fauzi Najjar. Toronto: Collier-McMacmillan, 1963, p. 112-122.

Imber, Colin. *The Ottoman Empire, 1300-1650: The Structure of Power*. New York: Palgrave McMacmillan, 2002.

Jairazbhoy, Hajj Qassim Ali. *Muhammad "A Mercy to All Nations."* London: Luzac & Co, Ltd., 1937.

Judycka, Joanna. *Wiara i rozum w filozofii Rajmunda Lulla*. Lublin: Wydawnictwo KUL, 2005.

Katsh, Abraham I. *Judaism in Islam: Biblical and Talmudic Backgrounds of the Koran and its Commentaries: Suras II and III*. New York: Bloch Pub., 1954.

Kedar, Benjamin Z. *Crusade and Mission: European Approaches towards the Muslims*. Princeton, NJ: Princeton University Press, 1984.

Kennedy, Hugh. *The Early Abbasid Caliphate: A Political History*. London–New York, Totowa, NJ: Barnes and Noble, 1981.

___________. *The Prophet and the Age of the Caliphates, 600-1050*. London and New York: Barnes and Noble, 1981.

________. *The Prophet and the Age of the Caliphates, 600-1050*. London: Longman, 1986.

Khoury, Adel Théodore. *Polémique byzatine contre l'Islam (VIIIe-XIIIe s.)*. Leiden: Brill 1972.

_________________. *Les théologiens byzantins et l'Islam: Textes et auteurs (VIIIe-XIIIe s.)*. Louvain–Paris: Beatrice-Nauwelaerts, 1969.

Kościelniak, Krzysztof. *Grecy i Arabowie. Historia Kościoła melkickiego (katolickiego) na ziemiach zdobytych przez muzułmanów (634-1516)*. Kraków: Wydawnictwo UNUM, 2004.

Kraemer, Jörg. *Das Problem der islamischen Kulturgeschichte*. Tübingen: M. Niemeyer, 1959.

Kramers, Johannes H. "Muḥammad ʻAlī ʻPasha." In: *The Encyclopaedia of Islam*. Vol. III, p. 681-684.

Kritzek, James. *Peter the Venerable and Islam*. Princeton, NJ: Princeton University Press, 1964.

Kubiak, Władysław B. *Al-Fustat, It's Early Foundation and Early Urban Development*, Cairo: American University of Cairo Press, 1987.

Küng, Hans ed. [et al.]. *Christianity and the World Religions: Paths of Dialogue with Islam, Hinduism, and Buddhism*. Translated by Peter Heinegg. Garden City, NY: Doubleday, 1986.

Lammens, Henri. "L'age de Mahomet et la chronologie de la Sirā." *Journal Asiatique*, Tenth Series, 17 (IV 1911), p. 209-250.

____________. "Qoran et tradition: comment fut composée la vie de Mahomet." *Revue de Recherches de Sciences Religieuse*, vol. 1 (1910), p. 26-51.

Lamoreaux, John C. "Early Christian Responses to Islam." In: John V. Tolan ed. *Medieval Christian Perceptions of Islam: A Book of Essays*. Garland Medieval Case Books 10. Garland Reference Library of Humanities 1786. New York–London: Garland, 1994, p. 3-28.

Lane-Poole, Stanley. *Cairo: Sketches of its History, Monuments, and Social Life*. London: J. S. Virtue, 1898.

Lapidus, Ira M. "Mamlūk Patronage of the Arts in Egypt: Concluding Remarks." *Muqarnas*, vol. 2 (1984), p. 173-181.

___________. *Muslim Cities in the Later Middle Ages*. Cambridge, MA: Harvard University Press, 1967.

Lassner, Jacob. *The Shaping of 'Abbāsid Rule*. Princeton, NJ: Princeton University Press, 1980.

Lawson, Fred. "Economic and Social Foundations of Egyptian Expansionism: The Invasion of Syria in 1831." *International History Review*, vol. 10 (1988), p. 71-89.

__________. *The Social Origins of Egyptian Expansionism during the Muhammad Ali Period*. New York: Columbia University Press, 1992.

Lelong, Michel. *L'Eglise catholique et l'Islam*. Paris: Maisonneuve & Larose, 1993.

Lerner, Ralph and Mahdi, Muhsin eds. *Medieval Political Philosophy: A Sourcebook*. New York: Free Press of Glencoe,1963.

Lewis, Bernard. *Faith and Power: Religion and Politics in the Middle East*. New York: Oxford University Press, 2010.

__________. *Islam and the West*. New York: Oxford University Press, 1993.

__________. *The Arabs in History*. New York: Oxford University Press, 1993.

__________. *The End of Modern History in the Middle East*. Stanford, CA: Hoover Institution Press, 2011.

__________. *The Middle East: 2000 Years of History from the Rise of Christianity to the Present Day*. London: Weidenfeld & Nicolson, 1995.

__________. *The Muslim Discovery of Europe*. New York: W.W. Norton & Company, 1982.

Lings, Martin. *Muhammad: His Life Based on the Earliest Sources*. Rochester, VT: Inner Traditions, 2006.

Little, Donald P. *A Catalogue of Islamic Documents from al-Ḥaram aš-Šarīf in Jerusalem*. Beirut–Wiesbaden: Orient-Institut der Deutschen Morgenländischen Gesellschaft, 1984.

__________. "Ḥaram Documents Related to the Jews of the Late Fourteenth-Century." *Journal of Semitic Studies*, vol. 30, 2 (1985), p. 227-264.

__________. *History and Historiography of the Mamlūks*. London: Variorum Reprints, 1986.

__________. "The Ḥaram Documents as Sources for the Arts and Architecture of the Mamlūk Period." *Muqarnas*, vol. 2 (1984), p. 61-73.

__________. "The Judicial Documents from al-Ḥaram al-Sharīf as Sources for the History of Palestine Under the Mamlūks." In: *The Third International Conference on Bilad al-Shām: Palestine (19-24 April, 1980)*, vol. I: *Jerusalem*, Amman: University of Jordan–Yarmouk University, 1983, p. 117-125.

__________. "The Significance of the *Ḥaram* Documents for the Study of Medieval Islamic History." *Der Islam*, vol. 57 (1980), p. 189-219.

__________. "Two Fourteenth-Century Court Records from Jerusalem Concerning the Disposition of Slaves by Minors." *Arabica*, vol. 29 (1982), p. 16-49.

__________. "Six Fourteenth-Century Purchase Deeds for Slaves from al-Ḥaram *aš-Šarīf*." *Zeitschrift der Deutschen Morgenländischen Gesellschaft*, vol. 131 (2), Wiesbaden, 1981, p. 297-337.

Llull Ramon. *Libre del gentil e dels tres savis*. Patronat Ramon Llull. Nova edicio de les obres de Ramón Llull, vol. 2. Edited by Antoni Bonner. Palma de Mallorca: Publicacions de I'Abadia de Montserrat, 2001.

__________. *Nova edicio de les obres de Ramón Llull: NEORL*. Palma de Mallorca: Patronat Ramón Llull, 1990<2010>.

__________. "Pieśń Rajmunda." In: Józef S. Kafel ed. *Antologia mistyków franciszkańskich*. Vol. 2: *Wiek XIII-XIV*. Warszawa: Akademia Teologii Katolickiej, 1986.

Lomax, John Ph. "Frederick II, His Saracens and the Papacy." In: John V. Tolan ed. *Medieval Christian Perceptions of Islam: A Book of Essays*. Garland Medieval Case Books 10, Garland Reference Library of Humanities 1786. New York–London: Garland, 1994, p. 175-197.

Lutfi, Huda. *Al-Quds al-Mamlūkiyya: A History of Mamlūk Jerusalem Based on the Ḥaram Documents*. Berlin: K. Schwarz Verlag, 1985.

_________. "A Study of the Fourteenth Century *Iqrārs* from al-Quds Relating to Muslim Women." *Journal of the Economic and Social History of the Orient*, vol. 26, no. 3 (1983), p. 246-294.

_________ and Little, Donald P. "Iqrārs from Al-Quds: Emendations." *Journal of the Economic and Social History of the Orient*, vol. 28 (1985), p. 326-330.

Madeyska, Danuta. *Historia świata arabskiego: Okres klasyczny od starożytności do końca epoki Umajjadów (750)*. Warszawa: Wydawnictwa Uniwersytetu Warszawskiego, 1999.

Mahdi, Muhsin S. *Alfarabi and the Foundation of Islamic Political Philosophy*. Chicago: University of Chicago Press, 2001.

Makdisi, Georges. "Muslim Institutions of Learning in Eleventh-Century in Baghdad." *Bulletin of the School of Oriental and African Studies*, vol. 24, no. 1 (1961), p. 1-56.

____________. *The Rise of the Colleges: Institutions of Learning in Islam and the West*. Edinburgh: Edinburgh University Press, 1981.

Mansfield, Peter. *A History of the Middle East*. New York: Penguin Books, 1992.

____________. "Muhammad 'Ali's Egypt: Ottoman Rival." In: *A History of the Middle East*. New York: Penguin Books, 1992, p. 46-63.

Marçais, George. *L'art musulman*. Les Neuf muses. Paris: Presses Universitaires de France, 1962.

Marcel, Jean-Joseph. *Égypte depuis la conquête des arabes jusqu'à la domination française*. Paris: Firmin Didot, 1848.

Marmura, Michael E. "Falsafa." In: Mircea Eliade, Charles J. Adams eds. [et al.]. *The Encyclopedia of Religion*. Vol. 5. New York: Macmillan, 1987, p. 267-276.

_______________ ed. *Islamic Theology and Philosophy: Studies in Honour of George F. Hourani*. Albany, NY: State University of New York Press, 1984

_______________. *Probing in Islamic Philosophy: Studies in the Philosophies of Ibn Sīnā, Al-Ghazālī, and Major Muslim Thinkers*. Binghamton: Global Academic Pub., Binghamton University, 2005.

Mastnak, Tomaž. *Crusading Peace: Christendom, the Muslim World, and Western Political Order*. Berkeley, CA–London: University of California Press, 2002.

McGinnis, Jon. *Avicenna*. Great Medieval Thinkers. New York–Oxford: Oxford University Press, 2010.

Meinecke-Berg, Viktoria. "Quellen zu Topographie und Baugeschichte in Kairo unter Sulṭān an-Nāṣir Muḥammad b. Qalā' ūn." *Deutscher Orientalistentag*, vol. 19 (1975), p. 538-550.

Menocal, Maria Rosa. *The Ornamant of the World: How Muslims, Jews, and Christians Created a Culture of Tolerance in Medieval Spain*. Boston: Little Brown & Co. (Inc.), 2002.

Meyendorff, John. "Byzantine Views of Islam." *Dumbarton Oaks Papers* 18 (1964), p. 113-132.

Migeon, Gaston and Saladin, Henri. *Art of Islam*. New York: Parkstone International, 2009.

Mitha, Farouk. *Al-Ghazālī and the Ismailis: A Debate on Reason and Authority in Medieval Islam.* Ismaili heritage series, 5. London: I. B. Tauris, in association with the Institute of Ismaili Studies, 2001.

Montgomery, James E. ed. *Arabic Theology, Arabic Philosophy: From the Many to the One: Essays in Celebration of Richard M. Frank.* Orientalia Lovaniensia Analecta 152. Leuven–Dudley, MA: Peeters Publishers, 2006.

Myers, Eugene A. *Arabic Thought and the Western World in the Golden Age of Islam.* New York: Ungar, 1964.

Nasr, Sayyed Hossein. *Islamic Philosophy from its Origin to the Present: Philosophy in the Land of Prophecy.* SUNY Series in Islam. Albany, NY: State Univeristy of New York Press, 2006.

Northrup, Linda S. and Abul-Hajj, Amal A. "A Collection of Medieval Arabic Documents in the Islamic Museum at the Ḥaram al-Sharīf." *Arabica*, vol. 25 (1979), p. 282-291.

Noth, A. "The Image in the Latin Middle Ages." In: *The Encyclopaedia of Islam.* New Edition. Vol. 7, p. 377-381.

Ormsby, Eric L. *Ghazali: The Revival of Islam.* Oxford: Oneworld, 2008.

Owen, Robert. *Cotton and the Egyptian Economy 1820-1914.* Oxford: Clarendon P., 1969.

Penn, Michael. "Syriac Sources for the Study of Early Christian-Muslim Relations." *Islamochristiana*, vol. 29 (2003), p. 72-73.

Prejs, Roland and Kijas, Zdzisław eds. *Źródła Franciszkańskie: Pisma św. Franciszka, Źródła biograficzne św. Franciszka, Pisma św. Klary i źródła biograficzne, Teksty ustalające normy dla braci i sióstr od pokuty.* Translated by Kajetan Ambrożkiewicz, Bruno A. Gancarz [et al.]. Kraków: Wydawnictwo OO. Franciszkanów "Bratni Zew," 2005.

Rafi'i, 'Abd al-Rahman. *'Asr Muhammad 'Ali.* Cairo: Maktabat al-Nahdah al-Misriyyah, 1951.

Ramadan, Tariq. *The Messenger: The Meaning of the Life of Muhammad.* London: Allen Lane, 2007.

Raven, Wim. "Sīra and the Qur'ān – Ibn Isḥāq and his Editors." In: Jane D. McAuliffe ed. *Encyclopaedia of the Qur'an.* Vol. 5. Leiden: Brill, 2006, p. 29-51.

Raymond, André. "Cairo's Area and Population in the Early Fifteenth Century." *Muqarnas*, vol. 2 (1984), p. 21-33.

Rice, David T. *Islamic Art.* London: Thames and Hudson, 1975.

Riley-Smith, Jonathan S. *The Oxford History of the Crusades.* New York: Oxford University Press, 2002.

___________________. *Historia krucjat.* Translated by Katarzyna Pachniak with an appendix to Polish edition by Jerzy Hauziński. Warszawa: Oficyna Wydawnicz "Vocatio," 2005.

Ritter, Helmut and Radtke, Bernd. *The Ocean of the Soul: Man, the World, and God in the Stories of Farīd al-Dīn 'Aṭṭār.* Handbuch der Orientalistik. Erste abteilung, Der Nahe und Mitlere Osten; Handbook of oriental studies. Translated by John O'Kane. Leiden–Boston: Brill, 2003.

Rivlin, Helen Anne B. *The Agricultural Policy of Muhammad 'Ali in Egypt.* Cambridge, MA: Harvard University Press, 1961.

R.L. Hl. "Mohammad 'Ali." In: *The Encyclopaedia Britannica.* Vol. XV, p. 645.

Rodinson, Maxime. *Muhammad.* Translated by Anne Carter. New York: Pantheon Books, 1980.

_______________. *Mahomet.* Translated by E. Michalska-Nowak. Warszawa: Państwowy Instytut Wydawniczy, 1991.

Rogers, Michael. "Al-Ḳāhira." In: *The Encyclopaedia of Islam.* New Edition. Vol. 4, p. 424.

Roggema, Barbara. *The Legend of Sergius Baḥīrā: Eastern Christian Apologetics and Apocalyptic in Response to Islam.* Leiden–Boston: Brill, 2009.

Ronart, Stephan and Ronart, Nandy. *Concise Encyclopaedia of Arabic Civilization.* Amsterdam: Djambatan, 1959.

Rosenthal, Erwin Isak J. "The Theory of the Power-State: Ibn Khaldun's Study of Civilization." In: *Political Thought in Medieval Islam: An Introductory Outline.* Cambridge: University Press, 1958, p. 84-109.

Ross, Alexander. *Pansebeia: or, A view of all religions in the world: with the several church-governments, from the creation, till these times. Also, a discovery of all known heresies, in all ages and places: and choice observations and reflections throughout the whole.* London: Printed for M. Gillyflower and W. Freeman, 1696.

Rudnicka-Kassem, Dorota. *John Paul II, Islam and the Middle East: The Pope's Spiritual Leadership in Developing a Dialogical Path for the New History od Christian-Muslim Relations.* Krakow: Księgarnia Akademicka, 2012.

Russell, Dorothea M. *Medieval Cairo and the Monasteries of Wādī Natrūn.* London: Weidenfeld and Nicolson, 1962.

Sage, Carleton M. *Paul Albar of Cordoba: Studies on his Life and Writings.* Washington, DC: Catholic Univeristy of America Press, 1943.

Sahas, Daniel J. *John of Damascus: The "Heresy of Ishmaelites."* Leiden: Brill, 1972.

Said, Yazeed. *Ghazālī's Politics in Context.* Abingdon–Oxon–New York: Routledge, 2013.

Salahi, Adil M. *Muhammad: Man and Prophet: A Complete Study of the Life of the Prophet of Islam.* Shaftesbury, Dorset–Rockport, MA: Element, 1995.

Sarwar, Hafiz Ghulam. *Muḥammad the Holy Prophet.* Lahore: Ashraf, 1949.

Savary, Claude E. ed. *Le Koran, traduit de l'arabe, accompagné de notes, précédé d'un abrégé de la vie de Mahomet par Savary.* Paris: Garnier, 1951.

Sawicka Anna, *Drogi i rozdroża kultury katalońskiej*, Kraków: Księgarnia Akademicka, 2007.

Sayyid-Marsot, Afaf L. *Egypt in the Reign of Muhammad 'Ali.* Cambridge–New York: Cambridge University Press, 1984.

Schimmel, Annemarie. *Islam: An Introduction.* Albany: State University of New York Press, 1992.

Sharif, Mian Muhammad. ed. *History of Muslim Philosophy: With Short Accounts of Other Disciplines and the Modern Renaissance in Muslim Lands.* Karachi: Royal Book Co., 1983.

Siddiqi, Zafar A. *Philosophy of Ibn Tufayl.* Faculty of Arts Publication Series, no. 18. Aligarh: Aligarh Muslim University, 1965.

Sourdel, Dominique. "Aḥmad B. Ṭūlūn." In: *The Encyclopaedia of Islam.* New Edition. Vol. 1, p. 278-279.

Southern, Richard William. *Western Views of Islam in the Middle Ages.* Cambridge, MA: Harvard University Press, 1962.

Sprenger, Aloys. *Das Leben und die Lehre des Mohammad.* Berlin: Verlagsbuchhandlung, 1861-1865.

Streusand, Douglas E. *Islamic Gunpowder Empires: Ottomans, Safavids, and Mughals.* Boulder, CO: Westview Press, 2011.

Tezcan, Baki. *The Second Ottoman Empire: Political and Social Transformation in the Early Modern World.* Cambridge–New York: Cambridge University Press, 2010.

Tolan, John V. ed. *Medieval Christian Perceptions of Islam: A Book of Essays*. Garland Medieval Case Books 10, Garland Reference Library of Humanities 1786. New York–London: Garland, 1994.

Toledano, Ehud R. "Muḥammad 'Alī Pasha." In: *The Encyclopaedia of Islam*. New Edition. Vol. 7, p. 423-431.

_____________. *State and Society in Mid-nineteenth Century Egypt*. Cambridge Middle East Library (22). Cambridge–New York: Cambridge University Press, 1989.

Torrey, Charles C. *The Jewish Foundation of Islam*. The Hilda Stich Stroock Lectures ... at the Jewish Institute of Religion. New York: Jewish Institute of Religion Press, 1933.

Treiger, Alexander. *Inspired Knowledge in Islamic Thought: Al-Ghazālī's Theory of Mystical Cognition and its Avicennian Foundation*. London–New York: Routledge, 2012.

Troll, Christian W. "Mission and Dialogue: The Example of Islam." *Encounter: Documents for Muslim-Christian Understanding*, no. 189-190 (November-December 1992), p. 3-14.

Tyan, Emile. *Le notariat et la régime de la preuve par écrit dans la practique du droit Musulman*. Beyrouth, 1945.

Ufford, Letitia Wheeler. *The Pasha. How Mehemet Ali Defied the West: 1839-1841*. Jefferson, NC: McFarland & Company, 2007.

Unknown Autor. *Dzieje Błogosławionego Franciszka i jego towarzyszy*. In: Prejs, Roland and Kijas, Zdzisław eds. *Źródła Franciszkańskie:Pisma św. Franciszka, Źródła biograficzne św. Franciszka, Pisma św. Klary i źródła biograficzne, Teksty ustalające normy dla braci i sióstr od pokuty*. Translated by Kajetan Ambrożkiewicz, Bruno A. Gancarz [et al.]. Kraków: Wydawnictwo OO. Franciszkanów "Bratni Zew," 2005, p. 1197-1198.

Urvoy, Dominique. "Ramon Lull et l'Islam." *Islamochristiana*, vol. 7 (1981), p. 127-146.

Waardenburg, Jean J. *Islam and Christianity: Mutual Perceptions since the Mid-20th Century*. Leuven: Peeters, 1998.

_________________. "Islamic Studies." In: Mircea Eliade, Charles J. Adams eds. [et al.]. In: *Encyclopedia of Religion*. Vol. 7. New York: Macmillan, 1987, p. 457-458.

Wakin, Jeanette A. *The Function of Documents in Islamic Law. The Chapters on Sales from Ṭahāwī's Kitāb al-Shurūṭ al-Kabīr*. Albany: State University of New York Press, 1972.

Waltz, James. "Muhammad and the Muslims in St. Thomas Aquinas." *The Muslim World*, vol. 66/2, April (1976), p. 81-95.

_________. "The Significance of the Voluntary Martyrs of Ninth-Century Cordoba." *Muslim World*, vol. 60 (1970), p. 143-159.

Walzer, Richard. *Greek into Arabic: Essays on Islamic Philosophy*. Cambridge, MA: Harvard University Press, 1962.

Warner, Nicholas. *The Monuments of Historic Cairo: A Map and Descriptive Catalogue*. Cairo: American University in Cairo Press, 2005.

Watt, William Montgomery. *Islamic Philosophy and Theology*. Edinburgh: University Press, 1962.

____________________. *Muhammad at Mecca*. Oxford: Clarendon Press, 1953.

____________________. *Muhammad at Medina*. Oxford: Clarendon Press, 1956.

____________________. *Muhammad: Prophet and Statesman*. London: Oxford University Press, 1961.

____________________. *Muslim Intellectual: A Study of Al-Ghazali*. Edinburgh: Edinburg University Press, 1963.

____________________. *The Formative Period of Islamic Thought*. Edinburgh: Edinburg University Press, 1973.

_____________________. *The Influence of Islam on Medieval Europe*. Edinburgh: Edinburg University Press, 1972.

Wellhausen, Julius. *The Arab Kingdom and its Fall*. Translated by Margaret Graham Weir. Calcutta: University of Calcutta, 1927.

Wiet, Gaston. *Cairo: City of Art and Commerce. Centers of Civilization Series*. Translated by Seymour Feiler. Norman, OA: University of Oklahoma Press, 1964.

__________. *Muhammad 'Ali et les beaux-arts*. Le Caire: Dar al Maaref [1949?].

Williams, John A. "Urbanization and Monument Construction in Mamlūk Cairo." *Muqarnas*, vol. 2 (1984), p. 33-45.

Wolf, Kenneth B. "Christian Views of Islam in Early Medieval Spain." In: John V. Tolan ed. *Medieval Christian Perceptions of Islam. A Book of Essays*. Garland Medieval Case Books 10, Garland Reference Library of Humanities 1786. New York–London: Garland, 1994. p. 85-108.

Wolfson, Harry A. *The Philosophy of the Kalam*. Cambridge, MA: Harvard University Press, 1976.

Yeomans, Richard. *The Art and Architecture of Islamic Cairo*. New York: New York University Press, 2000.

Zebiri, Kate. *Muslims and Christians Face to Face*. Oxford–Rockport, MA: Oneworld Publications, 1997.

Zwemer, Samuel M. *Raymund Lull: First Missionary to the Moslems*. Three Rivers: Diggory Press, 2006.

Żebrowski, Janusz. *Dzieje Syrii*. Warszawa: Wydawnictwo Akademickie Dialog, 2006.

Index

The books published in the *Societas* Series (Bogdan Szlachta, Editor) are:

1. Grzybek Dariusz, *Nauka czy ideologia. Biografia intelektualna Adama Krzyżanowskiego*, 2005.
2. Drzonek Maciej, *Między integracją a europeizacją. Kościół katolicki w Polsce wobec Unii Europejskiej w latach 1997-2003*, 2006.
3. Chmieliński Maciej, *Max Stirner. Jednostka, społeczeństwo, państwo*, 2006.
4. Nieć Mateusz, *Rozważania o pojęciu polityki w kręgu kultury attyckiej. Studium z historii polityki i myśli politycznej*, 2006.
5. Sokołów Florian, *Nahum Sokołów. Życie i legenda*, oprac. Andrzej A. Zięba, 2006.
6. Porębski Leszek, *Między przemocą a godnością. Teoria polityczna Harolda D. Laswella*, 2007.
7. Mazur Grzegorz, *Życie polityczne polskiego Lwowa 1918-1939*, 2007.
8. Węc Janusz Józef, *Spór o kształt instytucjonalny Wspólnot Europejskich i Unii Europejskiej 1950-2005. Między ideą ponadnarodowości a współpracą międzyrządową. Analiza politologiczna*, 2006.
9. Karas Marcin, *Integryzm Bractwa Kapłańskiego św. Piusa X. Historia i doktryna rzymskokatolickiego ruchu tradycjonalistycznego*, 2008.
10. *European Ideas on Tolerance*, red. Guido Naschert, Marcin Rebes, 2009.
11. Gacek Łukasz, *Chińskie elity polityczne w XX wieku*, 2009.
12. Zemanek Bogdan S., *Tajwańska tożsamość narodowa w publicystyce politycznej*, 2009.
13. Lencznarowicz Jan, *Jałta. W kręgu mitów założycielskich polskiej emigracji politycznej 1944-1956*, 2009.
14. Grabowski Andrzej, *Prawnicze pojęcie obowiązywania prawa stanowionego. Krytyka niepozytywistycznej koncepcji prawa*, 2009.
15. Kich-Masłej Olga, *Ukraina w opinii elit Krakowa końca XIX – pierwszej połowy XX wieku*, 2009.
16. Citkowska-Kimla Anna, *Romantyzm polityczny w Niemczech. Reprezentanci, idee, model*, 2010.
17. Mikuli Piotr, *Sądy a parlament w ustrojach Australii, Kanady i Nowej Zelandii (na tle rozwiązań brytyjskich)*, 2010.
18. Kubicki Paweł, *Miasto w sieci znaczeń. Kraków i jego tożsamości*, 2010.
19. Żurawski Jakub, *Internet jako współczesny środek elektronicznej komunikacji wyborczej i jego zastosowanie w polskich kampaniach parlamentarnych*, 2010.
20. *Polscy eurodeputowani 2004-2009. Uwarunkowania działania i ocena skuteczności*, red. K. Szczerski, 2010.
21. Bojko Krzysztof, *Stosunki dyplomatyczne Moskwy z Europą Zachodnią w czasach Iwana III*, 2010.
22. *Studia nad wielokulturowością*, red. Dorota Pietrzyk-Reeves, Małgorzata Kułakowska, Elżbieta Żak, 2010.
23. Bartnik Anna, *Emigracja latynoska w USA po II wojnie światowej na przykładzie Portorykańczyków, Meksykanów i Kubańczyków*, 2010.
24. *Transformacje w Ameryce Łacińskiej*, red. Adam Walaszek, Aleksandra Giera, 2011.
25. Praszałowicz Dorota, *Polacy w Berlinie. Strumienie migracyjne i społeczności imigrantów. Przegląd badań*, 2010.
26. Głogowski Aleksander, *Pakistan. Historia i współczesność*, 2011.
27. Brążkiewicz Bartłomiej, *Choroba psychiczna w literaturze i kulturze rosyjskiej*, 2011.

28. Bojenko-Izdebska Ewa, *Przemiany w Niemczech Wschodnich 1989-2010. Polityczne aspekty transformacji*, 2011.
29. Kołodziej Jacek, *Wartości polityczne. Rozpoznanie, rozumienie, komunikowanie*, 2011.
30. *Nacjonalizmy różnych narodów. Perspektywa politologiczno-religioznawcza*, red. Bogumił Grott, Olgierd Grott, 2012.
31. Matyasik Michał, *Realizacja wolności wypowiedzi na podstawie przepisów i praktyki w USA*, 2011.
32. Grzybek Dariusz, *Polityczne konsekwencje idei ekonomicznych w myśli polskiej 1869--1939*, 2012.
33. Woźnica Rafał, *Bułgarska polityka wewnętrzna a proces integracji z Unią Europejską*, 2012.
34. Ślufińska Monika, *Radykałowie francuscy. Koncepcje i działalność polityczna w XX wieku*, 2012.
35. Fyderek Łukasz, *Pretorianie i technokraci w reżimie politycznym Syrii*, 2012.
36. Węc Janusz Józef, *Traktat lizboński. Polityczne aspekty reformy ustrojowej Unii Europejskiej w latach 2007-2009*, 2011.
37. Rudnicka-Kassem Dorota, *John Paul II, Islam and the Middle East. The Pope's Spiritual Leadership in Developing a Dialogical Path for the New History of Christian-Muslim Relations*, 2012.
38. Bujwid-Kurek Ewa, *Serbia w nowej przestrzeni ustrojowej. Dzieje, ustrój, konstytucja*, 2012.
39. Cisek Janusz, *Granice Rzeczpospolitej i konflikt polsko-bolszewicki w świetle amerykańskich raportów dyplomatycznych i wojskowych*, 2012.
40. Gacek Łukasz, *Bezpieczeństwo energetyczne Chin. Aktywność państwowych przedsiębiorstw na rynkach zagranicznych*, 2012.
41. Węc Janusz Józef, *Spór o kształt ustrojowy Wspólnot Europejskich i Unii Europejskiej w latach 1950-2010. Między ideą ponadnarodowości a współpracą międzyrządową. Analiza politologiczna*, 2012.
42. *Międzycywilizacyjny dialog w świecie słowiańskim w XX i XX wieku. Historia – religia – kultura – polityka*, red. Irena Stawowy-Kawka, 2012.
43. *Ciekawość świata, ludzi, kultury... Księga jubileuszowa ofiarowana Profesorowi Ryszardowi Kantorowi z okazji czterdziestolecia pracy naukowej*, red. Renata Hołda, Tadeusz Paleczny, 2012.
44. Węc Janusz Józef, *Pierwsza polska prezydencja w Unii Europejskiej. Uwarunkowania – procesy decyzyjne – osiągnięcia i niepowodzenia*, 2012.
45. Zemanek Adina, *Córki Chin i obywatelki świata. Obraz kobiety w chińskich czasopismach o modzie*, 2012.
46. Kamińska Ewa, *Rezeption japanischer Kultur in Deutschland. Zeitgenössische Keramik als Fallstudie*, 2012.
47. Obeidat Hassaym, *Stabilność układu naftowego w warunkach zagrożeń konfliktami w świetle kryzysu w latach siedemdziesiątych XX i na progu XXI wieku*, 2012.
48. Ścigaj Paweł, *Tożsamość narodowa. Zarys problematyki*, 2012.
49. Głogowski Aleksander, *Af-Pak. Znaczenie zachodniego pogranicza pakistańsko-afgańskiego dla bezpieczeństwa regionalnego w latach 1947-2011*, 2012.
50. Miżejewski Maciej, *Ochrona pluralizmu w polityce medialnej Włoch*, 2012.
51. Jakubiak Łukasz, *Referendum jako narzędzie polityki. Francuskie doświadczenia ustrojowe*, 2013.

52. *Skuteczność polskiej prezydencji w Unii Europejskiej. Założone cele i ich realizacja*, red. Krzysztof Szczerski, 2013.
53. *Stosunki państwo–Kościół w Polsce 1944-2010*, red. Rafał Łatka, 2013.
54. Gacek Łukasz, Trojnar Ewa, *Pokojowe negocjacje czy twarda gra? Rozwój stosunków ponad cieśniną tajwańską*, 2012.
55. Sondel-Cedarmas Joanna, *Nacjonalizm włoski. Geneza i ewolucja doktryny politycznej (1896-1923)*, 2013.